HOLT SCIENCE & TECHNOLOGY

Forces, Motion, and Energy

HOLT, RINEHART AND WINSTON

A Harcourt Education Company

Orlando • **Austin** • New York • San Diego • Toronto • London

Acknowledgments

Contributing Authors

Leila Dumas, MA
Former Physics Teacher
Lago Vista, Texas

William G. Lamb, Ph.D.
Winningstad Chair in the Physical Sciences
Oregon Episcopal School
Portland, Oregon

Inclusion and Special Needs Consultant

Ellen McPeek Glisan
Special Needs Consultant
San Antonio, Texas

Safety Reviewer

Jack Gerlovich, Ph.D.
Associate Professor
School of Education
Drake University
Des Moines, Iowa

Academic Reviewers

Howard L. Brooks, Ph.D.
Professor of Physics & Astronomy
Department of Physics & Astronomy
DePauw University
Greencastle, Indiana

Simonetta Frittelli, Ph.D.
Associate Professor
Department of Physics
Duquesne University
Pittsburgh, Pennsylvania

David S. Hall, Ph.D.
Assistant Professor of Physics
Department of Physics
Amherst College
Amherst, Massachusetts

William H. Ingham, Ph.D.
Professor of Physics
James Madison University
Harrisonburg, Virginia

David Lamp, Ph.D.
Associate Professor of Physics
Physics Department
Texas Tech University
Lubbock, Texas

Mark Mattson, Ph.D.
Director, College of Science and Mathematics Learning Center
James Madison University
Harrisonburg, Virginia

H. Michael Sommermann, Ph.D.
Professor of Physics
Physics Department
Westmont College
Santa Barbara, California

Lab Testing

Barry L. Bishop
Science Teacher and Department Chair
San Rafael Junior High School
Ferron, Utah

Vicky Farland
Science Teacher
Crane Junior High School
Yuma, Arizona

Rebecca Ferguson
Science Teacher
North Ridge Middle School
North Richland Hills, Texas

Jennifer Ford
Science Teacher and Dept. Chair
North Ridge Middle School
North Richland Hills, Texas

C. John Graves
Science Teacher
Monforton Middle School
Bozeman, Montana

Dennis Hanson
Science Teacher and Dept. Chair
Big Bear Middle School
Big Bear Lake, California

Norman E. Holcomb
Science Teacher
Marion Elementary School
Marion, Ohio

Edith C. McAlanis
Science Teacher and Department Chair
Socorro Middle School
El Paso, Texas

Terry J. Rakes
Science Teacher
Elmwood Junior High School
Rogers, Arkansas

David M. Sparks
Science Teacher
Redwater Junior High School
Redwater, Texas

Larry Tackett
Science Teacher and Department Chair
Andrew Jackson Middle School
Cross Lanes, West Virginia

Elsie N. Waynes
Science Teacher and Department Chair
R. H. Terrell Junior High School
Washington, D.C.

Sharon L. Woolf
Science Teacher
Langston Hughes Middle School
Reston, Virginia

John Zambo
Science Teacher
Elizabeth Ustach Middle School
Modesto, California

Printed in the United States of America
ISBN-13: 978-0-03-050112-8
ISBN-10: 0-03-050112-1

11 0868 12 11   4500327471

Forces, Motion, and Energy

Safety First! x

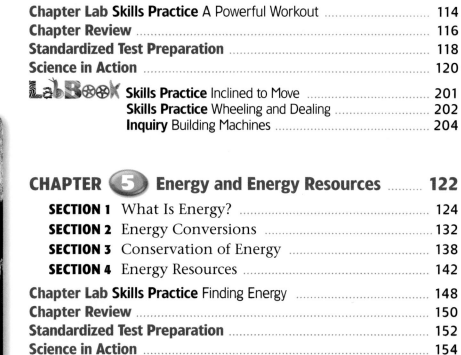

Contents **v**

Labs and Activities

How to Use Your Textbook

Your Roadmap for Success with Holt Science and Technology

What You Will Learn

At the beginning of every section you will find the section's objectives and vocabulary terms. The objectives tell you what you'll need to know after you finish reading the section.

Vocabulary terms are listed for each section. Learn the definitions of these terms because you will most likely be tested on them. Each term is highlighted in the text and is defined at point of use and in the margin. You can also use the glossary to locate definitions quickly.

STUDY TIP Reread the objectives and the definitions to the terms when studying for a test to be sure you know the material.

Get Organized

A Reading Strategy at the beginning of every section provides tips to help you organize and remember the information covered in the section. Keep a science notebook so that you are ready to take notes when your teacher reviews the material in class. Keep your assignments in this notebook so that you can review them when studying for the chapter test.

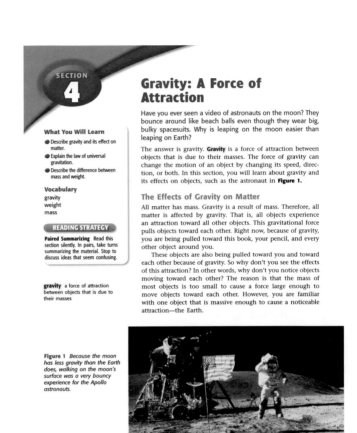

SECTION 4

Gravity: A Force of Attraction

Have you ever seen a video of astronauts on the moon? They bounce around like beach balls even though they wear big, bulky spacesuits. Why is leaping on the moon easier than leaping on Earth?

The answer is gravity. **Gravity** is a force of attraction between objects that is due to their masses. The force of gravity can change the motion of an object by changing its speed, direction, or both. In this section, you will learn about gravity and its effects on objects, such as the astronaut in **Figure 1.**

The Effects of Gravity on Matter

All matter has mass. Gravity is a result of mass. Therefore, all matter is affected by gravity. That is, all objects experience an attraction toward all other objects. This gravitational force pulls objects toward each other. Right now, because of gravity, you are being pulled toward this book, your pencil, and every other object around you.

These objects are also being pulled toward you and toward each other because of gravity. So why don't you see the effects of this attraction? In other words, why don't you notice objects moving toward each other? The reason is that the mass of most objects is too small to cause a force large enough to move objects toward each other. However, you are familiar with one object that is massive enough to cause a noticeable attraction—the Earth.

What You Will Learn
- Describe gravity and its effect on matter.
- Explain the law of universal gravitation.
- Describe the difference between mass and weight.

Vocabulary
gravity
weight
mass

READING STRATEGY

Paired Summarizing Read this section silently. In pairs, take turns summarizing the material. Stop to discuss ideas that seem confusing.

gravity a force of attraction between objects that is due to their masses

Figure 1 Because the moon has less gravity than the Earth does, walking on the moon's surface was a very bouncy experience for the Apollo astronauts.

134   Chapter 5   Matter in Motion

Be Resourceful—Use the Web

SciLinks boxes in your textbook take you to resources that you can use for science projects, reports, and research papers. Go to **scilinks.org** and type in the **SciLinks code** to find information on a topic.

Visit **go.hrw.com**
Check out the **Current Science®** magazine articles and other materials that go with your textbook at **go.hrw.com**. Click on the textbook icon and the table of contents to see all of the resources for each chapter.

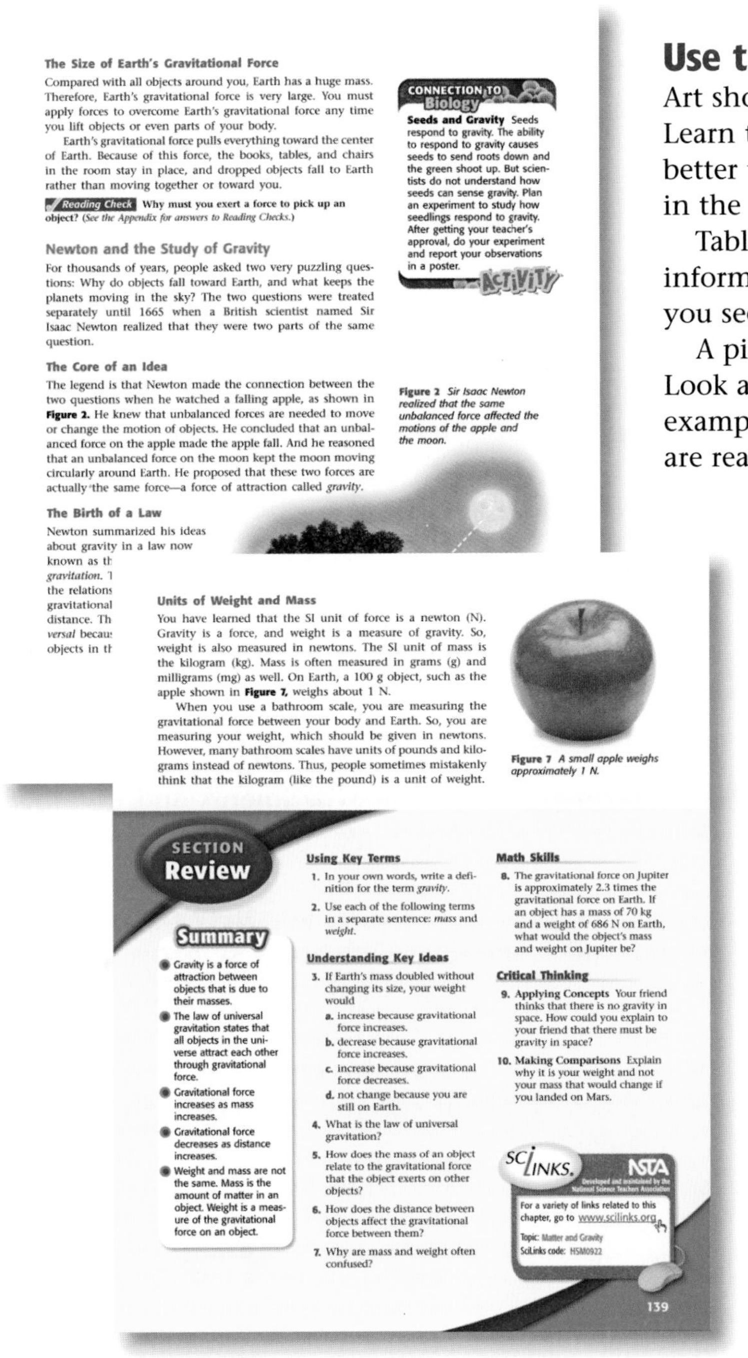

The Size of Earth's Gravitational Force

Compared with all objects around you, Earth has a huge mass. Therefore, Earth's gravitational force is very large. You must apply forces to overcome Earth's gravitational force any time you lift objects or even parts of your body.

Earth's gravitational force pulls everything toward the center of Earth. Because of this force, the books, tables, and chairs in the room stay in place, and dropped objects fall to Earth rather than moving together or toward you.

Reading Check Why must you exert a force to pick up an object? *(See the Appendix for answers to Reading Checks.)*

Newton and the Study of Gravity

For thousands of years, people asked two very puzzling questions: Why do objects fall toward Earth, and what keeps the planets moving in the sky? The two questions were treated separately until 1665 when a British scientist named Sir Isaac Newton realized that they were two parts of the same question.

The Core of an Idea

The legend is that Newton made the connection between the two questions when he watched a falling apple, as shown in **Figure 2**. He knew that unbalanced forces are needed to move or change the motion of objects. He concluded that an unbalanced force on the apple made the apple fall. And he reasoned that an unbalanced force on the moon kept the moon moving circularly around Earth. He proposed that these two forces are actually the same force—a force of attraction called *gravity*.

The Birth of a Law

Newton summarized his ideas about gravity in a law now known as th[...]
gravitation. [...]
the relations[...]
gravitational[...]
distance. Th[...]
versal becaus[...]
objects in th[...]

CONNECTION TO Biology

Seeds and Gravity Seeds respond to gravity. The ability to respond to gravity causes seeds to send roots down and the green shoot up. But scientists do not understand how seeds can sense gravity. Plan an experiment to study how seedlings respond to gravity. After getting your teacher's approval, do your experiment and report your observations in a poster.

ACTIVITY

Figure 2 Sir Isaac Newton realized that the same unbalanced force affected the motions of the apple and the moon.

Units of Weight and Mass

You have learned that the SI unit of force is a newton (N). Gravity is a force, and weight is a measure of gravity. So, weight is also measured in newtons. The SI unit of mass is the kilogram (kg). Mass is often measured in grams (g) and milligrams (mg) as well. On Earth, a 100 g object, such as the apple shown in **Figure 7**, weighs about 1 N.

When you use a bathroom scale, you are measuring the gravitational force between your body and Earth. So, you are measuring your weight, which should be given in newtons. However, many bathroom scales have units of pounds and kilograms instead of newtons. Thus, people sometimes mistakenly think that the kilogram (like the pound) is a unit of weight.

Figure 7 A small apple weighs approximately 1 N.

SECTION Review

Summary

- Gravity is a force of attraction between objects that is due to their masses.
- The law of universal gravitation states that all objects in the universe attract each other through gravitational force.
- Gravitational force increases as mass increases.
- Gravitational force decreases as distance increases.
- Weight and mass are not the same. Mass is the amount of matter in an object. Weight is a measure of the gravitational force on an object.

Using Key Terms

1. In your own words, write a definition for the term *gravity*.

2. Use each of the following terms in a separate sentence: *mass* and *weight*.

Understanding Key Ideas

3. If Earth's mass doubled without changing its size, your weight would
   a. increase because gravitational force increases.
   b. decrease because gravitational force increases.
   c. increase because gravitational force decreases.
   d. not change because you are still on Earth.

4. What is the law of universal gravitation?

5. How does the mass of an object relate to the gravitational force that the object exerts on other objects?

6. How does the distance between objects affect the gravitational force between them?

7. Why are mass and weight often confused?

Math Skills

8. The gravitational force on Jupiter is approximately 2.3 times the gravitational force on Earth. If an object has a mass of 70 kg and a weight of 686 N on Earth, what would the object's mass and weight on Jupiter be?

Critical Thinking

9. **Applying Concepts** Your friend thinks that there is no gravity in space. How could you explain to your friend that there must be gravity in space?

10. **Making Comparisons** Explain why it is your weight and not your mass that would change if you landed on Mars.

SciLINKS. NSTA *Developed and maintained by the National Science Teachers Association*

For a variety of links related to this chapter, go to www.scilinks.org

Topic: Matter and Gravity
SciLinks code: HSM0922

139

Use the Illustrations and Photos

Art shows complex ideas and processes. Learn to analyze the art so that you better understand the material you read in the text.

Tables and graphs display important information in an organized way to help you see relationships.

A picture is worth a thousand words. Look at the photographs to see relevant examples of science concepts that you are reading about.

Answer the Section Reviews

Section Reviews test your knowledge of the main points of the section. Critical Thinking items challenge you to think about the material in greater depth and to find connections that you infer from the text.

STUDY TIP When you can't answer a question, reread the section. The answer is usually there.

Do Your Homework

Your teacher may assign worksheets to help you understand and remember the material in the chapter.

STUDY TIP Don't try to answer the questions without reading the text and reviewing your class notes. A little preparation up front will make your homework assignments a lot easier. Answering the items in the Chapter Review will help prepare you for the chapter test.

Visit Holt Online Learning

If your teacher gives you a special password to log onto the **Holt Online Learning** site, you'll find your complete textbook on the Web. In addition, you'll find some great learning tools and practice quizzes. You'll be able to see how well you know the material from your textbook.

SAFETY FIRST!

Exploring, inventing, and investigating are essential to the study of science. However, these activities can also be dangerous. To make sure that your experiments and explorations are safe, you must be aware of a variety of safety guidelines. You have probably heard of the saying, "It is better to be safe than sorry." This is particularly true in a science classroom where experiments and explorations are being performed. Being uninformed and careless can result in serious injuries. Don't take chances with your own safety or with anyone else's.

The following pages describe important guidelines for staying safe in the science classroom. Your teacher may also have safety guidelines and tips that are specific to your classroom and laboratory. Take the time to be safe.

Safety Rules!

Start Out Right

Always get your teacher's permission before attempting any laboratory exploration. Read the procedures carefully, and pay particular attention to safety information and caution statements. If you are unsure about what a safety symbol means, look it up or ask your teacher. You cannot be too careful when it comes to safety. If an accident does occur, inform your teacher immediately regardless of how minor you think the accident is.

Safety Symbols

All of the experiments and investigations in this book and their related worksheets include important safety symbols to alert you to particular safety concerns. Become familiar with these symbols so that when you see them, you will know what they mean and what to do. It is important that you read this entire safety section to learn about specific dangers in the laboratory.

If you are instructed to note the odor of a substance, wave the fumes toward your nose with your hand. Never put your nose close to the source.

Eye protection

Clothing protection

Hand safety

Heating safety

Electric safety

Chemical safety

Animal safety

Sharp object

Plant safety

Eye Safety

Wear safety goggles when working around chemicals, acids, bases, or any type of flame or heating device. Wear safety goggles any time there is even the slightest chance that harm could come to your eyes. If any substance gets into your eyes, notify your teacher immediately and flush your eyes with running water for at least 15 minutes. Treat any unknown chemical as if it were a dangerous chemical. Never look directly into the sun. Doing so could cause permanent blindness.

Avoid wearing contact lenses in a laboratory situation. Even if you are wearing safety goggles, chemicals can get between the contact lenses and your eyes. If your doctor requires that you wear contact lenses instead of glasses, wear eye-cup safety goggles in the lab.

Safety Equipment

Know the locations of the nearest fire alarms and any other safety equipment, such as fire blankets and eyewash fountains, as identified by your teacher, and know the procedures for using the equipment.

Neatness

Keep your work area free of all unnecessary books and papers. Tie back long hair, and secure loose sleeves or other loose articles of clothing, such as ties and bows. Remove dangling jewelry. Don't wear open-toed shoes or sandals in the laboratory. Never eat, drink, or apply cosmetics in a laboratory setting. Food, drink, and cosmetics can easily become contaminated with dangerous materials.

Certain hair products (such as aerosol hair spray) are flammable and should not be worn while working near an open flame. Avoid wearing hair spray or hair gel on lab days.

Sharp/Pointed Objects

Use knives and other sharp instruments with extreme care. Never cut objects while holding them in your hands. Place objects on a suitable work surface for cutting.

Be extra careful when using any glassware. When adding a heavy object to a graduated cylinder, tilt the cylinder so that the object slides slowly to the bottom.

Heat

Wear safety goggles when using a heating device or a flame. Whenever possible, use an electric hot plate as a heat source instead of using an open flame. When heating materials in a test tube, always angle the test tube away from yourself and others. To avoid burns, wear heat-resistant gloves whenever instructed to do so.

Electricity

Be careful with electrical cords. When using a microscope with a lamp, do not place the cord where it could trip someone. Do not let cords hang over a table edge in a way that could cause equipment to fall if the cord is accidentally pulled. Do not use equipment with damaged cords. Be sure that your hands are dry and that the electrical equipment is in the "off" position before plugging it in. Turn off and unplug electrical equipment when you are finished.

Chemicals

Wear safety goggles when handling any potentially dangerous chemicals, acids, or bases. If a chemical is unknown, handle it as you would a dangerous chemical. Wear an apron and protective gloves when you work with acids or bases or whenever you are told to do so. If a spill gets on your skin or clothing, rinse it off immediately with water for at least 5 minutes while calling to your teacher.

Never mix chemicals unless your teacher tells you to do so. Never taste, touch, or smell chemicals unless you are specifically directed to do so. Before working with a flammable liquid or gas, check for the presence of any source of flame, spark, or heat.

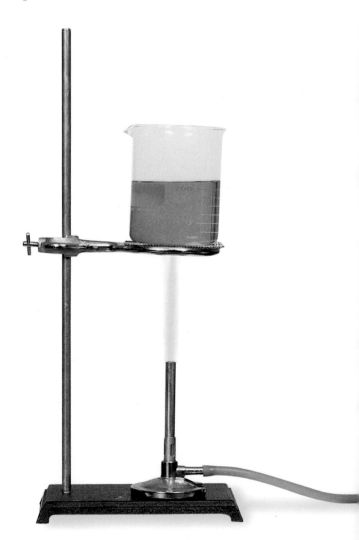

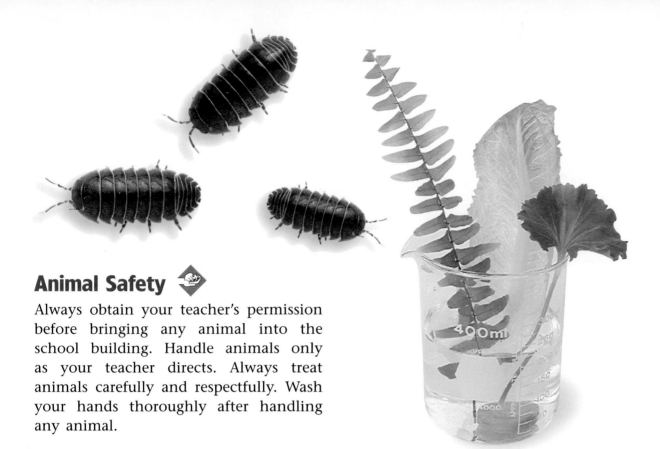

Animal Safety

Always obtain your teacher's permission before bringing any animal into the school building. Handle animals only as your teacher directs. Always treat animals carefully and respectfully. Wash your hands thoroughly after handling any animal.

Plant Safety

Do not eat any part of a plant or plant seed used in the laboratory. Wash your hands thoroughly after handling any part of a plant. When in nature, do not pick any wild plants unless your teacher instructs you to do so.

Glassware

Examine all glassware before use. Be sure that glassware is clean and free of chips and cracks. Report damaged glassware to your teacher. Glass containers used for heating should be made of heat-resistant glass.

1

Matter in Motion

The Big Idea
Forces act on objects and can produce motion.

About the PHOTO

Speed skaters are fast. In fact, some skaters can skate at a rate of 12 m/s! That's equal to a speed of 27 mi/h. To reach such a speed, skaters must exert large forces. They must also use friction to turn corners on the slippery surface of the ice.

PRE-READING ACTIVITY

FOLDNOTES **Four-Corner Fold**
Before you read the chapter, create the FoldNote entitled "Four-Corner Fold" described in the **Study Skills** section of the Appendix. Label the flaps of the four-corner fold with "Motion," "Forces," "Friction," and "Gravity." Write what you know about each topic under the appropriate flap. As you read the chapter, add other information that you learn.

The Domino Derby

Speed is the distance traveled by an object in a certain amount of time. In this activity, you will observe one factor that affects the speed of falling dominoes.

Procedure

1. Set up **25 dominoes** in a straight line. Try to keep equal spacing between the dominoes.

2. Use a **meterstick** to measure the total length of your row of dominoes, and record the length.

3. Use a **stopwatch** to time how long it takes for the dominoes to fall. Record this measurement.

4. Predict what would happen to that amount of time if you changed the distance between the dominoes. Write your predictions.

5. Repeat steps 2 and 3 several times using distances between the dominoes that are smaller and larger than the distance used in your first setup. Use the same number of dominoes in each trial.

Analysis

1. Calculate the average speed for each trial by dividing the total distance (the length of the domino row) by the time the dominoes take to fall.

2. How did the spacing between dominoes affect the average speed? Is this result what you expected? If not, explain.

Measuring Motion

Look around you—you are likely to see something in motion. Your teacher may be walking across the room, or perhaps your friend is writing with a pencil.

Even if you don't see anything moving, motion is still occurring all around you. Air particles are moving, the Earth is circling the sun, and blood is traveling through your blood vessels!

Observing Motion by Using a Reference Point

You might think that the motion of an object is easy to detect—you just watch the object. But you are actually watching the object in relation to another object that appears to stay in place. The object that appears to stay in place is a *reference point*. When an object changes position over time relative to a reference point, the object is in **motion**. You can describe the direction of the object's motion with a reference direction, such as north, south, east, west, up, or down.

✔ **Reading Check** What is a reference point? (*See the Appendix for answers to Reading Checks.*)

Common Reference Points

The Earth's surface is a common reference point for determining motion, as shown in **Figure 1.** Nonmoving objects, such as trees and buildings, are also useful reference points.

A moving object can also be used as a reference point. For example, if you were on the hot-air balloon shown in **Figure 1,** you could watch a bird fly by and see that the bird was changing position in relation to your moving balloon.

What You Will Learn

- Describe the motion of an object by the position of the object in relation to a reference point.
- Identify the two factors that determine speed.
- Explain the difference between speed and velocity.
- Analyze the relationship between velocity and acceleration.
- Demonstrate that changes in motion can be measured and represented on a graph.

Vocabulary

motion   velocity
speed   acceleration

READING STRATEGY

Discussion Read this section silently. Write down questions that you have about this section. Discuss your questions in a small group.

Figure 1 *During the interval between the times that these pictures were taken, the hot-air balloon changed position relative to a reference point—the mountain.*

Speed Depends on Distance and Time

Speed is the distance traveled by an object divided by the time taken to travel that distance. Look again at **Figure 1**. Suppose the time interval between the pictures was 10 s and that the balloon traveled 50 m in that time. The speed of the balloon is (50 m)/(10 s), or 5 m/s.

The SI unit for speed is meters per second (m/s). Kilometers per hour (km/h), feet per second (ft/s), and miles per hour (mi/h) are other units commonly used to express speed.

Determining Average Speed

Most of the time, objects do not travel at a constant speed. For example, you probably do not walk at a constant speed from one class to the next. So, it is very useful to calculate *average speed* using the following equation:

$$average\ speed = \frac{total\ distance}{total\ time}$$

Recognizing Speed on a Graph

Suppose a person drives from one city to another. The blue line in the graph in **Figure 2** shows the total distance traveled during a 4 h period. Notice that the distance traveled during each hour is different. The distance varies because the speed is not constant. The driver may change speed because of weather, traffic, or varying speed limits. The average speed for the entire trip can be calculated as follows:

$$average\ speed = \frac{360\ km}{4\ h} = 90\ km/h$$

The red line on the graph shows how far the driver must travel each hour to reach the same city if he or she moved at a constant speed. The slope of this line is the average speed.

motion an object's change in position relative to a reference point

speed the distance traveled divided by the time interval during which the motion occurred

What's Your Speed?

Measure a distance of 5 m or a distance of 25 ft inside or outside. Ask a family member to use a stopwatch or a watch with a second hand to time you as you travel the distance you measured. Then, find your average speed. Find the average speed of other members of your family in the same way.

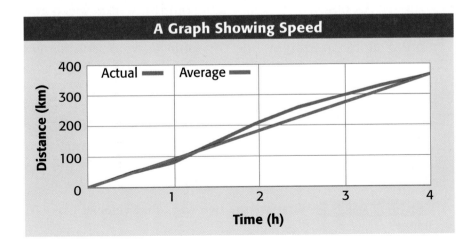

A Graph Showing Speed

Figure 2 *Speed can be shown on a graph of distance versus time.*

Calculating Average Speed   An athlete swims a distance from one end of a 50 m pool to the other end in a time of 25 s. What is the athlete's average speed?

Step 1: Write the equation for average speed.

$$average\ speed = \frac{total\ distance}{total\ time}$$

Step 2: Replace the total distance and total time with the values given, and solve.

$$average\ speed = \frac{50\ m}{25\ s} = 2\ m/s$$

Now It's Your Turn

1. Kira jogs to a store 72 m away in a time of 36 s. What is Kira's average speed?
2. If you travel 7.5 km and walk for 1.5 h, what is your average speed?
3. An airplane traveling from San Francisco to Chicago travels 1,260 km in 3.5 h. What is the airplane's average speed?

Velocity: Direction Matters

Imagine that two birds leave the same tree at the same time. They both fly at 10 km/h for 5 min, 12 km/h for 8 min, and 5 km/h for 10 min. Why don't they end up at the same place?

Have you figured out the answer? The birds went in different directions. Their speeds were the same, but they had different velocities. **Velocity** (vuh LAHS uh tee) is the speed of an object in a particular direction.

Be careful not to confuse the terms *speed* and *velocity*. They do not have the same meaning. Velocity must include a reference direction. If you say that an airplane's velocity is 600 km/h, you would not be correct. But you could say the plane's velocity is 600 km/h south. **Figure 3** shows an example of the difference between speed and velocity.

Changing Velocity

You can think of velocity as the rate of change of an object's position. An object's velocity is constant only if its speed and direction don't change. Therefore, constant velocity is always motion along a straight line. An object's velocity changes if either its speed or direction changes. For example, as a bus traveling at 15 m/s south speeds up to 20 m/s south, its velocity changes. If the bus continues to travel at the same speed but changes direction to travel east, its velocity changes again. And if the bus slows down at the same time that it swerves north to avoid a cat, the velocity of the bus changes, too.

Reading Check   What are the two ways that velocity can change?

Figure 3 *The speeds of these cars may be similar, but the velocities of the cars differ because the cars are going in different directions.*

Figure 4 **Finding Resultant Velocity**

When you combine two velocities that are **in the same direction,** add them together to find the resultant velocity.

Person's resultant velocity
15 m/s east + 1 m/s east = 16 m/s east

When you combine two velocities that are **in opposite directions,** subtract the smaller velocity from the larger velocity to find the resultant velocity. The resultant velocity is in the direction of the larger velocity.

Combining Velocities

Imagine that you are riding in a bus that is traveling east at 15 m/s. You and the other passengers are also traveling at a velocity of 15 m/s east. But suppose you stand up and walk down the bus's aisle while the bus is moving. Are you still moving at the same velocity as the bus? No! **Figure 4** shows how you can combine velocities to find the *resultant velocity.*

Acceleration

Although the word *accelerate* is commonly used to mean "speed up," the word means something else in science. **Acceleration** (ak SEL uhr AY shuhn) is the rate at which velocity changes. Velocity changes if speed changes, if direction changes, or if both change. So, an object accelerates if its speed, its direction, or both change.

An increase in velocity is commonly called *positive acceleration.* A decrease in velocity is commonly called *negative acceleration,* or *deceleration.* Keep in mind that acceleration is not only how much velocity changes but also how fast velocity changes. The faster the velocity changes, the greater the acceleration is.

velocity the speed of an object in a particular direction

acceleration the rate at which velocity changes over time; an object accelerates if its speed, direction, or both change

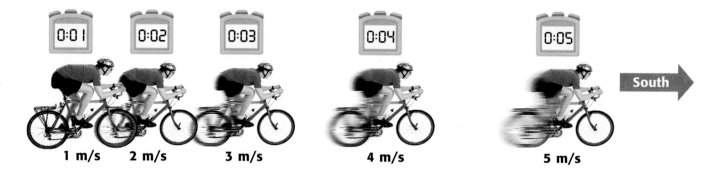

0:01   0:02   0:03   0:04   0:05

South

1 m/s   **2 m/s**   **3 m/s**   **4 m/s**   **5 m/s**

Figure 5 *This cyclist is accelerating at 1 m/s² south.*

Calculating Average Acceleration

You can find average acceleration by using the equation:

$$average\ acceleration = \frac{final\ velocity - starting\ velocity}{time\ it\ takes\ to\ change\ velocity}$$

Velocity is expressed in meters per second (m/s), and time is expressed in seconds (s). So acceleration is expressed in meters per second per second, or (m/s)/s, which equals m/s². For example, look at **Figure 5.** Every second, the cyclist's southward velocity increases by 1 m/s. His average acceleration can be calculated as follows:

$$average\ acceleration = \frac{5\ m/s - 1\ m/s}{4\ s} = 1\ m/s^2\ south$$

✓ **Reading Check** What are the units of acceleration?

Recognizing Acceleration on a Graph

Suppose that you are riding a roller coaster. The roller-coaster car moves up a hill until it stops at the top. Then, you are off! The graph in **Figure 6** shows your acceleration for the next 10 s. During the first 8 s, you move down the hill. You can tell from the graph that your acceleration is positive for the first 8 s because your velocity increases as time passes. During the last 2 s, your car starts climbing the next hill. Your acceleration is negative because your velocity decreases as time passes.

MATH PRACTICE

Calculating Acceleration

Use the equation for average acceleration to do the following problem.

A plane passes over point A at a velocity of 240 m/s north. Forty seconds later, it passes over point B at a velocity of 260 m/s north. What is the plane's average acceleration?

Figure 6 *Acceleration can be shown on a graph of velocity versus time.*

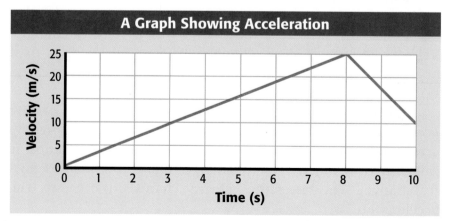

A Graph Showing Acceleration

Circular Motion: Continuous Acceleration

You may be surprised to know that even when you are completely still, you are experiencing acceleration. You may not seem to be changing speed or direction, but you are! You are traveling in a circle as the Earth rotates. An object traveling in a circular motion is always changing its direction. Therefore, its velocity is always changing, so it is accelerating. The acceleration that occurs in circular motion is known as *centripetal acceleration* (sen TRIP uht uhl ak SEL uhr AY shuhn). Centripetal acceleration occurs on a Ferris wheel at an amusement park or as the moon orbits Earth. Another example of centripetal acceleration is shown in **Figure 7.**

Figure 7 *The blades of these windmills are constantly changing direction. Thus, centripetal acceleration is occurring.*

SECTION Review

Summary

- An object is in motion if it changes position over time in relation to a reference point.
- Speed is the distance traveled by an object divided by the time the object takes to travel that distance.
- Velocity is speed in a given direction.
- Acceleration is the rate at which velocity changes.
- An object can accelerate by changing speed, direction, or both.
- Speed can be represented on a graph of distance versus time.
- Acceleration can be represented by graphing velocity versus time.

Using Key Terms

1. In your own words, write definitions for each of the following terms: *motion* and *acceleration*.

2. Use each of the following terms in a separate sentence: *speed* and *velocity*.

Understanding Key Ideas

3. Which of the following is NOT an example of acceleration?
   a. a person jogging at 3 m/s along a winding path
   b. a car stopping at a stop sign
   c. a cheetah running 27 m/s east
   d. a plane taking off

4. Which of the following would be a good reference point to describe the motion of a dog?
   a. the ground
   b. another dog running
   c. a tree
   d. All of the above

5. Explain the difference between speed and velocity.

6. What two things must you know to determine speed?

7. How are velocity and acceleration related?

Math Skills

8. Find the average speed of a person who swims 105 m in 70 s.

9. What is the average acceleration of a subway train that speeds up from 9.6 m/s to 12 m/s in 0.8 s on a straight section of track?

Critical Thinking

10. **Applying Concepts** Why is it more helpful to know a tornado's velocity rather than its speed?

11. **Evaluating Data** A wolf is chasing a rabbit. Graph the wolf's motion using the following data: 15 m/s at 0 s, 10 m/s at 1 s, 5 m/s at 2 s, 2.5 m/s at 3 s, 1 m/s at 4 s, and 0 m/s at 5 s. What does the graph tell you?

9

What Is a Force?

You have probably heard the word **force** in everyday conversation. People say things such as "That storm had a lot of force" or "Our football team is a force to be reckoned with." But what, exactly, is a force?

In science, a **force** is simply a push or a pull. All forces have both size and direction. A force can change the acceleration of an object. This acceleration can be a change in the speed or direction of the object. In fact, any time you see a change in an object's motion, you can be sure that the change in motion was created by a force. Scientists express force using a unit called the **newton** (N).

Forces Acting on Objects

All forces act on objects. For any push to occur, something has to receive the push. You can't push nothing! The same is true for any pull. When doing schoolwork, you use your fingers to pull open books or to push the buttons on a computer keyboard. In these examples, your fingers are exerting forces on the books and the keys. So, the forces act on the books and keys. Another example of a force acting on an object is shown in **Figure 1.**

However, just because a force acts on an object doesn't mean that motion will occur. For example, you are probably sitting on a chair. But the force you are exerting on the chair does not cause the chair to move. The chair doesn't move because the floor is also exerting a force on the chair.

What You Will Learn

● Describe forces, and explain how forces act on objects.
● Determine the net force when more than one force is acting on an object.
● Compare balanced and unbalanced forces.
● Describe ways that unbalanced forces cause changes in motion.

Vocabulary

force
newton
net force

READING STRATEGY

Reading Organizer As you read this section, make a table comparing balanced forces and unbalanced forces.

Figure 1 *The bulldozer is exerting a force on the pile of soil. But the pile of soil also exerts a force by just sitting on the ground!*

Unseen Sources and Receivers of Forces

It is not always easy to tell what is exerting a force or what is receiving a force, as shown in **Figure 2.** You cannot see what exerts the force that pulls magnets to refrigerators. And you cannot see that the air around you is held near Earth's surface by a force called *gravity.*

Determining Net Force

Usually, more than one force is acting on an object. The **net force** is the combination all of the forces acting on an object. So, how do you determine the net force? The answer depends on the directions of the forces.

Forces in the Same Direction

Suppose the music teacher asks you and a friend to move a piano. You pull on one end and your friend pushes on the other end, as shown in **Figure 3.** The forces you and your friend exert on the piano act in the same direction. The two forces are added to determine the net force because the forces act in the same direction. In this case, the net force is 45 N. This net force is large enough to move the piano—if it is on wheels, that is!

✓ Reading Check How do you determine the net force on an object if all forces act in the same direction? (*See the Appendix for answers to Reading Checks.*)

Figure 2 *Something that you cannot see exerts a force that makes this cat's fur stand up.*

force a push or a pull exerted on an object in order to change the motion of the object; force has size and direction

newton the SI unit for force (symbol, N)

net force the combination of all of the forces acting on an object

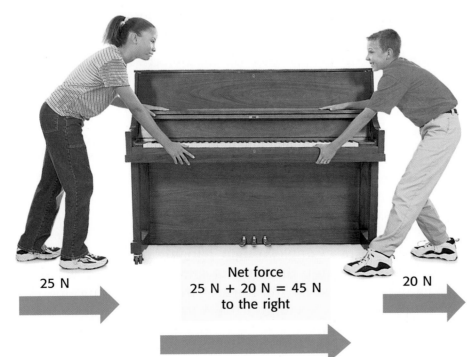

25 N

Net force
25 N + 20 N = 45 N
to the right

20 N

Figure 3 *When forces act in the same direction, you add the forces to determine the net force. The net force will be in the same direction as the individual forces.*

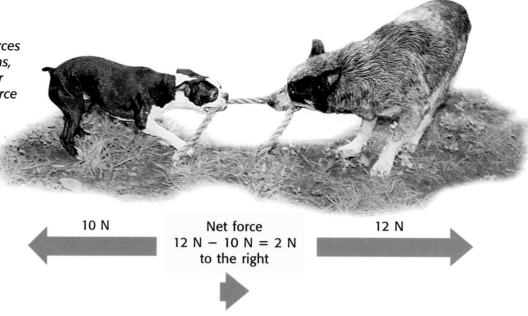

Figure 4 *When two forces act in opposite directions, you subtract the smaller force from the larger force to determine the net force. The net force will be in the same direction as the larger force.*

10 N

Net force
12 N − 10 N = 2 N
to the right

12 N

Forces in Different Directions

Look at the two dogs playing tug of war in **Figure 4.** Each dog is exerting a force on the rope. But the forces are in opposite directions. Which dog will win the tug of war?

Because the forces are in opposite directions, the net force on the rope is found by subtracting the smaller force from the larger one. In this case, the net force is 2 N in the direction of the dog on the right. Give that dog a dog biscuit!

✓ Reading Check What is the net force on an object when you combine a force of 7 N north with a force of 5 N south?

Balanced and Unbalanced Forces

If you know the net force on an object, you can determine the effect of the net force on the object's motion. Why? The net force tells you whether the forces on the object are balanced or unbalanced.

Balanced Forces

When the forces on an object produce a net force of 0 N, the forces are *balanced*. Balanced forces will not cause a change in the motion of a moving object. And balanced forces do not cause a nonmoving object to start moving.

Many objects around you have only balanced forces acting on them. For example, a light hanging from the ceiling does not move because the force of gravity pulling down on the light is balanced by the force of the cord pulling upward. A bird's nest in a tree and a hat resting on your head are also examples of objects that have only balanced forces acting on them. **Figure 5** shows another example of balanced forces.

Figure 5 *Because all the forces on this house of cards are balanced, none of the cards move.*

Unbalanced Forces

When the net force on an object is not 0 N, the forces on the object are *unbalanced*. Unbalanced forces produce a change in motion, such as a change in speed or a change in direction. Unbalanced forces are necessary to cause a nonmoving object to start moving.

Unbalanced forces are also necessary to change the motion of moving objects. For example, consider the soccer game shown in **Figure 6.** The soccer ball is already moving when it is passed from one player to another. When the ball reaches another player, that player exerts an unbalanced force—a kick—on the ball. After the kick, the ball moves in a new direction and has a new speed.

An object can continue to move when the unbalanced forces are removed. For example, when it is kicked, a soccer ball receives an unbalanced force. The ball continues to roll on the ground long after the force of the kick has ended.

Figure 6 *The soccer ball moves because the players exert an unbalanced force on the ball each time they kick it.*

SECTION Review

Summary

- A force is a push or a pull. Forces have size and direction and are expressed in newtons.
- Force is always exerted by one object on another object.
- Net force is determined by combining forces. Forces in the same direction are added. Forces in opposite directions are subtracted.
- Balanced forces produce no change in motion. Unbalanced forces produce a change in motion.

Using Key Terms

1. In your own words, write a definition for each of the following terms: *force* and *net force*.

Understanding Key Ideas

2. Which of the following may happen when an object receives unbalanced forces?
   a. The object changes direction.
   b. The object changes speed.
   c. The object starts to move.
   d. All of the above

3. Explain the difference between balanced and unbalanced forces.

4. Give an example of an unbalanced force causing a change in motion.

5. Give an example of an object that has balanced forces acting on it.

6. Explain the meaning of the phrase "Forces act on objects."

Math Skills

7. A boy pulls a wagon with a force of 6 N east as another boy pushes it with a force of 4 N east. What is the net force?

Critical Thinking

8. **Making Inferences** When finding net force, why must you know the directions of the forces acting on an object?

9. **Applying Concepts** List three forces that you exert when riding a bicycle.

For a variety of links related to this chapter, go to www.scilinks.org

Topic: Forces
SciLinks code: HSM0604

Friction: A Force That Opposes Motion

While playing ball, your friend throws the ball out of your reach. Rather than running for the ball, you walk after it. You know that the ball will stop. But do you know why?

You know that the ball is slowing down. An unbalanced force is needed to change the speed of a moving object. So, what force is stopping the ball? The force is called friction. **Friction** is a force that opposes motion between two surfaces that are in contact. Friction can cause a moving object, such as a ball, to slow down and eventually stop.

The Source of Friction

Friction occurs because the surface of any object is rough. Even surfaces that feel smooth are covered with microscopic hills and valleys. When two surfaces are in contact, the hills and valleys of one surface stick to the hills and valleys of the other surface, as shown in **Figure 1.** This contact causes friction.

The amount of friction between two surfaces depends on many factors. Two factors include the force pushing the surfaces together and the roughness of the surfaces.

The Effect of Force on Friction

The amount of friction depends on the force pushing the surfaces together. If this force increases, the hills and valleys of the surfaces can come into closer contact. The close contact increases the friction between the surfaces. Objects that weigh less exert less downward force than objects that weigh more do, as shown in **Figure 2.** But changing how much of the surfaces come in contact does not change the amount of friction.

What You Will Learn

● Explain why friction occurs.
● List the two types of friction, and give examples of each type.
● Explain how friction can be both harmful and helpful.

Vocabulary
friction

READING STRATEGY

Brainstorming The key idea of this section is friction. Brainstorm words and phrases related to friction.

friction a force that opposes motion between two surfaces that are in contact

Figure 1 *When the hills and valleys of one surface stick to the hills and valleys of another surface, friction is created.*

Figure 2 **Force and Friction**

ⓐ There is more friction between the book with more weight and the table than there is between the book with less weight and the table. A harder push is needed to move the heavier book.

ⓑ Turning a book on its edge does not change the amount of friction between the table and the book.

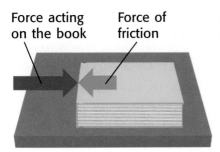

Force acting on the book   Force of friction

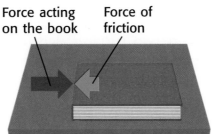

Force acting on the book   Force of friction

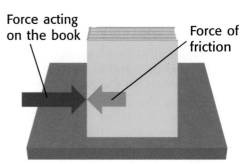

Force acting on the book   Force of friction

The Effect of Rougher Surfaces on Friction

Rough surfaces have more microscopic hills and valleys than smooth surfaces do. So, the rougher the surface is, the greater the friction is. For example, a ball rolling on the ground slows down because of the friction between the ball and the ground. A large amount of friction is produced because the ground has a rough surface. But imagine that you were playing ice hockey. If the puck passed out of your reach, it would slide across the ice for a long while before stopping. The reason the puck would continue to slide is that the ice is a smooth surface that has very little friction.

✓ **Reading Check** **Why is friction greater between surfaces that are rough?** (*See the Appendix for answers to Reading Checks.*)

The Friction 500

1. Make a short ramp out of **a piece of cardboard** and **one or two books** on a table.

2. Put a **toy car** at the top of the ramp, and let go of the car. If necessary, adjust the ramp height so that your car does not roll off the table.

3. Put the car at the top of the ramp again, and let go of the car. Record the distance the car travels after leaving the ramp.

4. Repeat step 3 two more times, and calculate the average for your results.

5. Change the surface of the table by covering the table with **sandpaper.** Repeat steps 3 and 4.

6. Change the surface of the table one more time by covering the table with **cloth.** Repeat steps 3 and 4 again.

7. Which surface had the most friction? Why? What do you predict would happen if the car were heavier?

Types of Friction

There are two types of friction. The friction you observe when sliding books across a tabletop is called *kinetic friction*. The other type of friction is *static friction*. You observe static friction when you push on a piece of furniture and it does not move.

Kinetic Friction

The word *kinetic* means "moving." So, kinetic friction is friction between moving surfaces. The amount of kinetic friction between two surfaces depends in part on how the surfaces move. Surfaces can slide past each other. Or a surface can roll over another surface. Usually, the force of sliding kinetic friction is greater than the force of rolling kinetic friction. Thus, it is usually easier to move objects on wheels than to slide the objects along the floor, as shown in **Figure 3.**

Kinetic friction is very useful in everyday life. You use sliding kinetic friction when you apply the brakes on a bicycle and when you write with a pencil or a piece of chalk. You also use sliding kinetic friction when you scratch a part of your body that is itchy!

Rolling kinetic friction is an important part of almost all means of transportation. Anything that has wheels—bicycles, in-line skates, cars, trains, and planes—uses rolling kinetic friction.

Figure 3 Comparing Kinetic Friction

ⓐ Moving a heavy piece of furniture in your room can be hard work because **the force of sliding kinetic friction is large.**

ⓑ Moving a heavy piece of furniture is easier if you put it on wheels. **The force of rolling kinetic friction is smaller** and easier to overcome.

Figure 4   Static Friction

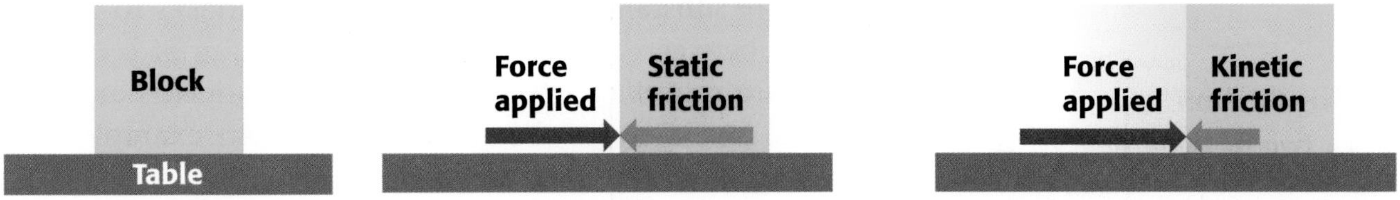

Block
Table

a There is no friction between the block and the table when no force is applied to the block.

Force applied   **Static friction**

b If a small force (purple arrow) is exerted on the block, the block does not move. The force of static friction (green arrow) balances the force applied.

Force applied   **Kinetic friction**

c When the force exerted on the block is greater than the force of static friction, the block starts moving. When the block starts moving, all static friction is gone, and only kinetic friction (green arrow) opposes the force applied.

Static Friction

When a force is applied to an object but does not cause the object to move, *static friction* occurs. The word *static* means "not moving." The object does not move because the force of static friction balances the force applied. Static friction can be overcome by applying a large enough force. Static friction disappears as soon as an object starts moving, and then kinetic friction immediately occurs. Look at **Figure 4** to understand under what conditions static friction affects an object.

✓ *Reading Check*   What does the word *static* mean?

Friction: Harmful and Helpful

Think about how friction affects a car. Without friction, the tires could not push against the ground to move the car forward, and the brakes could not stop the car. Without friction, a car is useless. However, friction can also cause problems in a car. Friction between moving engine parts increases their temperature and causes the parts to wear down. A liquid coolant is added to the engine to keep the engine from overheating. And engine parts need to be changed as they wear out.

Friction is both harmful and helpful to you and the world around you. Friction can cause holes in your socks and in the knees of your jeans. Friction by wind and water can cause erosion of the topsoil that nourishes plants. On the other hand, friction between your pencil and your paper is necessary to allow the pencil to leave a mark. Without friction, you would just slip and fall when you tried to walk. Because friction can be both harmful and helpful, it is sometimes necessary to decrease or increase friction.

INTERNET ACTIVITY

For another activity related to this chapter, go to **go.hrw.com** and type in the keyword **HP5MOTW**.

CONNECTION TO Social Studies

WRITING SKILL   **Invention of the Wheel** Archeologists have found evidence that the first vehicles with wheels were used in ancient Mesopotamia sometime between 3500 and 3000 BCE. Before wheels were invented, people used planks or sleds to carry loads. In your **science journal,** write a paragraph about how your life would be different if wheels did not exist.

Section 3   Friction: A Force That Opposes Motion   **17**

Some Ways to Reduce Friction

One way to reduce friction is to use lubricants (LOO bri kuhnts). *Lubricants* are substances that are applied to surfaces to reduce the friction between the surfaces. Some examples of common lubricants are motor oil, wax, and grease. Lubricants are usually liquids, but they can be solids or gases. An example of a gas lubricant is the air that comes out of the tiny holes of an air-hockey table. **Figure 5** shows one use of a lubricant.

Friction can also be reduced by switching from sliding kinetic friction to rolling kinetic friction. Ball bearings placed between the wheels and axles of in-line skates and bicycles make it easier for the wheels to turn by reducing friction.

Another way to reduce friction is to make surfaces that rub against each other smoother. For example, rough wood on a park bench is painful to slide across because there is a large amount of friction between your leg and the bench. Rubbing the bench with sandpaper makes the bench smoother and more comfortable to sit on. The reason the bench is more comfortable is that the friction between your leg and the bench is reduced.

Reading Check List three common lubricants.

Figure 5 *When you work on a bicycle, watch out for the chain! You might get dirty from the grease or oil that keeps the chain moving freely. Without this lubricant, friction between the sections of the chain would quickly wear the chain out.*

Some Ways to Increase Friction

One way to increase friction is to make surfaces rougher. For example, sand scattered on icy roads keeps cars from skidding. Baseball players sometimes wear textured batting gloves to increase the friction between their hands and the bat so that the bat does not fly out of their hands.

Another way to increase friction is to increase the force pushing the surfaces together. For example, if you are sanding a piece of wood, you can sand the wood faster by pressing harder on the sandpaper. Pressing harder increases the force pushing the sandpaper and wood together. So, the friction between the sandpaper and wood increases. **Figure 6** shows another example of friction increased by pushing on an object.

Figure 6 *No one likes cleaning dirty pans. To get this chore done quickly, press down with the scrubber to increase friction.*

SECTION Review

Summary

- Friction is a force that opposes motion.
- Friction is caused by hills and valleys on the surfaces of two objects touching each other.
- The amount of friction depends on factors such as the roughness of the surfaces and the force pushing the surfaces together.
- Two kinds of friction are kinetic friction and static friction.
- Friction can be helpful or harmful.

Using Key Terms

1. In your own words, write a definition for the term *friction*.

Understanding Key Ideas

2. Why is it easy to slip when there is water on the floor?
   a. The water is a lubricant and reduces the friction between your feet and the floor.
   b. The friction between your feet and the floor changes from kinetic to static friction.
   c. The water increases the friction between your feet and the floor.
   d. The friction between your feet and the floor changes from sliding kinetic friction to rolling kinetic friction.

3. Explain why friction occurs.

4. How does the roughness of surfaces that are touching affect the friction between the surfaces?

5. Describe how the amount of force pushing two surfaces together affects friction.

6. Name two ways in which friction can be increased.

7. List the two types of friction, and give an example of each.

Interpreting Graphics

8. Why do you think the sponge shown below has a layer of plastic bristles attached to it?

Critical Thinking

9. **Applying Concepts** Name two ways that friction is harmful and two ways that friction is helpful to you when riding a bicycle.

10. **Making Inferences** Describe a situation in which static friction is useful.

SCiLINKS®

NSTA
Developed and maintained by the National Science Teachers Association

For a variety of links related to this chapter, go to www.scilinks.org

Topic: Force and Friction
SciLinks code: HSM0601

Gravity: A Force of Attraction

gravity a force of attraction between objects that is due to their masses

Have you ever seen a video of astronauts on the moon? They bounce around like beach balls even though they wear big, bulky spacesuits. Why is leaping on the moon easier than leaping on Earth?

The answer is gravity. **Gravity** is a force of attraction between objects that is due to their masses. The force of gravity can change the motion of an object by changing its speed, direction, or both. In this section, you will learn about gravity and its effects on objects, such as the astronaut in **Figure 1.**

The Effects of Gravity on Matter

All matter has mass. Gravity is a result of mass. Therefore, all matter is affected by gravity. That is, all objects experience an attraction toward all other objects. This gravitational force pulls objects toward each other. Right now, because of gravity, you are being pulled toward this book, your pencil, and every other object around you.

These objects are also being pulled toward you and toward each other because of gravity. So why don't you see the effects of this attraction? In other words, why don't you notice objects moving toward each other? The reason is that the mass of most objects is too small to cause a force large enough to move objects toward each other. However, you are familiar with one object that is massive enough to cause a noticeable attraction—the Earth.

Figure 1 *Because the moon has less gravity than the Earth does, walking on the moon's surface was a very bouncy experience for the Apollo astronauts.*

The Size of Earth's Gravitational Force

Compared with all objects around you, Earth has a huge mass. Therefore, Earth's gravitational force is very large. You must apply forces to overcome Earth's gravitational force any time you lift objects or even parts of your body.

Earth's gravitational force pulls everything toward the center of Earth. Because of this force, the books, tables, and chairs in the room stay in place, and dropped objects fall to Earth rather than moving together or toward you.

✓ Reading Check **Why must you exert a force to pick up an object?** (*See the Appendix for answers to Reading Checks.*)

Newton and the Study of Gravity

For thousands of years, people asked two very puzzling questions: Why do objects fall toward Earth, and what keeps the planets moving in the sky? The two questions were treated separately until 1665 when a British scientist named Sir Isaac Newton realized that they were two parts of the same question.

The Core of an Idea

The legend is that Newton made the connection between the two questions when he watched a falling apple, as shown in **Figure 2.** He knew that unbalanced forces are needed to change the motion of objects. He concluded that an unbalanced force on the apple made the apple fall. And he reasoned that an unbalanced force on the moon kept the moon moving circularly around Earth. He proposed that these two forces are actually the same force—a force of attraction called *gravity*.

The Birth of a Law

Newton summarized his ideas about gravity in a law now known as the *law of universal gravitation*. This law describes the relationships between gravitational force, mass, and distance. The law is called *universal* because it applies to all objects in the universe.

Figure 2 *Sir Isaac Newton realized that the same unbalanced force affected the motions of the apple and the moon.*

The Law of Universal Gravitation

The law of universal gravitation is the following: All objects in the universe attract each other through gravitational force. The size of the force depends on the masses of the objects and the distance between the objects. Understanding the law is easier if you consider it in two parts.

Part 1: Gravitational Force Increases as Mass Increases

Imagine an elephant and a cat. Because an elephant has a larger mass than a cat does, the amount of gravity between an elephant and Earth is greater than the amount of gravity between a cat and Earth. So, a cat is much easier to pick up than an elephant! There is also gravity between the cat and the elephant, but that force is very small because the cat's mass and the elephant's mass are so much smaller than Earth's mass. **Figure 3** shows the relationship between mass and gravitational force.

This part of the law of universal gravitation also explains why the astronauts on the moon bounce when they walk. The moon has less mass than Earth does. Therefore, the moon's gravitational force is less than Earth's. The astronauts bounced around on the moon because they were not being pulled down with as much force as they would have been on Earth.

✔ **Reading Check** How does mass affect gravitational force?

CONNECTION TO Astronomy

WRITING SKILL **Black Holes** Black holes are 4 times to 1 billion times as massive as our sun. So, the gravitational effects around a black hole are very large. The gravitational force of a black hole is so large that objects that enter a black hole can never get out. Even light cannot escape from a black hole. Because black holes do not emit light, they cannot be seen. Research how astronomers can detect black holes without seeing them. Write a one-page paper that details the results of your research.

Figure 3 **How Mass Affects Gravitational Force**

The gravitational force between objects increases as the masses of the objects increase. The arrows indicate the gravitational force between two objects. The length of the arrows indicates the strength of the force.

ⓐ Gravitational force is small between objects that have small masses.

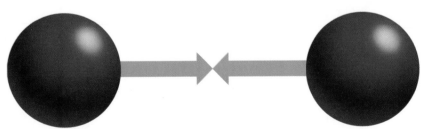

ⓑ Gravitational force is large when the mass of one or both objects is large.

Part 2: Gravitational Force Decreases as Distance Increases

The gravitational force between you and Earth is large. Whenever you jump up, you are pulled back down by Earth's gravitational force. On the other hand, the sun is more than 300,000 times more massive than Earth. So why doesn't the sun's gravitational force affect you more than Earth's does? The reason is that the sun is so far away.

You are about 150 million kilometers (93 million miles) away from the sun. At this distance, the gravitational force between you and the sun is very small. If there were some way you could stand on the sun, you would find it impossible to move. The gravitational force acting on you would be so great that you could not move any part of your body!

Although the sun's gravitational force on your body is very small, the force is very large on Earth and the other planets, as shown in **Figure 4.** The gravity between the sun and the planets is large because the objects have large masses. If the sun's gravitational force did not have such an effect on the planets, the planets would not stay in orbit around the sun. **Figure 5** will help you understand the relationship between gravitational force and distance.

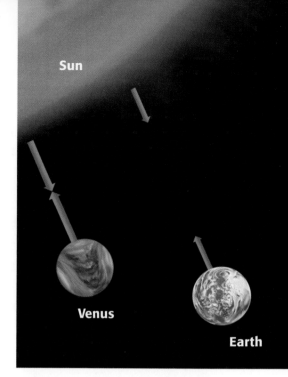

Figure 4 *Venus and Earth have approximately the same mass. But because Venus is closer to the sun, the gravitational force between Venus and the sun is greater than the gravitational force between Earth and the sun.*

Figure 5 **How Distance Affects Gravitational Force**

The gravitational force between objects decreases as the distance between the objects increases. The length of the arrows indicates the strength of the gravitational force between two objects.

ⓐ Gravitational force is strong when the distance between two objects is small.

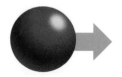 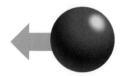

ⓑ If the distance between two objects increases, the gravitational force pulling them together decreases rapidly.

weight a measure of the gravitational force exerted on an object; its value can change with the location of the object in the universe

mass a measure of the amount of matter in an object

Weight as a Measure of Gravitational Force

Gravity is a force of attraction between objects. **Weight** is a measure of the gravitational force on an object. When you see or hear the word *weight*, it usually refers to Earth's gravitational force on an object. But weight can also be a measure of the gravitational force exerted on objects by the moon or other planets.

The Differences Between Weight and Mass

Weight is related to mass, but they are not the same. Weight changes when gravitational force changes. **Mass** is the amount of matter in an object. An object's mass does not change. Imagine that an object is moved to a place that has a greater gravitational force—such as the planet Jupiter. The object's weight will increase, but its mass will remain the same. **Figure 6** shows the weight and mass of an astronaut on Earth and on the moon. The moon's gravitational force is about one-sixth of Earth's gravitational force.

Gravitational force is about the same everywhere on Earth. So, the weight of any object is about the same everywhere. Because mass and weight are constant on Earth, the terms *weight* and *mass* are often used to mean the same thing. This can be confusing. Be sure you understand the difference!

✓ **Reading Check** How is gravitational force related to the weight of an object?

Figure 6 *The astronaut's weight on the moon is about one-sixth of his weight on Earth, but his mass remains constant.*

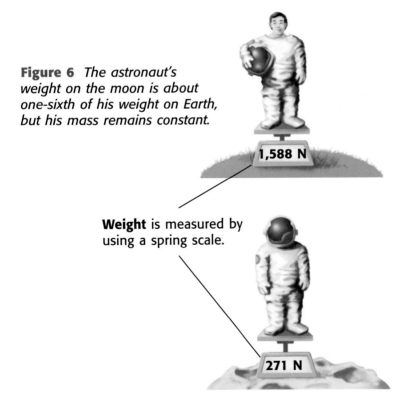

Weight is measured by using a spring scale.

1,588 N

271 N

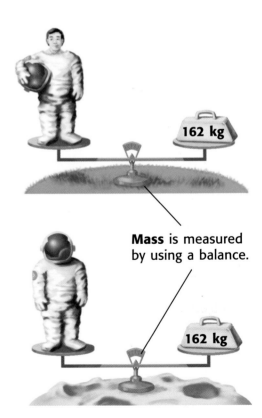

162 kg

Mass is measured by using a balance.

162 kg

Units of Weight and Mass

You have learned that the SI unit of force is a newton (N). Gravity is a force, and weight is a measure of gravity. So, weight is also measured in newtons. The SI unit of mass is the kilogram (kg). Mass is often measured in grams (g) and milligrams (mg) as well. On Earth, a 100 g object, such as the apple shown in **Figure 7,** weighs about 1 N.

When you use a bathroom scale, you are measuring the gravitational force between your body and Earth. So, you are measuring your weight, which should be given in newtons. However, many bathroom scales have units of pounds and kilograms instead of newtons. Thus, people sometimes mistakenly think that the kilogram (like the pound) is a unit of weight.

Figure 7 *A small apple weighs approximately 1 N.*

SECTION Review

Summary

- Gravity is a force of attraction between objects that is due to their masses.

- The law of universal gravitation states that all objects in the universe attract each other through gravitational force.

- Gravitational force increases as mass increases.

- Gravitational force decreases as distance increases.

- Weight and mass are not the same. Mass is the amount of matter in an object. Weight is a measure of the gravitational force on an object.

Using Key Terms

1. In your own words, write a definition for the term *gravity*.

2. Use each of the following terms in a separate sentence: *mass* and *weight*.

Understanding Key Ideas

3. If Earth's mass doubled without changing its size, your weight would
   a. increase because gravitational force increases.
   b. decrease because gravitational force increases.
   c. increase because gravitational force decreases.
   d. not change because you are still on Earth.

4. What is the law of universal gravitation?

5. How does the mass of an object relate to the gravitational force that the object exerts on other objects?

6. How does the distance between objects affect the gravitational force between them?

7. Why are mass and weight often confused?

Math Skills

8. The gravitational force on Jupiter is approximately 2.3 times the gravitational force on Earth. If an object has a mass of 70 kg and a weight of 686 N on Earth, what would the object's mass and weight on Jupiter be?

Critical Thinking

9. **Applying Concepts** Your friend thinks that there is no gravity in space. How could you explain to your friend that there must be gravity in space?

10. **Making Comparisons** Explain why it is your weight and not your mass that would change if you landed on Mars.

SCiLINKS®

NSTA
Developed and maintained by the National Science Teachers Association

For a variety of links related to this chapter, go to www.scilinks.org

Topic: Matter and Gravity
SciLinks code: HSM0922

Skills Practice Lab

OBJECTIVES

Build an accelerometer.

Explain how an accelerometer works.

MATERIALS

- container, 1 L, with watertight lid
- cork or plastic-foam ball, small
- modeling clay
- pushpin
- scissors
- string
- water

SAFETY

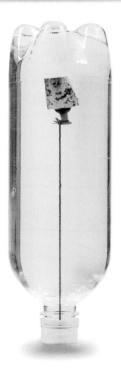

Detecting Acceleration

Have you ever noticed that you can "feel" acceleration? In a car or in an elevator, you may notice changes in speed or direction—even with your eyes closed! You are able to sense these changes because of tiny hair cells in your ears. These cells detect the movement of fluid in your inner ear. The fluid accelerates when you do, and the hair cells send a message about the acceleration to your brain. This message allows you to sense the acceleration. In this activity, you will build a device that detects acceleration. This device is called an *accelerometer* (ak SEL uhr AHM uht uhr).

Procedure

1. Cut a piece of string that reaches three-quarters of the way into the container.

2. Use a pushpin to attach one end of the string to the cork or plastic-foam ball.

3. Use modeling clay to attach the other end of the string to the center of the inside of the container lid. The cork or ball should hang no farther than three-quarters of the way into the container.

4. Fill the container with water.

5. Put the lid tightly on the container. The string and cork or ball should be inside the container.

6. Turn the container upside down. The cork should float about three-quarters of the way up inside the container, as shown at left. You are now ready to detect acceleration by using your accelerometer and completing the following steps.

7. Put the accelerometer on a tabletop. The container lid should touch the tabletop. Notice that the cork floats straight up in the water.

8. Now, gently push the accelerometer across the table at a constant speed. Notice that the cork quickly moves in the direction you are pushing and then swings backward. If you did not see this motion, repeat this step until you are sure you can see the first movement of the cork.

9 After you are familiar with how to use your accelerometer, try the following changes in motion. For each change, record your observations of the cork's first motion.

a. As you move the accelerometer across the table, gradually increase its speed.

b. As you move the accelerometer across the table, gradually decrease its speed.

c. While moving the accelerometer across the table, change the direction in which you are pushing.

d. Make any other changes in motion you can think of. You should make only one change to the motion for each trial.

Analyze the Results

1 **Analyzing Results** When you move the bottle at a constant speed, why does the cork quickly swing backward after it moves in the direction of acceleration?

2 **Explaining Events** The cork moves forward (in the direction you were moving the bottle) when you speed up but moves backward when you slow down. Explain why the cork moves this way. (Hint: Think about the direction of acceleration.)

Draw Conclusions

3 **Making Predictions** Imagine you are standing on a corner and watching a car that is waiting at a stoplight. A passenger inside the car is holding some helium balloons. Based on what you observed with your accelerometer, what do you think will happen to the balloons when the car begins moving?

Applying Your Data

If you move the bottle in a circle at a constant speed, what do you predict the cork will do? Try it, and check your answer.

27

Chapter Review

USING KEY TERMS

Complete each of the following sentences by choosing the correct term from the word bank.

mass	gravity
friction	weight
speed	velocity
net force	newton

1 ___ opposes motion between surfaces that are touching.

2 The ___ is the unit of force.

3 ___ is determined by combining forces.

4 Acceleration is the rate at which ___ changes.

5 ___ is a measure of the gravitational force on an object.

UNDERSTANDING KEY IDEAS

Multiple Choice

6 If a student rides her bicycle on a straight road and does not speed up or slow down, she is traveling with a

a. constant acceleration.

b. constant velocity.

c. positive acceleration.

d. negative acceleration.

7 A force

a. is expressed in newtons.

b. can cause an object to speed up, slow down, or change direction.

c. is a push or a pull.

d. All of the above

8 If you are in a spacecraft that has been launched into space, your weight would

a. increase because gravitational force is increasing.

b. increase because gravitational force is decreasing.

c. decrease because gravitational force is decreasing.

d. decrease because gravitational force is increasing.

9 The gravitational force between 1 kg of lead and Earth is ___ the gravitational force between 1 kg of marshmallows and Earth.

a. greater than   c. the same as

b. less than   d. None of the above

10 Which of the following is a measurement of velocity?

a. 16 m east   c. 55 m/h south

b. 25 m/s^2 d. 60 km/h

Short Answer

11 Describe the relationship between motion and a reference point.

12 How is it possible to be accelerating and traveling at a constant speed?

13 Explain the difference between mass and weight.

Math Skills

14 A kangaroo hops 60 m to the east in 5 s. Use this information to answer the following questions.

   a. What is the kangaroo's average speed?

   b. What is the kangaroo's average velocity?

   c. The kangaroo stops at a lake for a drink of water and then starts hopping again to the south. Each second, the kangaroo's velocity increases 2.5 m/s. What is the kangaroo's acceleration after 5 s?

CRITICAL THINKING

15 Concept Mapping Use the following terms to create a concept map: *speed, velocity, acceleration, force, direction,* and *motion.*

16 Applying Concepts Your family is moving, and you are asked to help move some boxes. One box is so heavy that you must push it across the room rather than lift it. What are some ways you could reduce friction to make moving the box easier?

17 Analyzing Ideas Considering the scientific meaning of the word *acceleration,* how could using the term *accelerator* when talking about a car's gas pedal lead to confusion?

18 Identifying Relationships Explain why it is important for airplane pilots to know wind velocity and not just wind speed during a flight.

INTERPRETING GRAPHICS

Use the figures below to answer the questions that follow.

19 Is the graph below showing positive acceleration or negative acceleration? How can you tell?

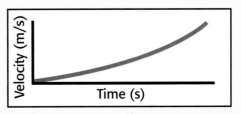

20 You know how to combine two forces that act in one or two directions. The same method can be used to combine several forces acting in several directions. Look at the diagrams, and calculate the net force in each diagram. Predict the direction each object will move.

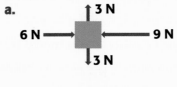

a.
   3 N
6 N ← → 9 N
   3 N

b.
5 N → ← 5 N
   5 N

c.
   4 N
8 N →
   4 N

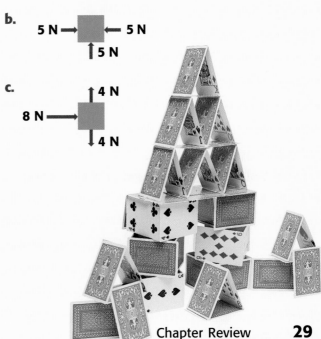

Standardized Test Preparation

Read each of the passages below. Then, answer the questions that follow each passage.

Passage 1 If you look closely at the surface of a golf ball, you'll see dozens of tiny dimples. When air flows past these dimples, the air is stirred up and stays near the surface of the ball. By keeping air moving near the surface of the ball, the dimples help the golf ball move faster and farther through the air. Jeff DiTullio, a teacher at MIT in Cambridge, Massachusetts, decided to apply this principle to a baseball bat. When DiTullio tested his dimpled bat in a <u>wind tunnel</u>, he found that the bat could be swung 3% to 5% faster than a bat without dimples. That increase may not seem like much, but the dimpled bat could add about 5 m of distance to a fly ball!

1. Who is Jeff DiTullio?
   A the inventor of the dimpled golf ball
   B a teacher at Cambridge University
   C the inventor of the dimpled bat
   D a professional baseball player

2. Which of the following ideas is NOT stated in the passage?
   F Dimples make DiTullio's bat move faster.
   G MIT is in Cambridge, Massachusetts.
   H Air that is stirred up near the surface of DiTullio's bat makes it easier to swing the bat faster.
   I DiTullio will make a lot of money from his invention.

3. In the passage, what does *wind tunnel* mean?
   A a place to practice batting
   B a place to test the speed of objects in the air
   C a baseball stadium
   D a passageway that is shielded from the wind

Passage 2 The Golden Gate Bridge in San Francisco, California, is one of the most famous <u>landmarks</u> in the world. Approximately 9 million people from around the world visit the bridge each year.

The Golden Gate Bridge is a suspension bridge. A suspension bridge is one in which the roadway is hung, or suspended, from huge cables that extend from one end of the bridge to the other. The main cables on the Golden Gate Bridge are 2.33 km long. Many forces act on the main cables. For example, smaller cables pull down on the main cables to connect the roadway to the main cables. And two towers that are 227 m tall push up on the main cables. The forces on the main cable must be balanced, or the bridge will collapse.

1. In this passage, what does *landmarks* mean?
   A large areas of land
   B well-known places
   C street signs
   D places where people meet

2. Which of the following statements is a fact from the passage?
   F The roadway of the Golden Gate Bridge is suspended from huge cables.
   G The towers of the Golden Gate Bridge are 2.33 km tall.
   H The main cables connect the roadway to the towers.
   I The forces on the cables are not balanced.

3. According to the passage, why do people from around the world visit the Golden Gate Bridge?
   A It is the longest bridge in the world.
   B It is a suspension bridge.
   C It is the only bridge that is painted orange.
   D It is a famous landmark.

The graph below shows the data collected by a student as she watched a squirrel running on the ground. Use the graph below to answer the questions that follow.

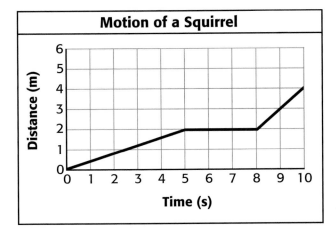

Motion of a Squirrel

1. Which of the following best describes the motion of the squirrel between 5 s and 8 s?

   A The squirrel's speed increased.

   B The squirrel's speed decreased.

   C The squirrel's speed did not change.

   D The squirrel moved backward.

2. Which of the following statements about the motion of the squirrel is true?

   F The squirrel moved with the greatest speed between 0 s and 5 s.

   G The squirrel moved with the greatest speed between 8 s and 10 s.

   H The squirrel moved with a constant speed between 0 s and 8 s.

   I The squirrel moved with a constant speed between 5 s and 10 s.

3. What is the average speed of the squirrel between 8 s and 10 s?

   A 0.4 m/s

   B 1 m/s

   C 2 m/s

   D 4 m/s

Read each question below, and choose the best answer.

1. The distance between Cedar Rapids, Iowa, and Sioux Falls, South Dakota, is about 660 km. How long will it take a car traveling with an average speed of 95 km/h to drive from Cedar Rapids to Sioux Falls?

   A less than 1 h

   B about 3 h

   C about 7 h

   D about 10 h

2. Martha counted the number of people in each group that walked into her school's cafeteria. In the first 10 groups, she counted the following numbers of people: 6, 4, 9, 6, 4, 10, 9, 5, 9, and 8. What is the mode of this set of data?

   F 6

   G 7

   H 9

   I 10

3. Which of the following terms describes the angle marked in the triangle below.

   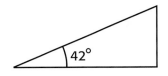

   A acute

   B obtuse

   C right

   D None of the above

4. Donnell collected money for a charity fundraiser. After one hour, he counted the money and found that he had raised $10.00 in bills and $3.74 in coins. Which of the following represents the number of coins he collected?

   F 4 pennies, 9 nickels, 18 dimes, and 6 quarters

   G 9 pennies, 7 nickels, 18 dimes, and 6 quarters

   H 6 pennies, 7 nickels, 15 dimes, and 8 quarters

   I 9 pennies, 8 nickels, 12 dimes, and 3 quarters

Standardized Test Preparation

Science in Action

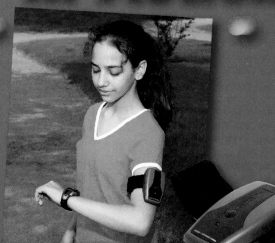

Science, Technology, and Society

GPS Watch System

Some athletes are concerned about knowing their speed during training. To calculate speed, they need to know distance and time. Finding time by using a watch is easy to do. But determining distance is more difficult. However, a GPS watch system is now available to help with this problem. *GPS* stands for *global positioning system*. A GPS unit, which is worn on an athlete's upper arm, monitors the athlete's position by using signals from satellites. As the athlete moves, the GPS unit calculates the distance traveled. The GPS unit sends a signal to the watch, which keeps the athlete's time, and the watch displays the athlete's speed.

Weird Science

The Segway™ Human Transporter

In November 2002, a new people-moving machine was introduced, and people have been fascinated by the odd-looking device ever since. The device is called the *Segway Human Transporter*. The Segway is a two-wheeled device that is powered by a rechargeable battery. To move forward, the rider simply leans forward. Sensors detect this motion and send signals to the on-board computer. The computer, in turn, tells the motor to start going. To slow down, the rider leans backward, and to stop, the rider stands straight up. The Segway has a top speed of 20 km/h (about 12.5 mi/h) and can travel up to 28 km (about 17.4 mi) on a single battery charge.

Math ACTIVITY

Suppose an athlete wishes to finish a 5 K race in under 25 min. The distance of a 5 K is 5 km. (Remember that 1 km = 1,000 m.) If the athlete runs the race at a constant speed of 3.4 m/s, will she meet her goal?

Language Arts ACTIVITY

WRITING SKILL The inventor of the Segway thinks that the machine will make a good alternative to walking and bicycle riding. Write a one-page essay explaining whether you think using a Segway is better or worse than riding a bicycle.

Victor Petrenko

Snowboard and Ski Brakes Have you ever wished for emergency brakes on your snowboard or skis? Thanks to Victor Petrenko and the Ice Research Lab of Dartmouth College, snowboards and skis that have braking systems may soon be available.

Not many people know more about the properties of ice and ice-related technologies than Victor Petrenko does. He has spent most of his career researching the electrical and mechanical properties of ice. Through his research, Petrenko learned that ice can hold an electric charge. He used this property to design a braking system for snowboards. The system is a form of electric friction control.

The power source for the brakes is a battery. The battery is connected to a network of wires embedded on the bottom surface of a snowboard. When the battery is activated, the bottom of the snowboard gains a negative charge. This negative charge creates a positive charge on the surface of the snow. Because opposite charges attract, the snowboard and the snow are pulled together. The force that pulls the surfaces together increases friction, and the snowboard slows down.

Social Studies ACTIVITY

Research the history of skiing. Make a poster that includes a timeline of significant dates in the history of skiing. Illustrate your poster with photos or drawings.

go.hrw.com

To learn more about these Science in Action topics, visit go.hrw.com and type in the keyword HP5MOTF.

Current Science

Check out Current Science® articles related to this chapter by visiting go.hrw.com. Just type in the keyword HP5CS05.

2

Forces and Motion

The Big Idea
Unbalanced forces cause changes in motion that can be predicted and described.

About the PHOTO

To train for space flight, astronauts fly in a modified KC-135 cargo airplane. The airplane first flies upward at a steep angle. Then, it flies downward at a 45° angle, which causes the feeling of reduced gravity inside. Under these conditions, the astronauts in the plane can float and can practice carrying out tasks that they will need to perform when they are in orbit. Because the floating makes people queasy, this KC-135 is nicknamed the "Vomit Comet."

PRE-READING ACTIVITY

Graphic Organizer

Spider Map Before you read the chapter, create the graphic organizer entitled "Spider Map" described in the **Study Skills** section of the Appendix. Label the circle "Motion." Create a leg for each law of motion, a leg for gravity, and a leg for momentum. As you read the chapter, fill in the map with details about how motion is related to the laws of motion, gravity, and momentum.

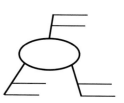

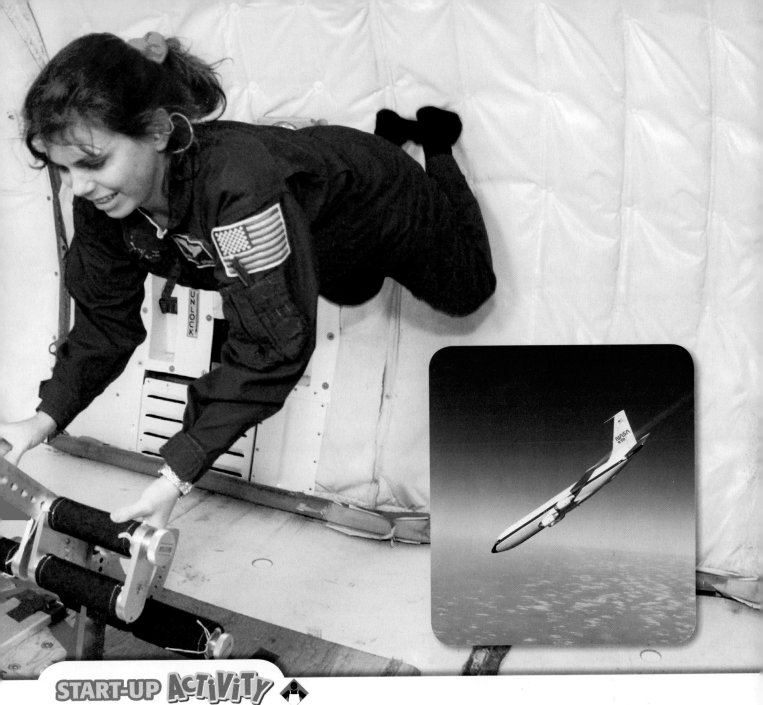

START-UP ACTIVITY

Falling Water

Gravity is one of the most important forces in your life. In this activity, you will observe the effect of gravity on a falling object.

Procedure

1. Place a **wide plastic tub** on the floor. Punch a small hole in the side of a **paper cup,** near the bottom.

2. Hold your finger over the hole, and fill the cup with **water.** Keep your finger over the hole, and hold the cup waist-high above the tub.

3. Uncover the hole. Record your observations as Trial 1.

4. Predict what will happen to the water if you drop the cup at the same time you uncover the hole.

5. Cover the hole, and refill the cup with water.

6. Uncover the hole, and drop the cup at the same time. Record your observations as Trial 2.

7. Clean up any spilled water with **paper towels.**

Analysis

1. What differences did you observe in the behavior of the water during the two trials?

2. In Trial 2, how fast did the cup fall compared with how fast the water fell?

3. How did the results of Trial 2 compare with your prediction?

Gravity and Motion

Suppose you dropped a baseball and a marble at the same time from the top of a tall building. Which do you think would land on the ground first?

In ancient Greece around 400 BCE, a philosopher named Aristotle (AR is TAWT uhl) thought that the rate at which an object falls depended on the object's mass. If you asked Aristotle whether the baseball or the marble would land first, he would have said the baseball. But Aristotle never tried dropping objects with different masses to test his idea about falling objects.

Gravity and Falling Objects

In the late 1500s, a young Italian scientist named Galileo Galilei (GAL uh LAY oh GAL uh LAY) questioned Aristotle's idea about falling objects. Galileo argued that the mass of an object does not affect the time the object takes to fall to the ground. According to one story, Galileo proved his argument by dropping two cannonballs of different masses from the top of the Leaning Tower of Pisa in Italy. The people watching from the ground below were amazed to see the two cannonballs land at the same time. Whether or not this story is true, Galileo's work changed people's understanding of gravity and falling objects.

What You Will Learn

● Explain the effect of gravity and air resistance on falling objects.
● Explain why objects in orbit are in free fall and appear to be weightless.
● Describe how projectile motion is affected by gravity.

Vocabulary

terminal velocity
free fall
projectile motion

READING STRATEGY

Reading Organizer As you read this section, create an outline of the section. Use the headings from the section in your outline.

Gravity and Acceleration

Objects fall to the ground at the same rate because the acceleration due to gravity is the same for all objects. Why is this true? Acceleration depends on both force and mass. A heavier object experiences a greater gravitational force than a lighter object does. But a heavier object is also harder to accelerate because it has more mass. The extra mass of the heavy object exactly balances the additional gravitational force. **Figure 1** shows objects that have different masses falling with the same acceleration.

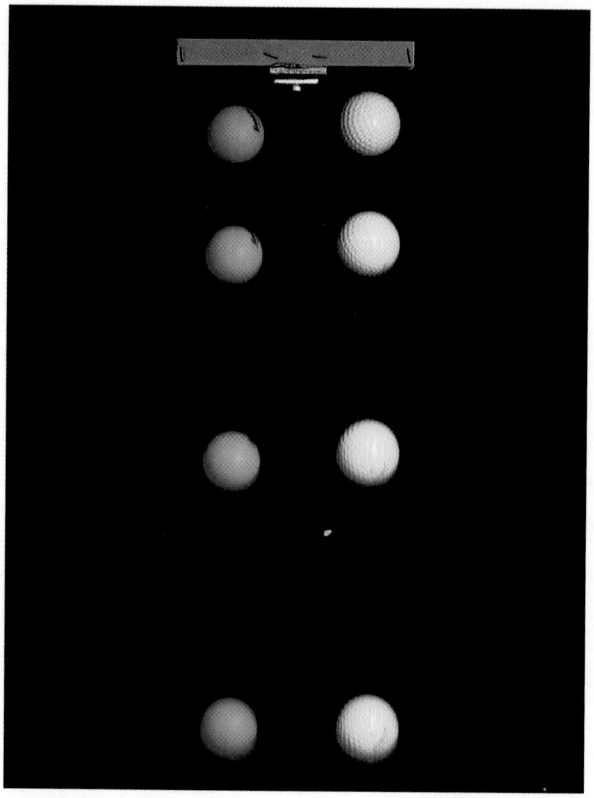

Figure 1 *This stop-action photo shows that a table-tennis ball and a golf ball fall at the same rate even though they have different masses.*

Acceleration Due to Gravity

Acceleration is the rate at which velocity changes over time. So, the acceleration of an object is the object's change in velocity divided by the amount of time during which the change occurs. All objects accelerate toward Earth at a rate of 9.8 meters per second per second. This rate is written as 9.8 m/s/s, or 9.8 m/s^2. So, for every second that an object falls, the object's downward velocity increases by 9.8 m/s, as shown in **Figure 2.**

Reading Check What is the acceleration due to gravity? (*See the Appendix for answers to Reading Checks.*)

Velocity of Falling Objects

You can calculate the change in velocity (Δv) of a falling object by using the following equation:

$$\Delta v = g \times t$$

In this equation, g is the acceleration due to gravity on Earth (9.8 m/s^2), and t is the time the object takes to fall (in seconds). The change in velocity is the difference between the final velocity and the starting velocity. If the object starts at rest, this equation yields the velocity of the object after a certain time period.

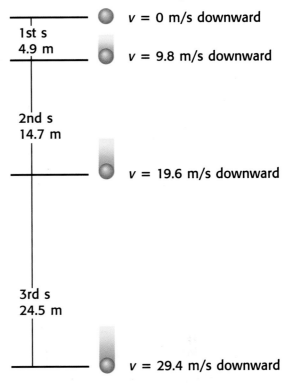

Figure 2 *A falling object accelerates at a constant rate. The object falls faster and farther each second than it did the second before.*

MATH FOCUS

Calculating the Velocity of Falling Objects A stone at rest is dropped from a cliff, and the stone hits the ground after a time of 3 s. What is the stone's velocity when it hits the ground?

Step 1: Write the equation for change in velocity.

$$\Delta v = g \times t$$

Step 2: Replace g with its value and t with the time given in the problem, and solve.

$$\Delta v = 9.8 \, \frac{m/s}{s} \times 3 \, s$$
$$= 29.4 \, m/s$$

To rearrange the equation to find time, divide by the acceleration due to gravity:

$$t = \frac{\Delta v}{g}$$

Now It's Your Turn

1. A penny at rest is dropped from the top of a tall stairwell. What is the penny's velocity after it has fallen for 2 s?

2. The same penny hits the ground in 4.5 s. What is the penny's velocity as it hits the ground?

3. A marble at rest is dropped from a tall building. The marble hits the ground with a velocity of 98 m/s. How long was the marble in the air?

4. An acorn at rest falls from an oak tree. The acorn hits the ground with a velocity of 14.7 m/s. How long did it take the acorn to land?

Figure 3 **Effect of Air Resistance on a Falling Object**

a The **force of gravity** is pulling down on the apple. If gravity were the only force acting on the apple, the apple would accelerate at a rate of 9.8 m/s².

b The **force of air resistance** is pushing up on the apple. This force is subtracted from the force of gravity to yield the net force.

c The **net force** on the apple is equal to the force of air resistance subtracted from the force of gravity. Because the net force is not 0 N, the apple accelerates downward. But the apple does not accelerate as fast as it would without air resistance.

Air Resistance and Falling Objects

Try dropping two sheets of paper—one crumpled in a tight ball and the other kept flat. What happened? Does this simple experiment seem to contradict what you just learned about falling objects? The flat paper falls more slowly than the crumpled paper because of *air resistance*. Air resistance is the force that opposes the motion of objects through air.

The amount of air resistance acting on an object depends on the size, shape, and speed of the object. Air resistance affects the flat sheet of paper more than the crumpled one. The larger surface area of the flat sheet causes the flat sheet to fall slower than the crumpled one. **Figure 3** shows the effect of air resistance on the downward acceleration of a falling object.

✓ *Reading Check* Will air resistance have more effect on the acceleration of a falling leaf or the acceleration of a falling acorn?

Acceleration Stops at the Terminal Velocity

As the speed of a falling object increases, air resistance increases. The upward force of air resistance continues to increase until it is equal to the downward force of gravity. At this point, the net force is 0 N and the object stops accelerating. The object then falls at a constant velocity called the **terminal velocity.**

Terminal velocity can be a good thing. Every year, cars, buildings, and vegetation are severely damaged in hailstorms. The terminal velocity of hailstones is between 5 and 40 m/s, depending on their size. If there were no air resistance, hailstones would hit the ground at velocities near 350 m/s! **Figure 4** shows another situation in which terminal velocity is helpful.

Figure 4 *The parachute increases the air resistance of this sky diver and slows him to a safe terminal velocity.*

terminal velocity the constant velocity of a falling object when the force of air resistance is equal in magnitude and opposite in direction to the force of gravity

Free Fall Occurs When There Is No Air Resistance

Sky divers are often described as being in free fall before they open their parachutes. However, that is an incorrect description, because air resistance is always acting on the sky diver.

An object is in **free fall** only if gravity is pulling it down and no other forces are acting on it. Because air resistance is a force, free fall can occur only where there is no air. Two places that have no air are in space and in a vacuum. A vacuum is a place in which there is no matter. **Figure 5** shows objects falling in a vacuum. Because there is no air resistance in a vacuum, the two objects are in free fall.

Orbiting Objects Are in Free Fall

Look at the astronaut in **Figure 6.** Why is the astronaut floating inside the space shuttle? You may be tempted to say that she is weightless in space. However, it is impossible for any object to be weightless anywhere in the universe.

Weight is a measure of gravitational force. The size of the force depends on the masses of objects and the distances between them. Suppose you traveled in space far away from all the stars and planets. The gravitational force acting on you would be very small because the distance between you and other objects would be very large. But you and all the other objects in the universe would still have mass. Therefore, gravity would attract you to other objects—even if just slightly—so you would still have weight.

Astronauts float in orbiting spacecrafts because of free fall. To better understand why astronauts float, you need to know what *orbiting* means.

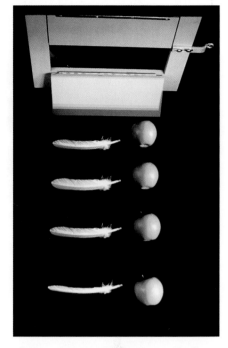

Figure 5 *Air resistance usually causes a feather to fall more slowly than an apple falls. But in a vacuum, a feather and an apple fall with the same acceleration because both are in free fall.*

free fall the motion of a body when only the force of gravity is acting on the body

Figure 6 *Astronauts appear to be weightless while they are floating inside the space shuttle—but they are not weightless!*

Figure 7 **How an Orbit Is Formed**

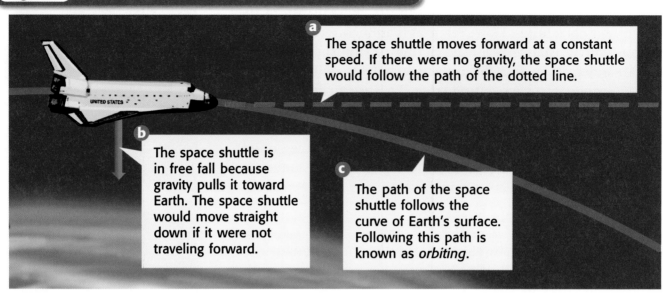

a The space shuttle moves forward at a constant speed. If there were no gravity, the space shuttle would follow the path of the dotted line.

b The space shuttle is in free fall because gravity pulls it toward Earth. The space shuttle would move straight down if it were not traveling forward.

c The path of the space shuttle follows the curve of Earth's surface. Following this path is known as *orbiting*.

Two Motions Combine to Cause Orbiting

An object is orbiting when it is traveling around another object in space. When a spacecraft orbits Earth, it is moving forward. But the spacecraft is also in free fall toward Earth. **Figure 7** shows how these two motions combine to cause orbiting.

As you can see in **Figure 7,** the space shuttle is always falling while it is in orbit. So why don't astronauts hit their heads on the ceiling of the falling shuttle? Because they are also in free fall—they are always falling, too. Because astronauts are in free fall, they float.

Orbiting and Centripetal Force

Besides spacecrafts and satellites, many other objects in the universe are in orbit. The moon orbits the Earth. Earth and the other planets orbit the sun. In addition, many stars orbit large masses in the center of galaxies. Many of these objects are traveling in a circular or nearly circular path. Any object in circular motion is constantly changing direction. Because an unbalanced force is necessary to change the motion of any object, there must be an unbalanced force working on any object in circular motion.

The unbalanced force that causes objects to move in a circular path is called a *centripetal force* (sen TRIP uht uhl FOHRS). Gravity provides the centripetal force that keeps objects in orbit. The word *centripetal* means "toward the center." As you can see in **Figure 8,** the centripetal force on the moon points toward the center of the moon's circular orbit.

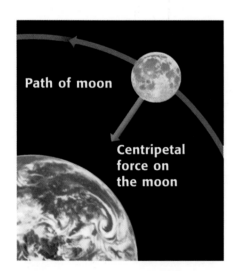

Path of moon

Centripetal force on the moon

Figure 8 *The moon stays in orbit around Earth because Earth's gravitational force provides a centripetal force on the moon.*

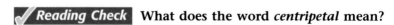

Reading Check What does the word *centripetal* mean?

Projectile Motion and Gravity

The motion of a hopping grasshopper is an example of projectile motion (proh JEK tuhl MOH shuhn). **Projectile motion** is the curved path an object follows when it is thrown or propelled near the surface of the Earth. Projectile motion has two components—horizontal motion and vertical motion. The two components are independent, so they have no effect on each other. When the two motions are combined, they form a curved path, as shown in **Figure 9.** Some examples of projectile motion include the following:

- a frog leaping
- water sprayed by a sprinkler
- a swimmer diving into water
- balls being juggled
- an arrow shot by an archer

Horizontal Motion

When you throw a ball, your hand exerts a force on the ball that makes the ball move forward. This force gives the ball its horizontal motion, which is motion parallel to the ground.

After you release the ball, no horizontal forces are acting on the ball (if you ignore air resistance). Even gravity does not affect the horizontal component of projectile motion. So, there are no forces to change the ball's horizontal motion. Thus, the horizontal velocity of the ball is constant after the ball leaves your hand, as shown in **Figure 9.**

projectile motion the curved path that an object follows when thrown, launched, or otherwise projected near the surface of Earth

---

Figure 9 Projectile Motion

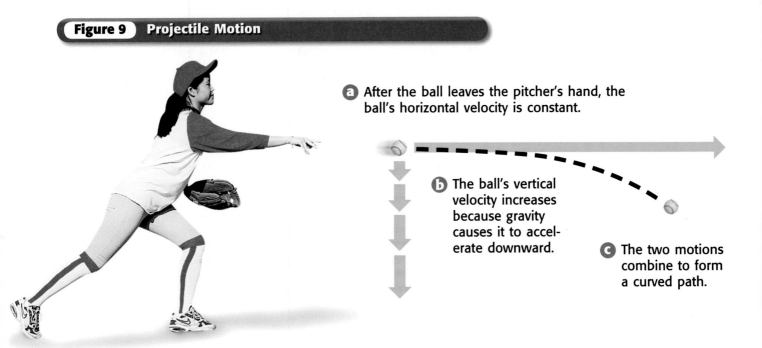

a After the ball leaves the pitcher's hand, the ball's horizontal velocity is constant.

b The ball's vertical velocity increases because gravity causes it to accelerate downward.

c The two motions combine to form a curved path.

For another activity related to this chapter, go to **go.hrw.com** and type in the keyword **HP5FORW.**

Figure 10 Projectile Motion and Acceleration Due to Gravity

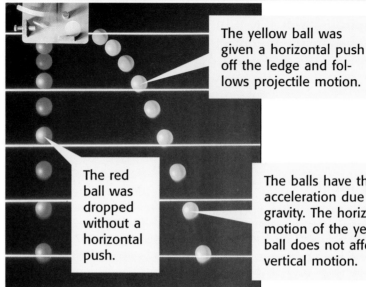

The yellow ball was given a horizontal push off the ledge and follows projectile motion.

The red ball was dropped without a horizontal push.

The balls have the same acceleration due to gravity. The horizontal motion of the yellow ball does not affect its vertical motion.

Vertical Motion

Gravity pulls everything on Earth downward toward the center of Earth. A ball in your hand is prevented from falling by your hand. After you throw the ball, gravity pulls it downward and gives the ball vertical motion. Vertical motion is motion that is perpendicular to the ground. Gravity pulls objects in projectile motion down at an acceleration of 9.8 m/s^2 (if air resistance is ignored). This rate is the same for all falling objects. **Figure 10** shows that the downward acceleration of a thrown object and a falling object are the same.

Because objects in projectile motion accelerate downward, you always have to aim above a target if you want to hit it with a thrown or propelled object. That's why when you aim an arrow directly at a bull's-eye, your arrow strikes the bottom of the target rather than the middle of the target.

✓ **Reading Check** What gives an object in projectile motion its vertical motion?

Penny Projectile Motion

1. Position a **flat ruler** and **two pennies** on a **desk or table** as shown below.

2. Hold the ruler by the end that is on the desk. Move the ruler quickly in the direction shown so that the ruler knocks the penny off the table and so that the other penny also drops. Repeat this step several times.

3. Which penny travels with projectile motion? In what order do the pennies hit the ground? Record and explain your answers.

Summary

- Gravity causes all objects to accelerate toward Earth at a rate of 9.8 m/s².

- Air resistance slows the acceleration of falling objects. An object falls at its terminal velocity when the upward force of air resistance equals the downward force of gravity.

- An object is in free fall if gravity is the only force acting on it.

- Objects in orbit appear to be weightless because they are in free fall.

- A centripetal force is needed to keep objects in circular motion. Gravity acts as a centripetal force to keep objects in orbit.

- Projectile motion is the curved path an object follows when thrown or propelled near the surface of Earth.

- Projectile motion has two components—horizontal motion and vertical motion. Gravity affects only the vertical motion of projectile motion.

Using Key Terms

1. Use each of the following terms in a separate sentence: *terminal velocity* and *free fall*.

Understanding Key Ideas

2. Which of the following is in projectile motion?
   a. a feather falling in a vacuum
   b. a cat leaping on a toy
   c. a car driving up a hill
   d. a book laying on a desk

3. How does air resistance affect the acceleration of falling objects?

4. How does gravity affect the two components of projectile motion?

5. How is the acceleration of falling objects affected by gravity?

6. Why is the acceleration due to gravity the same for all objects?

Math Skills

7. A rock at rest falls off a tall cliff and hits the valley below after 3.5 s. What is the rock's velocity as it hits the ground?

Critical Thinking

8. **Applying Concepts** Think about a sport that uses a ball. Identify four examples from that sport in which an object is in projectile motion.

9. **Making Inferences** The moon has no atmosphere. Predict what would happen if an astronaut on the moon dropped a hammer and a feather at the same time from the same height.

Interpreting Graphics

10. Whenever Jon delivers a newspaper to the Zapanta house, the newspaper lands in the bushes, as shown below. What should Jon do to make sure the newspaper lands on the porch?

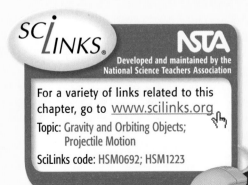

For a variety of links related to this chapter, go to www.scilinks.org

Topic: Gravity and Orbiting Objects; Projectile Motion

SciLinks code: HSM0692; HSM1223

Developed and maintained by the National Science Teachers Association

Newton's Laws of Motion

Imagine that you are playing baseball. The pitch comes in, and—crack—you hit the ball hard! But instead of flying off the bat, the ball just drops to the ground. Is that normal?

You would probably say no. You know that force and motion are related. When you exert a force on a baseball by hitting it with a bat, the baseball should move. In 1686, Sir Isaac Newton explained this relationship between force and the motion of an object with his three laws of motion.

Newton's First Law of Motion

An object at rest remains at rest, and an object in motion remains in motion at constant speed and in a straight line unless acted on by an unbalanced force.

Newton's first law of motion describes the motion of an object that has a net force of 0 N acting on it. This law may seem complicated when you first read it. But, it is easy to understand when you consider its two parts separately.

Part 1: Objects at Rest

An object that is not moving is said to be at rest. A chair on the floor and a golf ball balanced on a tee are examples of objects at rest. Newton's first law says that objects at rest will stay at rest unless they are acted on by an unbalanced force. For example, objects will not start moving until a push or a pull is exerted on them. So, a chair won't slide across the room unless you push the chair. And, a golf ball won't move off the tee unless the ball is struck by a golf club, as shown in **Figure 1.**

Figure 1 *A golf ball will remain at rest on a tee until it is acted on by the unbalanced force of a moving club.*

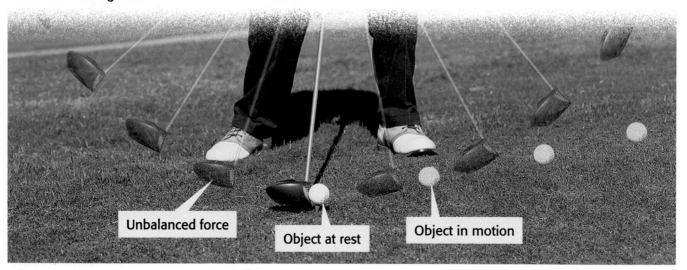

Unbalanced force

Object at rest

Object in motion

Part 2: Objects in Motion

The second part of Newton's first law is about objects moving with a certain velocity. Such objects will continue to move forever with the same velocity unless an unbalanced force acts on them.

Think about driving a bumper car at an amusement park. Your ride is pleasant as long as you are driving in an open space. But the name of the game is bumper cars! Sooner or later you are likely to run into another car, as shown in **Figure 2.** Your bumper car stops when it hits another car. But, you continue to move forward until the force from your seat belt stops you.

Friction and Newton's First Law

An object in motion will stay in motion forever unless it is acted on by an unbalanced force. So, you should be able to give your desk a push and send it sliding across the floor. If you push your desk, the desk quickly stops. Why?

There must be an unbalanced force that acts on the desk to stop its motion. That unbalanced force is friction. The friction between the desk and the floor works against the motion of the desk. Because of friction, observing the effects of Newton's first law is often difficult. For example, friction will cause a rolling ball to slow down and stop. Friction will also make a car slow down if the driver lets up on the gas pedal. Because of friction, the motion of objects changes.

Reading Check When you ride a bus, why do you fall forward when the bus stops moving? (*See the Appendix for answers to Reading Checks.*)

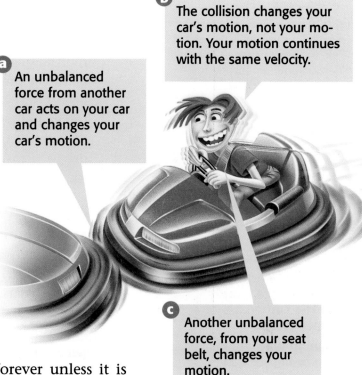

b The collision changes your car's motion, not your motion. Your motion continues with the same velocity.

a An unbalanced force from another car acts on your car and changes your car's motion.

c Another unbalanced force, from your seat belt, changes your motion.

Figure 2 *Bumper cars let you have fun with Newton's first law.*

First Law Skateboard

1. Place an **empty soda can** on top of a **skateboard.**

2. Ask a friend to catch the skateboard after you push it. Now, give the skateboard a quick, firm push. What happened to the soda can?

3. Put the can on the skateboard again. Push the skateboard gently so that the skateboard moves quickly but so that the can does not fall.

4. Ask your friend to stop the skateboard after he or she allows it to travel a short distance. What happened to the can?

5. Explain how Newton's first law applies to what happened.

Inertia and Newton's First Law

Newton's first law of motion is sometimes called the *law of inertia*. **Inertia** (in UHR shuh) is the tendency of all objects to resist any change in motion. Because of inertia, an object at rest will remain at rest until a force makes it move. Likewise, inertia is the reason a moving object stays in motion with the same velocity unless a force changes its speed or direction. For example, because of inertia, you slide toward the side of a car when the driver turns a corner. Inertia is also why it is impossible for a plane, car, or bicycle to stop immediately.

Mass and Inertia

Mass is a measure of inertia. An object that has a small mass has less inertia than an object that has a large mass. So, changing the motion of an object that has a small mass is easier than changing the motion of an object that has a large mass. For example, a softball has less mass and therefore less inertia than a bowling ball. Because the softball has a small amount of inertia, it is easy to pitch a softball and to change its motion by hitting it with a bat. Imagine how difficult it would be to play softball with a bowling ball! **Figure 3** further shows the relationship between mass and inertia.

First-Law Magic

1. On a **table or desk**, place a **large, empty plastic cup** on top of a **paper towel.**

2. Without touching the cup or tipping it over, remove the paper towel from under the cup. How did you accomplish this? Repeat this step.

3. Fill the cup half full with **water,** and place the cup on the paper towel.

4. Once again, remove the paper towel from under the cup. Was it easier or harder to do this time?

5. Explain your observations in terms of mass, inertia, and Newton's first law of motion.

Figure 3 *Inertia makes it harder to accelerate a car than to accelerate a bicycle. Inertia also makes it easier to stop a moving bicycle than a car moving at the same speed.*

Newton's Second Law of Motion

The acceleration of an object depends on the mass of the object and the amount of force applied.

Newton's second law describes the motion of an object when an unbalanced force acts on the object. As with Newton's first law, you should consider the second law in two parts.

Part 1: Acceleration Depends on Mass

Suppose you are pushing an empty cart. You have to exert only a small force on the cart to accelerate it. But, the same amount of force will not accelerate the full cart as much as the empty cart. Look at the first two photos in **Figure 4.** They show that the acceleration of an object decreases as its mass increases and that its acceleration increases as its mass decreases.

Part 2: Acceleration Depends on Force

Suppose you give the cart a hard push, as shown in the third photo in **Figure 4.** The cart will start moving faster than if you gave it only a soft push. So, an object's acceleration increases as the force on the object increases. On the other hand, an object's acceleration decreases as the force on the object decreases.

The acceleration of an object is always in the same direction as the force applied. The cart in **Figure 4** moved forward because the push was in the forward direction.

✓ Reading Check What is the relationship between the force on an object and the object's acceleration?

CONNECTION TO Environmental Science

Car Sizes and Pollution

On average, newer cars pollute the air less than older cars do. One reason for this is that newer cars have less mass than older cars have. An object that has less mass requires less force to achieve the same acceleration as an object that has more mass. So, a small car can have a small engine and still have good acceleration. Because small engines use less fuel than large engines use, small engines create less pollution. Research three models of cars from the same year, and make a chart to compare the mass of the cars with the amount of fuel they use.

ACTIVITY

Figure 4 Mass, Force, and Acceleration

Acceleration

Acceleration

Acceleration

If the force applied to the carts is the same, the acceleration of the empty cart is greater than the acceleration of the loaded cart.

Acceleration will increase when a larger force is exerted.

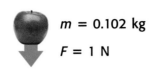 **Figure 5** **Newton's Second Law and Acceleration Due to Gravity**

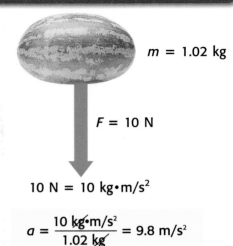

$m = 0.102$ kg

$F = 1$ N

$m = 1.02$ kg

$F = 10$ N

1 N = 1 kg•m/s²

$$a = \frac{1 \cancel{\text{kg}} \cdot \text{m/s}^2}{0.102 \cancel{\text{kg}}} = 9.8 \text{ m/s}^2$$

10 N = 10 kg•m/s²

$$a = \frac{10 \cancel{\text{kg}} \cdot \text{m/s}^2}{1.02 \cancel{\text{kg}}} = 9.8 \text{ m/s}^2$$

The apple has less mass than the watermelon does. So, less force is needed to give the apple the same acceleration that the watermelon has.

Expressing Newton's Second Law Mathematically

The relationship of acceleration (a) to mass (m) and force (F) can be expressed mathematically with the following equation:

$$a = \frac{F}{m}, \text{ or } F = m \times a$$

Notice that the equation can be rearranged to find the force applied. Both forms of the equation can be used to solve problems.

Newton's second law explains why objects fall to Earth with the same acceleration. In **Figure 5,** you can see how the large force of gravity on the watermelon is offset by its large mass. Thus, you find that the accelerations of the watermelon and the apple are the same when you solve for acceleration.

Second-Law Problems What is the acceleration of a 3 kg mass if a force of 14.4 N is used to move the mass? (Note: 1 N is equal to 1 kg•m/s²)

Step 1: Write the equation for acceleration.

$$a = \frac{F}{m}$$

Step 2: Replace F and m with the values given in the problem, and solve.

$$a = \frac{14.4 \text{ kg} \cdot \text{m/s}^2}{3 \text{ kg}} = 4.8 \text{ m/s}^2$$

Now It's Your Turn

1. What is the acceleration of a 7 kg mass if a force of 68.6 N is used to move it toward Earth?
2. What force is necessary to accelerate a 1,250 kg car at a rate of 40 m/s²?
3. Zookeepers carry a stretcher that holds a sleeping lion. The total mass of the lion and the stretcher is 175 kg. The lion's forward acceleration is 2 m/s². What is the force necessary to produce this acceleration?

Newton's Third Law of Motion

> *Whenever one object exerts a force on a second object, the second object exerts an equal and opposite force on the first.*

Newton's third law can be simply stated as follows: All forces act in pairs. If a force is exerted, another force occurs that is equal in size and opposite in direction. The law itself addresses only forces. But the way that force pairs interact affects the motion of objects.

How do forces act in pairs? Study **Figure 6** to learn how one force pair helps propel a swimmer through water. Action and reaction force pairs are present even when there is no motion. For example, you exert a force on a chair when you sit on it. Your weight pushing down on the chair is the action force. The reaction force is the force exerted by the chair that pushes up on your body. The force is equal to your weight.

✓ **Reading Check** How are the forces in each force pair related?

Force Pairs Do Not Act on the Same Object

A force is always exerted by one object on another object. This rule is true for all forces, including action and reaction forces. However, action and reaction forces in a pair do not act on the same object. If they did, the net force would always be 0 N and nothing would ever move! To understand how action and reaction forces act on objects, look at **Figure 6** again. The action force was exerted on the water by the swimmer's hands. But the reaction force was exerted on the swimmer's hands by the water. The forces did not act on the same object.

Newton Ball

Play catch with an adult. As you play, discuss how Newton's laws of motion are involved in the game. After you finish your game, make a list in your **science journal** of what you discussed.

ACTIVITY

Figure 6 *The action force and reaction force are a pair. The two forces are equal in size but opposite in direction.*

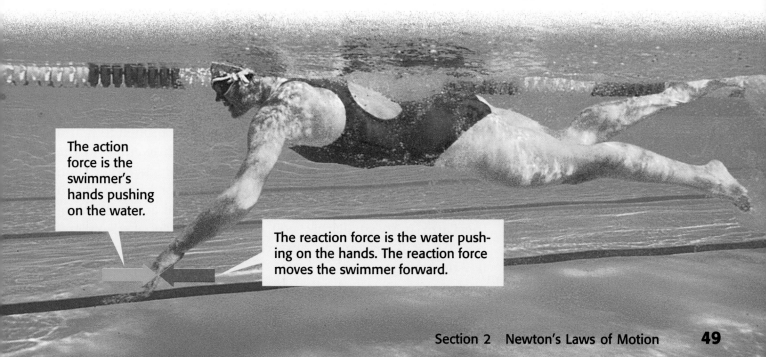

The action force is the swimmer's hands pushing on the water.

The reaction force is the water pushing on the hands. The reaction force moves the swimmer forward.

Figure 7 Examples of Action and Reaction Force Pairs

The space shuttle's thrusters push the exhaust gases downward as the gases push the shuttle upward with an equal force.

The rabbit's legs exert a force on Earth. Earth exerts an equal force on the rabbit's legs and causes the rabbit to accelerate upward.

The bat exerts a force on the ball and sends the ball flying. The ball exerts an equal force on the bat, but the bat does not move backward because the batter is exerting another force on the bat.

All Forces Act in Pairs—Action and Reaction

Newton's third law says that all forces act in pairs. When a force is exerted, there is always a reaction force. A force never acts by itself. **Figure 7** shows some examples of action and reaction force pairs. In each example, the action force is shown in yellow and the reaction force is shown in red.

The Effect of a Reaction Can Be Difficult to See

Another example of a force pair is shown in **Figure 8.** Gravity is a force of attraction between objects that is due to their masses. If you drop a ball, gravity pulls the ball toward Earth. This force is the action force exerted by Earth on the ball. But gravity also pulls Earth toward the ball. The force is the reaction force exerted by the ball on Earth.

It's easy to see the effect of the action force—the ball falls to Earth. Why don't you notice the effect of the reaction force—Earth being pulled upward? To find the answer to this question, think about Newton's second law. It states that the acceleration of an object depends on the force applied to it and on the mass of the object. The force on Earth is equal to the force on the ball. But the mass of Earth is much larger than the mass of the ball. Thus, the acceleration of Earth is much smaller than the acceleration of the ball. The acceleration of the Earth is so small that you can't see or feel the acceleration. So, it is difficult to observe the effect of Newton's third law on falling objects.

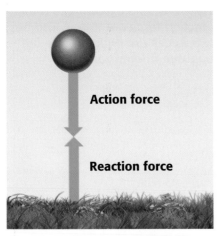

Action force

Reaction force

Figure 8 *The force of gravity between Earth and a falling object is a force pair.*

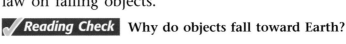
Reading Check Why do objects fall toward Earth?

Summary

- Newton's first law of motion states that the motion of an object will not change if no unbalanced forces act on it.
- Objects at rest will not move unless acted upon by an unbalanced force.
- Objects in motion will continue to move at a constant speed and in a straight line unless acted upon by an unbalanced force.
- Inertia is the tendency of matter to resist a change in motion. Mass is a measure of inertia.

- Newton's second law of motion states that the acceleration of an object depends on its mass and on the force exerted on it.
- Newton's second law is represented by the following equation: $F = m \times a$.
- Newton's third law of motion states that whenever one object exerts a force on a second object, the second object exerts an equal and opposite force on the first object.

Using Key Terms

1. In your own words, write a definition for the term *inertia*.

Understanding Key Ideas

2. Which of the following will increase the acceleration of an object that is pushed by a force?
   a. decreasing the mass of the object
   b. increasing the mass of the object
   c. increasing the force pushing the object
   d. Both (a) and (c)

3. Give three examples of force pairs that occur when you do your homework.

4. What does Newton's first law of motion say about objects at rest and objects in motion?

5. Use Newton's second law to describe the relationship between force, mass, and acceleration.

Math Skills

6. What force is necessary to accelerate a 70 kg object at a rate of 4.2 m/s²?

Critical Thinking

7. **Applying Concepts** When a truck pulls a trailer, the trailer and truck accelerate forward even though the action and reaction forces are the same size but are in opposite directions. Why don't these forces balance each other?

8. **Making Inferences** Use Newton's first law of motion to explain why airbags in cars are important during head-on collisions.

Interpreting Graphics

9. Imagine you accidentally bumped your hand against a table, as shown in the photo below. Your hand hurts after it happens. Use Newton's third law of motion to explain what caused your hand to hurt.

SCI LINKS®

NSTA

Developed and maintained by the
National Science Teachers Association

For a variety of links related to this chapter, go to www.scilinks.org

Topic: Newton's Laws of Motion
SciLinks code: HSM1028

Momentum

Imagine a compact car and a large truck traveling with the same velocity. The drivers of both vehicles put on the brakes at the same time. Which vehicle will stop first?

You would probably say that the compact car will stop first. You know that smaller objects are easier to stop than larger objects. But why? The answer is momentum (moh MEN tuhm).

Momentum, Mass, and Velocity

The **momentum** of an object depends on the object's mass and velocity. The more momentum an object has, the harder it is to stop the object or change its direction. In the example above, the truck has more mass and more momentum than the car has. So, a larger force is needed to stop the truck. Similarly, a fast-moving car has a greater velocity and thus more momentum than a slow-moving car of the same mass. So, a fast-moving car is harder to stop than a slow-moving car. **Figure 1** shows another example of an object that has momentum.

Calculating Momentum

Momentum (*p*) can be calculated with the equation below:

$$p = m \times v$$

In this equation, *m* is the mass of an object in kilograms and *v* is the object's velocity in meters per second. The units of momentum are kilograms multiplied by meters per second, or kg•m/s. Like velocity, momentum has a direction. Its direction is always the same as the direction of the object's velocity.

Figure 1 *The teen on the right has less mass than the teen on the left. But, the teen on the right can have a large momentum by moving quickly when she kicks.*

Momentum Calculations   What is the momentum of an ostrich with a mass of 120 kg that runs with a velocity of 16 m/s north?

Step 1: Write the equation for momentum.

$$p = m \times v$$

Step 2: Replace *m* and *v* with the values given in the problem, and solve.

$$p = 120 \text{ kg} \times 16 \text{ m/s north}$$
$$p = 19{,}200 \text{ kg} \bullet \text{m/s north}$$

Now It's Your Turn

1. What is the momentum of a 6 kg bowling ball that is moving at 10 m/s down the alley toward the pins?
2. An 85 kg man is jogging with a velocity of 2.6 m/s to the north. Nearby, a 65 kg person is skateboarding and is traveling with a velocity of 3 m/s north. Which person has greater momentum? Show your calculations.

The Law of Conservation of Momentum

When a moving object hits another object, some or all of the momentum of the first object is transferred to the object that is hit. If only some of the momentum is transferred, the rest of the momentum stays with the first object.

Imagine that a cue ball hits a billiard ball so that the billiard ball starts moving and the cue ball stops, as shown in **Figure 2.** The white cue ball had a certain amount of momentum before the collision. During the collision, all of the cue ball's momentum was transferred to the red billiard ball. After the collision, the billiard ball moved away with the same amount of momentum the cue ball had. This example shows the *law of conservation of momentum.* The law of conservation of momentum states that any time objects collide, the total amount of momentum stays the same. The law of conservation of momentum is true for any collision if no other forces act on the colliding objects. This law applies whether the objects stick together or bounce off each other after they collide.

✓ Reading Check What can happen to momentum when two objects collide? (*See the Appendix for answers to Reading Checks.*)

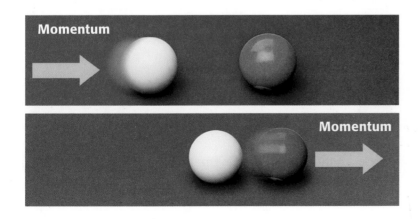

Figure 2 *The momentum before a collision is equal to the momentum after the collision.*

Objects Sticking Together

Sometimes, objects stick together after a collision. The football players shown in **Figure 3** are an example of such a collision. A dog leaping and catching a ball and a teen jumping on a skateboard are also examples. After two objects stick together, they move as one object. The mass of the combined objects is equal to the masses of the two objects added together. In a head-on collision, the combined objects move in the direction of the object that had the greater momentum before the collision. But together, the objects have a velocity that differs from the velocity of either object before the collision. The objects have a different velocity because momentum is conserved and depends on mass and velocity. So, when mass changes, the velocity must change, too.

Objects Bouncing Off Each Other

In some collisions, the objects bounce off each other. The bowling ball and bowling pins shown in **Figure 3** are examples of objects that bounce off each other after they collide. Billiard balls and bumper cars are other examples. During these types of collisions, momentum is usually transferred from one object to another object. The transfer of momentum causes the objects to move in different directions at different speeds. However, the total momentum of all the objects will remain the same before and after the collision.

✓ **Reading Check** What are two ways that objects may interact after a collision?

CONNECTION TO Language Arts

WRITING SKILL **Momentum and Language**
The word *momentum* is often used in everyday language. For example, a sports announcer may say that the momentum of a game has changed. Or you may read that an idea is gaining momentum. In your **science journal,** write a paragraph that explains how the everyday use of the word *momentum* differs from momentum in science.

Figure 3 **Examples of Conservation of Momentum**

When football players tackle another player, they stick together. The velocity of each player changes after the collision because of conservation of momentum.

Although the bowling ball and bowling pins bounce off each other and move in different directions after a collision, momentum is neither gained nor lost.

Conservation of Momentum and Newton's Third Law

Conservation of momentum can be explained by Newton's third law of motion. In the example of the billiard ball, the cue ball hit the billiard ball with a certain amount of force. This force was the action force. The reaction force was the equal but opposite force exerted by the billiard ball on the cue ball. The action force made the billiard ball start moving, and the reaction force made the cue ball stop moving, as shown in **Figure 4.** Because the action and reaction forces are equal and opposite, momentum is neither gained nor lost.

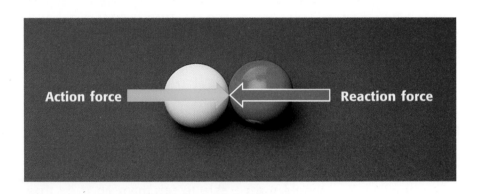

Figure 4 *The action force makes the billiard ball begin moving, and the reaction force stops the cue ball's motion.*

SECTION Review

Summary

● Momentum is a property of moving objects.

● Momentum is calculated by multiplying the mass of an object by the object's velocity.

● When two or more objects collide, momentum may be transferred, but the total amount of momentum does not change. This is the law of conservation of momentum.

Using Key Terms

1. Use the following term in a sentence: *momentum.*

Understanding Key Ideas

2. Which of the following has the smallest amount of momentum?
   a. a loaded truck driven at high-way speeds
   b. a track athlete running a race
   c. a baby crawling on the floor
   d. a jet airplane being towed toward an airport

3. Explain the law of conservation of momentum.

4. How is Newton's third law of motion related to the law of conservation of momentum?

Math Skills

5. Calculate the momentum of a 2.5 kg puppy that is running with a velocity of 4.8 m/s south.

Critical Thinking

6. **Applying Concepts** A car and a train are traveling with the same velocity. Do the two objects have the same momentum? Explain your answer.

7. **Analyzing Ideas** When you catch a softball, your hand and glove move in the same direction that the ball is moving. Analyze the motion of your hand and glove in terms of momentum.

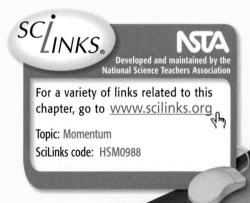

Skills Practice Lab

Inertia-Rama!

Inertia is a property of all matter, from small particles of dust to enormous planets and stars. In this lab, you will investigate the inertia of various shapes and kinds of matter. Keep in mind that each investigation requires you to either overcome or use the object's inertia.

Station 1: Magic Eggs

Procedure

1. There are two eggs at this station—one is hard-boiled (solid all the way through) and the other is raw (liquid inside). The masses of the two eggs are about the same. The eggs are not marked. You should not be able to tell them apart by their appearance. Without breaking them open, how can you tell which egg is raw and which egg is hard-boiled?

2. Before you do anything to either egg, make some predictions. Will there be any difference in the way the two eggs spin? Which egg will be the easier to stop?

3. First, spin one egg. Then, place your finger on it gently to make it stop spinning. Record your observations.

4. Repeat step 3 with the second egg.

5. Compare your predictions with your observations. (Repeat steps 3 and 4 if necessary.)

6. Which egg is hard-boiled and which one is raw? Explain.

Analyze the Results

1. **Explaining Events** Explain why the eggs behave differently when you spin them even though they should have the same inertia. (Hint: Think about what happens to the liquid inside the raw egg.)

Draw Conclusions

2. **Drawing Conclusions** Explain why the eggs react differently when you try to stop them.

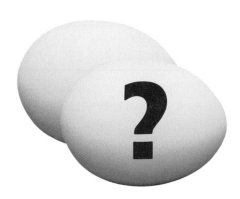

Station 2: Coin in a Cup

Procedure

1. At this station, you will find a coin, an index card, and a cup. Place the card over the cup. Then, place the coin on the card over the center of the cup, as shown below.

2. Write down a method for getting the coin into the cup without touching the coin and without lifting the card.

3. Try your method. If it doesn't work, try again until you find a method that does work.

Analyze the Results

1. **Describing Events** Use Newton's first law of motion to explain why the coin falls into the cup if you remove the card quickly.

Draw Conclusions

2. **Defending Conclusions** Explain why pulling on the card slowly will not work even though the coin has inertia. (Hint: Friction is a force.)

Station 3: The Magic Thread

Procedure

1. At this station, you will find a spool of thread and a mass hanging from a strong string. Cut a piece of thread about 40 cm long. Tie the thread around the bottom of the mass, as shown at right.

2. Pull gently on the end of the thread. Observe what happens, and record your observations.

3. Stop the mass from moving. Now hold the end of the thread so that there is a lot of slack between your fingers and the mass.

4. Give the thread a quick, hard pull. You should observe a very different event. Record your observations. Throw away the thread.

Analyze the Results

1. **Analyzing Results** Use Newton's first law of motion to explain why the result of a gentle pull is different from the result of a hard pull.

Draw Conclusions

2. **Applying Conclusions** Both moving and non-moving objects have inertia. Explain why throwing a bowling ball and catching a thrown bowling ball are hard.

3. **Drawing Conclusions** Why is it harder to run with a backpack full of books than to run with an empty backpack?

Chapter Review

USING KEY TERMS

Complete each of the following sentences by choosing the correct term from the word bank.

free fall   projectile motion
inertia   terminal velocity
momentum

1 An object in motion has ___, so it tends to stay in motion.

2 An object is falling at its ___ if it falls at a constant velocity.

3 ___ is the path that a thrown object follows.

4 ___ is a property of moving objects that depends on mass and velocity.

5 ___ occurs only when air resistance does not affect the motion of a falling object.

UNDERSTANDING KEY IDEAS

Multiple Choice

6 When a soccer ball is kicked, the action and reaction forces do not cancel each other out because
- **a.** the forces are not equal in size.
- **b.** the forces act on different objects.
- **c.** the forces act at different times.
- **d.** All of the above

7 An object is in projectile motion if it
- **a.** is thrown with a horizontal push.
- **b.** is accelerated downward by gravity.
- **c.** does not accelerate horizontally.
- **d.** All of the above

8 Newton's first law of motion applies to
- **a.** moving objects.
- **b.** objects that are not moving.
- **c.** objects that are accelerating.
- **d.** Both (a) and (b)

9 To accelerate two objects at the same rate, the force used to push the object that has more mass should be
- **a.** smaller than the force used to push the object that has less mass.
- **b.** larger than the force used to push the object that has less mass.
- **c.** the same as the force used to push the object that has less mass.
- **d.** equal to the object's weight.

10 A golf ball and a bowling ball are moving at the same velocity. Which of the two has more momentum?
- **a.** The golf ball has more momentum because it has less mass.
- **b.** The bowling ball has more momentum because it has more mass.
- **c.** They have the same momentum because they have the same velocity.
- **d.** There is not enough information to determine the answer.

Short Answer

11 Give an example of an object that is in free fall.

12 Describe how gravity and air resistance are related to an object's terminal velocity.

13 Why can friction make observing Newton's first law of motion difficult?

Math Skills

14 A 12 kg rock falls from rest off a cliff and hits the ground in 1.5 s.

  a. Without considering air resistance, what is the rock's velocity just before it hits the ground?

  b. What is the rock's momentum just before it hits the ground?

CRITICAL THINKING

15 Concept Mapping Use the following terms to create a concept map: *gravity, free fall, terminal velocity, projectile motion,* and *air resistance.*

16 Identifying Relationships During a space shuttle launch, about 830,000 kg of fuel is burned in 8 min. The fuel provides the shuttle with a constant thrust, or forward force. How does Newton's second law of motion explain why the shuttle's acceleration increases as the fuel is burned?

17 Analyzing Processes When using a hammer to drive a nail into wood, you have to swing the hammer through the air with a certain velocity. Because the hammer has both mass and velocity, it has momentum. Describe what happens to the hammer's momentum after the hammer hits the nail.

18 Applying Concepts Suppose you are standing on a skateboard or on in-line skates and you toss a backpack full of heavy books toward your friend. What do you think will happen to you? Explain your answer in terms of Newton's third law of motion.

INTERPRETING GRAPHICS

19 The picture below shows a common desk toy. If you pull one ball up and release it, it hits the balls at the bottom and comes to a stop. In the same instant, the ball on the other side swings up and repeats the cycle. How does conservation of momentum explain how this toy works?

Standardized Test Preparation

Read each of the passages below. Then, answer the questions that follow each passage.

Passage 1 How do astronauts prepare for trips in the space shuttle? One method is to use simulations on Earth that mimic the conditions in space. For example, underwater training lets astronauts experience reduced gravity. They can also ride on NASA's modified KC-135 airplane. NASA's KC-135 simulates how it feels to be in a space shuttle. How does this airplane work? It flies upward at a steep angle and then flies downward at a 45° angle. When the airplane flies downward, the effect of reduced gravity is produced. As the plane falls, the astronauts inside the plane can float like astronauts in the space shuttle do!

1. What is the purpose of this passage?
   A to explain how astronauts prepare for missions in space
   B to convince people to become astronauts
   C to show that space is similar to Earth
   D to describe what it feels like to float in space

2. What can you conclude about NASA's KC-135 from the passage?
   F NASA's KC-135 is just like other airplanes.
   G All astronauts train in NASA's KC-135.
   H NASA's KC-135 simulates the space shuttle by reducing the effects of gravity.
   I Being in NASA's KC-135 is not very much like being in the space shuttle.

3. Based on the passage, which of the following statements is a fact?
   A Astronauts always have to train underwater.
   B Flying in airplanes is similar to riding in the space shuttle.
   C People in NASA's KC-135 float at all times.
   D Astronauts use simulations to learn what reduced gravity is like.

Passage 2 There once was a game that could be played by as few as 5 or as many as 1,000 players. The game could be played on a small field for a few hours or on a huge tract of land for several days. The game was not just for fun—in fact, it was often used as a substitute for war. One of the few rules was that the players couldn't touch the ball with their hands—they had to use a special stick with webbing on one end. Would you believe that this game is the same as the game of lacrosse that is played today?

Lacrosse is a game that was originally played by Native Americans. They called the game *baggataway*, which means "little brother of war." Although lacrosse has changed and is now played all over the world, it still requires special, webbed sticks.

1. What is the purpose of this passage?
   A to explain the importance of rules in lacrosse
   B to explain why sticks are used in lacrosse
   C to describe the history of lacrosse
   D to describe the rules of lacrosse

2. Based on the passage, what does the word *substitute* mean?
   F something that occurs before war
   G something that is needed to play lacrosse
   H something that is of Native American origin
   I something that takes the place of something else

Read each question below, and choose the best answer.

1. Which of the following images shows an object with no momentum that is about to be set in motion by an unbalanced force?

A

B

C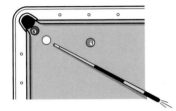

D

2. During a laboratory experiment, liquid was collected in a graduated cylinder. What is the volume of the liquid?

F 30 mL
G 35 mL
H 40 mL
I 45 mL

Read each question below, and choose the best answer.

1. The table below shows the accelerations produced by different forces for a 5 kg mass. Assuming that the pattern continues, use this data to predict what acceleration would be produced by a 100 N force.

Force	Acceleration
25 N	5 m/s^2
50 N	10 m/s^2
75 N	15 m/s^2

A 10 m/s^2
B 20 m/s^2
C 30 m/s^2
D 100 m/s^2

2. The average radius of the moon is 1.74×10^6 m. What is another way to express the radius of the moon?

F 0.00000174 m
G 0.000174 m
H 174,000 m
I 1,740,000 m

3. The half price bookstore is selling 4 paperback books for a total of $5.75. What would the price of 20 paperback books be?

A $23.00
B $24.75
C $28.75
D $51.75

4. A 75 kg speed skater is moving with a velocity of 16 m/s east. What is the speed skater's momentum? (Momentum is calculated with the equation: *momentum = mass × velocity*.)

F 91 kg•m/s
G 91 kg•m/s east
H 1,200 kg•m/s east
I 1,200 kg•m/s^2 east

Standardized Test Preparation

Science in Action

Scientific Discoveries

The Millennium Bridge

You may have heard the children's song, "London Bridge is falling down . . .". London Bridge never fell. But some people who walked on the Millennium Bridge thought that it might fall instead! The Millennium Bridge is a pedestrian bridge in London, England. The bridge opened on June 10, 2000, and more than 80,000 people crossed it that day. Immediately, people noticed something wrong—the bridge was swaying! The bridge was closed after two days so that engineers could determine what was wrong. After much research, the engineers learned that the force of the footsteps of the people crossing the bridge caused the bridge to sway.

Language Arts ACTiViTY

WRITING SKILL Imagine that you were in London on June 10, 2000 and walked across the Millennium Bridge. Write a one-page story about what you think it was like on the bridge that day.

Science, Technology, and Society

Power Suit for Lifting Patients

Imagine visiting a hospital and seeing someone who looked half human and half robot. No, it isn't a scene from a science fiction movie—it is a new invention that may some day help nurses lift patients easily. The invention, called a power suit, is a metal framework that a nurse would wear on his or her back. The suit calculates how much force a nurse needs to lift a patient, and then the robotic joints on the suit help the nurse exert the right amount of force. The suit will also help nurses avoid injuring their backs.

Math ACTiViTY

The pound (symbol £) is the currency in England. The inventor of the suit thinks that it will be sold for £1200. How much will the suit cost in dollars if $1 is equal to £0.60?

Steve Okamoto

Roller Coaster Designer Roller coasters have fascinated Steve Okamoto ever since his first ride on one. "I remember going to Disneyland as a kid. My mother was always upset with me because I kept looking over the sides of the rides, trying to figure out how they worked," he says. To satisfy his curiosity, Okamoto became a mechanical engineer. Today he uses his scientific knowledge to design and build machines, systems, and buildings. But his specialty is roller coasters.

Roller coasters really do coast along the track. A motor pulls the cars up a high hill to start the ride. After that, the cars are powered by only gravity. Designing a successful roller coaster is not a simple task. Okamoto has to calculate the cars' speed and acceleration on each part of the track. He must also consider the safety of the ride and the strength of the structure that supports the track.

Social Studies ACTIVITY

Research the history of roller coasters to learn how roller coaster design has changed over time. Make a poster to summarize your research.

To learn more about these Science in Action topics, visit **go.hrw.com** and type in the keyword **HP5FORF.**

Current Science

Check out Current Science® articles related to this chapter by visiting **go.hrw.com.** Just type in the keyword **HP5CS06.**

3

Forces in Fluids

The Big Idea

Forces in fluids are related to pressure and density and can affect the motion of objects in the fluid.

About the

As you race downhill on your bicycle, the air around you pushes on your body and slows you down. "What a drag!" you say. Well, actually, it is a drag. When designing bicycle gear and clothing, manufacturers consider more than just looks and comfort. They also try to decrease drag, a fluid force that opposes motion. This photo shows cyclists riding their bikes in a wind tunnel in a study of how a fluid—air—affects their ride.

PRE-READING ACTIVITY

FOLDNOTES

Booklet Before you read the chapter, create the FoldNote entitled "Booklet" described in the **Study Skills** section of the Appendix. Label each page of the booklet with a main idea from the chapter. As you read the chapter, write what you learn about each main idea on the appropriate page of the booklet.

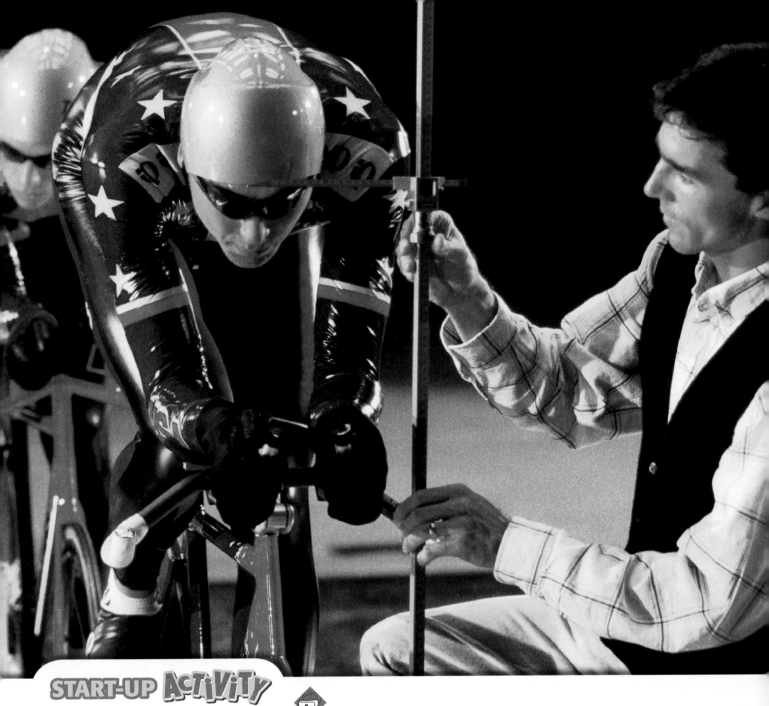

START-UP ACTIVITY

Taking Flight

In this activity, you will build a model airplane to learn how wing size affects flight.

Procedure

1. Fold a **sheet of paper** in half lengthwise. Then, open it. Fold the top corners toward the center crease. Keep the corners folded down, and fold the entire sheet in half along the center crease.

2. With the plane on its side, fold the top front edge down so that it meets the bottom edge. Fold the top edge down again so that it meets the bottom edge. Turn the plane over, and repeat.

3. Raise the wings so that they are perpendicular to the body.

4. Point the plane slightly upward, and gently throw it. Repeat several times. Describe what you see.

5. Make the wings smaller by folding them one more time. Gently throw the plane. Repeat several times. Describe what you see.

6. Using the smaller wings, try to achieve the same flight path you saw when the wings were bigger.

Analysis

1. What happened to the plane's flight when you reduced the size of its wings? What did you have to do to achieve the same flight path as when the wings were bigger?

2. What gave your plane its forward motion?

Fluids and Pressure

What does a dolphin have in common with a sea gull? What does a dog have in common with a fly? What do you have in common with all these living things?

One answer to these questions is that you and all these other living things spend a lifetime moving through fluids. A **fluid** is any material that can flow and that takes the shape of its container. Fluids include liquids and gases. Fluids can flow because the particles in fluids move easily past each other.

What You Will Learn

- Describe how fluids exert pressure.
- Analyze how atmospheric pressure varies with depth.
- Explain how depth and density affect water pressure.
- Give examples of fluids flowing from high to low pressure.

Vocabulary

fluid
pressure
pascal
atmospheric pressure

READING STRATEGY

Brainstorming The key idea of this section is pressure. Brainstorm words and phrases related to pressure.

Fluids Exert Pressure

You probably have heard the terms *air pressure* and *water pressure*. Air and water are fluids. All fluids exert pressure. So, what is pressure? Think about this example. When you pump up a bicycle tire, you push air into the tire. And like all matter, air is made of tiny particles that are constantly moving.

Look at **Figure 1.** Inside the tire, the air particles collide with each other and with the walls of the tire. Together, these collisions create a force on the tire. The amount of force exerted on a given area is **pressure.**

Calculating Pressure

Pressure can be calculated by using the following equation:

$$pressure = \frac{force}{area}$$

The SI unit for pressure is the **pascal.** One pascal (1 Pa) is the force of one newton exerted over an area of one square meter (1 N/m^2).

fluid a nonsolid state of matter in which the atoms or molecules are free to move past each other, as in a gas or liquid

pressure the amount of force exerted per unit area of a surface

pascal the SI unit of pressure (symbol, Pa)

atmospheric pressure the pressure caused by the weight of the atmosphere

Figure 1 *The force of the air particles hitting the inner surface of the tire creates pressure, which keeps the tire inflated.*

Pressure, Force, and Area What is the pressure exerted by a book that has an area of 0.2 m² and a weight of 10 N?

Step 1: Write the equation for pressure.

$$pressure = \frac{force}{area}$$

Step 2: Replace *force* and *area* with the values given, and solve. (Hint: Weight is a measure of gravitational force.)

$$pressure = \frac{10 \text{ N}}{0.2 \text{ m}^2} = 50 \text{ N/m}^2 = 50 \text{ Pa}$$

The equation for pressure can be rearranged to find force or area, as shown below.

force = pressure × area (*Rearrange by multiplying by area.*)

$$area = \frac{force}{pressure}$$ (*Rearrange by multiplying by area and then dividing by pressure.*)

Now It's Your Turn

1. Find the pressure exerted by a 3,000 N crate that has an area of 2 m².
2. Find the weight of a rock that has an area of 10 m² and that exerts a pressure of 250 Pa.

Pressure and Bubbles

When you blow a soap bubble, you blow in only one direction. So, why does the bubble get rounder instead of longer as you blow? The shape of the bubble partly depends on an important property of fluids: Fluids exert pressure evenly in all directions. The air you blow into the bubble exerts pressure evenly in all directions. So, the bubble expands in all directions to create a sphere.

Atmospheric Pressure

The *atmosphere* is the layer of nitrogen, oxygen, and other gases that surrounds Earth. Earth's atmosphere is held in place by gravity, which pulls the gases toward Earth. The pressure caused by the weight of the atmosphere is called **atmospheric pressure.**

Atmospheric pressure is exerted on everything on Earth, including you. At sea level, the atmosphere exerts a pressure of about 101,300 N on every square meter, or 101,300 Pa. So, there is a weight of about 10 N (about 2 lbs) on every square centimeter of your body. Why don't you feel this crushing pressure? Like the air inside a balloon, the fluids inside your body exert pressure. **Figure 2** can help you understand why you don't feel the pressure.

✓ Reading Check Name two gases in the atmosphere. (*See the Appendix for answers to Reading Checks.*)

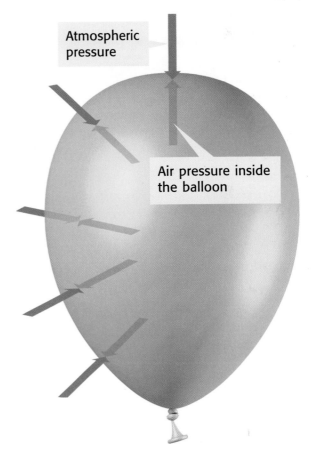

Atmospheric pressure

Air pressure inside the balloon

Figure 2 *The air inside a balloon exerts pressure that keeps the balloon inflated against atmospheric pressure. Similarly, fluid inside your body exerts pressure that works against atmospheric pressure.*

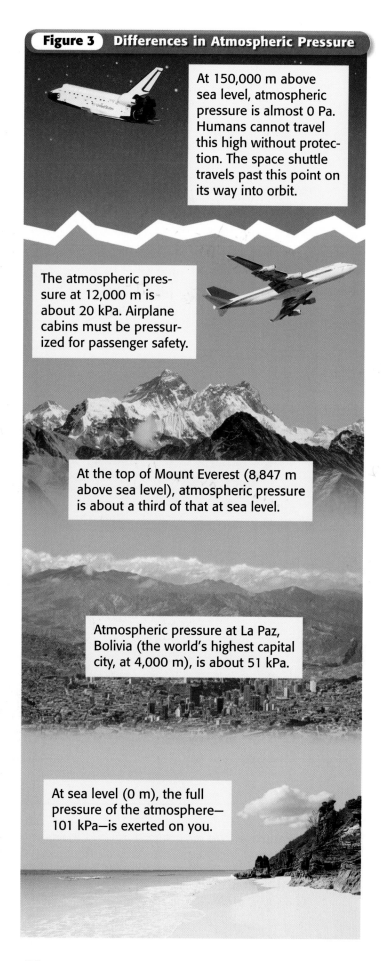

Figure 3 Differences in Atmospheric Pressure

At 150,000 m above sea level, atmospheric pressure is almost 0 Pa. Humans cannot travel this high without protection. The space shuttle travels past this point on its way into orbit.

The atmospheric pressure at 12,000 m is about 20 kPa. Airplane cabins must be pressurized for passenger safety.

At the top of Mount Everest (8,847 m above sea level), atmospheric pressure is about a third of that at sea level.

Atmospheric pressure at La Paz, Bolivia (the world's highest capital city, at 4,000 m), is about 51 kPa.

At sea level (0 m), the full pressure of the atmosphere—101 kPa—is exerted on you.

Variation of Atmospheric Pressure

The atmosphere stretches about 150 km above Earth's surface. However, about 80% of the atmosphere's gases are found within 10 km of Earth's surface. At the top of the atmosphere, pressure is almost nonexistent. The pressure is close to 0 Pa because the gas particles are far apart and rarely collide. Mount Everest in south-central Asia is the highest point on Earth. At the top of Mount Everest, atmospheric pressure is about 33,000 Pa, or 33 kilopascals (33 kPa). (Remember that the prefix *kilo-* means 1,000. So, 1 kPa is equal to 1,000 Pa.) At sea level, atmospheric pressure is about 101 kPa.

Atmospheric Pressure and Depth

Take a look at **Figure 3.** Notice how atmospheric pressure changes as you travel through the atmosphere. The further down through the atmosphere you go, the greater the pressure is. In other words, the pressure increases as the atmosphere gets "deeper." An important point to remember about fluids is that pressure varies depending on depth. At lower levels of the atmosphere, there is more fluid above that is being pulled by Earth's gravitational force. So, there is more pressure at lower levels of the atmosphere.

✓ **Reading Check** Describe how pressure changes with depth.

Pressure Changes and Your Body

So, what happens to your body when atmospheric pressure changes? If you travel to higher or lower points in the atmosphere, the fluids in your body have to adjust to maintain equal pressure. You may have experienced this adjustment if your ears have "popped" when you were in a plane taking off or in a car traveling down a steep mountain road. The "pop" happens because of pressure changes in pockets of air behind your eardrums.

Water Pressure

Water is a fluid. So, it exerts pressure like the atmosphere does. Water pressure also increases as depth increases, as shown in **Figure 4.** The deeper a diver goes in the water, the greater the pressure is. The pressure increases because more water above the diver is being pulled by Earth's gravitational force. In addition, the atmosphere presses down on the water, so the total pressure on the diver includes water pressure and atmospheric pressure.

Water Pressure and Depth

Like atmospheric pressure, water pressure depends on depth. Water pressure does not depend on the total amount of fluid present. A swimmer would feel the same pressure swimming at 3 m below the surface of a small pond and at 3 m below the surface of an ocean. Even though there is more water in the ocean than in the pond, the pressure on the swimmer in the pond would be the same as the pressure on the swimmer in the ocean.

Density Making a Difference

Water is about 1,000 times more dense than air. *Density* is the amount of matter in a given volume, or mass per unit volume. Because water is more dense than air, a certain volume of water has more mass—and weighs more—than the same volume of air. So, water exerts more pressure than air.

For example, if you climb a 10 m tree, the decrease in atmospheric pressure is too small to notice. But if you dive 10 m underwater, the pressure on you increases to 201 kPa, which is almost twice the atmospheric pressure at the surface!

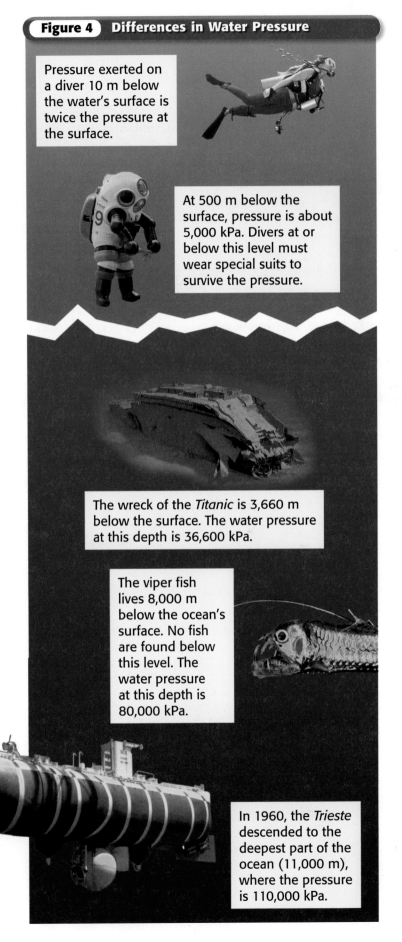

Figure 4 Differences in Water Pressure

Pressure exerted on a diver 10 m below the water's surface is twice the pressure at the surface.

At 500 m below the surface, pressure is about 5,000 kPa. Divers at or below this level must wear special suits to survive the pressure.

The wreck of the *Titanic* is 3,660 m below the surface. The water pressure at this depth is 36,600 kPa.

The viper fish lives 8,000 m below the ocean's surface. No fish are found below this level. The water pressure at this depth is 80,000 kPa.

In 1960, the *Trieste* descended to the deepest part of the ocean (11,000 m), where the pressure is 110,000 kPa.

Pressure Differences and Fluid Flow

When you drink through a straw, you remove some of the air in the straw. Because there is less air inside the straw, the pressure in the straw is reduced. But the atmospheric pressure on the surface of the liquid remains the same. Thus, there is a difference between the pressure inside the straw and the pressure outside the straw. The outside pressure forces the liquid up the straw and into your mouth. So, just by drinking through a straw, you can observe an important property of fluids: Fluids flow from areas of high pressure to areas of low pressure.

✓ **Reading Check** When drinking through a straw, how do you decrease the pressure inside the straw?

Pressure Differences and Breathing

Take a deep breath—fluid is flowing from high to low pressure! When you inhale, a muscle increases the space in your chest and gives your lungs room to expand. This expansion decreases the pressure in your lungs. The pressure in your lungs becomes lower than the air pressure outside your lungs. Air then flows into your lungs—from high to low pressure. This air carries oxygen that you need to live. **Figure 5** shows how exhaling also causes fluids to flow from high to low pressure. You can see a similar flow of fluid when you open a carbonated beverage or squeeze toothpaste onto your toothbrush.

Blown Away

1. Lay an **empty plastic soda bottle** on its side.
2. Wad a **small piece of paper** (about 4 × 4 cm) into a ball.
3. Place the paper ball just inside the bottle's opening.
4. Blow straight into the opening.
5. Record your observations.
6. Explain your results in terms of high and low fluid pressures.

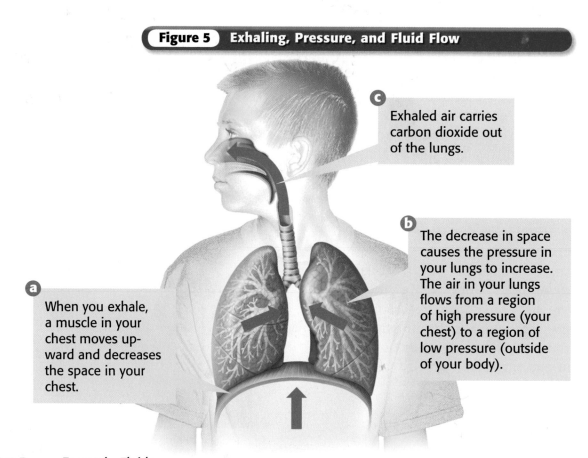

Figure 5 Exhaling, Pressure, and Fluid Flow

c Exhaled air carries carbon dioxide out of the lungs.

b The decrease in space causes the pressure in your lungs to increase. The air in your lungs flows from a region of high pressure (your chest) to a region of low pressure (outside of your body).

a When you exhale, a muscle in your chest moves upward and decreases the space in your chest.

Pressure Differences and Tornadoes

Look at the tornado in **Figure 6.** Some of the damaging winds caused by tornadoes are the result of pressure differences. The air pressure inside a tornado is very low. Because the air pressure outside of the tornado is higher than the pressure inside, air rushes into the tornado. The rushing air causes the tornado to be like a giant vacuum cleaner—objects are pushed into the tornado. The winds created are usually very strong and affect the area around the tornado. So, objects, such as trees and buildings, can be severely damaged by wind even if they are not in the direct path of a tornado.

Figure 6 *Tornadoes are like giant vacuum cleaners because of pressure differences.*

SECTION Review

Summary

- A fluid is any material that flows and takes the shape of its container.
- Pressure is force exerted on a given area.
- Moving particles of matter create pressure by colliding with one another and with the walls of their container.
- The pressure caused by the weight of the atmosphere is called *atmospheric pressure*.
- Fluid pressure increases as depth increases.
- As depth increases, water pressure increases faster than atmospheric pressure does because water is denser than air.
- Fluids flow from areas of high pressure to areas of low pressure.

Using Key Terms

1. In your own words, write a definition for each of the following terms: *fluid* and *atmospheric pressure*.

2. Use the following terms in the same sentence: *pressure* and *pascal*.

Understanding Key Ideas

3. Which of the following statements about fluids is true?
   a. Fluids rarely take the shape of their container.
   b. Fluids include liquids and gases.
   c. Fluids flow from low pressure to high pressure.
   d. Fluids exert the most pressure in the downward direction.

4. How do fluids exert pressure on a container?

5. Why are you not crushed by atmospheric pressure?

6. Explain why atmospheric pressure changes as depth changes.

7. Give three examples of fluids flowing from high pressure to low pressure in everyday life.

Math Skills

8. The water in a glass has a weight of 2.4 N. The bottom of the glass has an area of 0.012 m^2. What is the pressure exerted by the water on the bottom of the glass?

Critical Thinking

9. **Identifying Relationships** Mercury is a liquid that has a density of 13.5 g/mL. Water has a density of 1.0 g/mL. Equal volumes of mercury and water are in identical containers. Explain why the pressures exerted on the bottoms of the containers are different.

10. **Making Inferences** Why do airplanes need to be pressurized for passenger safety when flying high in the atmosphere?

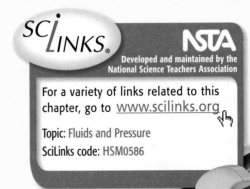

Buoyant Force

Why does an ice cube float on water? Why doesn't it sink to the bottom of your glass?

Imagine that you use a straw to push an ice cube under water. Then, you release the cube. A force pushes the ice back to the water's surface. The force, called **buoyant force** (BOY uhnt FAWRS), is the upward force that fluids exert on all matter.

Buoyant Force and Fluid Pressure

Look at **Figure 1.** Water exerts fluid pressure on all sides of an object. The pressure exerted horizontally on one side of the object is equal to the pressure exerted on the opposite side. These equal pressures cancel one another. So, the only fluid pressures affecting the net force on the object are at the top and at the bottom. Pressure increases as depth increases. So, the pressure at the bottom of the object is greater than the pressure at the top. The water exerts a net upward force on the object. This upward force is buoyant force.

Determining Buoyant Force

Archimedes (AHR kuh MEE deez), a Greek mathematician who lived in the third century BCE, discovered how to determine buoyant force. **Archimedes' principle** states that the buoyant force on an object in a fluid is an upward force equal to the weight of the fluid that the object takes the place of, or displaces. Suppose the object in **Figure 1** displaces 250 mL of water. The weight of that volume of displaced water is about 2.5 N. So, the buoyant force on the object is 2.5 N. Notice that only the weight of the displaced fluid determines the buoyant force on an object. The weight of the object does not affect buoyant force.

What You Will Learn

- Explain the relationship between fluid pressure and buoyant force.
- Predict whether an object will float or sink in a fluid.
- Analyze the role of density in an object's ability to float.
- Explain how the overall density of an object can be changed.

Vocabulary

buoyant force
Archimedes' principle

READING STRATEGY

Discussion Read this section silently. Write down questions that you have about this section. Discuss your questions in a small group.

buoyant force the upward force that keeps an object immersed in or floating on a liquid

Archimedes' principle the principle that states that the buoyant force on an object in a fluid is an upward force equal to the weight of the volume of fluid that the object displaces

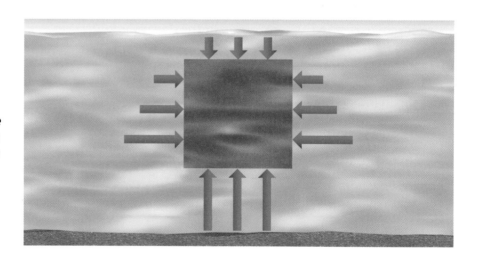

Figure 1 *There is more pressure at the bottom of an object because pressure increases with depth. This results in an upward buoyant force on the object.*

Weight Versus Buoyant Force

An object in a fluid will sink if its weight is greater than the buoyant force (the weight of the fluid it displaces). An object floats only when the buoyant force on the object is equal to the object's weight.

Sinking

The rock in **Figure 2** weighs 75 N. It displaces 5 L of water. Archimedes' principle says that the buoyant force is equal to the weight of the displaced water—about 50 N. The rock's weight is greater than the buoyant force. So, the rock sinks.

Floating

The fish in **Figure 2** weighs 12 N. It displaces a volume of water that weighs 12 N. Because the fish's weight is equal to the buoyant force, the fish floats in the water. In fact, the fish is suspended in the water as it floats. Now, look at the duck. The duck does not sink. So, the buoyant force on the duck must be equal to the duck's weight. But the duck isn't all the way underwater! Only the duck's feet, legs, and stomach have to be underwater to displace 9 N of water, which is equal to the duck's weight. So, the duck floats on the surface of the water.

Buoying Up

If the duck dove underwater, it would displace more than 9 N of water. So, the buoyant force on the duck would be greater than the duck's weight. When the buoyant force on an object is greater than the object's weight, the object is *buoyed up* (pushed up) in water. An object is buoyed up until the part of the object underwater displaces an amount of water that equals the object's entire weight. Thus, an ice cube pops to the surface when it is pushed to the bottom of a glass of water.

✓ Reading Check What causes an object to buoy up? (*See the Appendix for answers to Reading Checks.*)

Floating Fun

Fill a sink with water. Ask an adult to help you find five things that float in water and five things that sink in water. Discuss what the floating objects have in common and what the sinking objects have in common. In your **science journal,** list the objects, and summarize your discussion.

Figure 2 *Will an object sink or float? That depends on whether the buoyant force is less than or equal to the object's weight.*

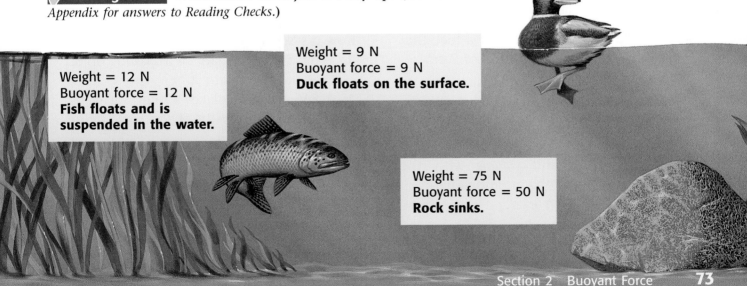

Weight = 9 N
Buoyant force = 9 N
Duck floats on the surface.

Weight = 12 N
Buoyant force = 12 N
Fish floats and is suspended in the water.

Weight = 75 N
Buoyant force = 50 N
Rock sinks.

Figure 3 *Helium in a balloon floats in air for the same reason an ice cube floats on water—helium is less dense than the surrounding fluid.*

Floating, Sinking, and Density

Think again about the rock in the lake. The rock displaces 5 L of water. But volumes of solids are measured in cubic centimeters (cm³). Because 1 mL is equal to 1 cm³, the volume of the rock is 5,000 cm³. But 5,000 cm³ of rock weighs more than an equal volume of water. So, the rock sinks.

Because mass is proportional to weight, you can say that the rock has more mass per volume than water has. Mass per unit volume is density. The rock sinks because it is more dense than water is. The duck floats because it is less dense than water is. The density of the fish is equal to the density of the water.

More Dense Than Air

Why does an ice cube float on water but not in air? An ice cube floats on water because it is less dense than water. But most substances are *more* dense than air. So, there are few substances that float in air. The ice cube is more dense than air, so the ice cube doesn't float in air.

Less Dense Than Air

One substance that is less dense than air is helium, a gas. In fact, helium has one-seventh the density of air under normal conditions. A given volume of helium displaces an equal volume of air that is much heavier than itself. So, helium floats in air. Because helium floats in air, it is used in parade balloons, such as the one shown in **Figure 3.**

✓ **Reading Check** Name a substance that is less dense than air.

Finding Density Find the density of a rock that has a mass of 10 g and a volume of 2 cm³.

Step 1: Write the equation for density. Density is calculated by using this equation:

$$density = \frac{mass}{volume}$$

Step 2: Replace *mass* and *volume* with the values in the problem, and solve.

$$density = \frac{10 \text{ g}}{2 \text{ cm}^3} = 5 \text{ g/cm}^3$$

Now It's Your Turn

1. What is the density of a 20 cm³ object that has a mass of 25 g?
2. A 546 g fish displaces 420 mL of water. What is the density of the fish? (Note: 1 mL = 1 cm³)
3. A beaker holds 50 mL of a slimy green liquid. The mass of the liquid is 163 g. What is the density of the liquid?

Changing Overall Density

Steel is almost 8 times denser than water. And yet huge steel ships cruise the oceans with ease. But hold on! You just learned that substances that are more dense than water will sink in water. So, how does a steel ship float?

Changing Shape

The secret of how a ship floats is in the shape of the ship. What if a ship were just a big block of steel, as shown in **Figure 4**? If you put that block into water, the block would sink because it is more dense than water. So, ships are built with a hollow shape. The amount of steel in the ship is the same as in the block. But the hollow shape increases the volume of the ship. Remember that density is mass per unit volume. So, an increase in the ship's volume leads to a decrease in its density. Thus, ships made of steel float because their *overall density* is less than the density of water.

Most ships are built to displace more water than is necessary for the ship to float. Ships are made this way so that they won't sink when people and cargo are loaded on the ship.

CONNECTION TO Geology

Floating Rocks The rock that makes up Earth's continents is about 15% less dense than the molten (melted) mantle rock below it. Because of this difference in density, the continents are floating on the mantle. Research the structure of Earth, and make a poster that shows Earth's interior layers.

ACTiViTY

Figure 4 Shape and Overall Density

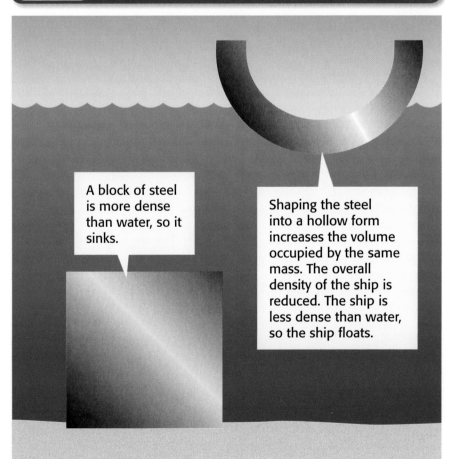

A block of steel is more dense than water, so it sinks.

Shaping the steel into a hollow form increases the volume occupied by the same mass. The overall density of the ship is reduced. The ship is less dense than water, so the ship floats.

INTERNET ACTiViTY

For another activity related to this chapter, go to **go.hrw.com** and type in the keyword **HP5FLUW**.

Ship Shape

1. Roll a **piece of clay** into a ball the size of a golf ball, and drop it into a **container of water.** Record your observations.

2. With your hands, flatten the ball of clay until it is a bit thinner than your little finger, and press it into the shape of a bowl or canoe.

3. Place the clay boat gently in the water. How does the change of shape affect the buoyant force on the clay? How is that change related to the overall density of the clay boat? Record your answers.

Changing Mass

A submarine is a special kind of ship that can travel both on the surface of the water and underwater. Submarines have *ballast tanks* that can be opened to allow sea water to flow in. As water is added, the submarine's mass increases, but its volume stays the same. The submarine's overall density increases so that it can dive under the surface. Crew members control the amount of water taken in. In this way, they control how dense the submarine is and how deep it dives. Compressed air is used to blow the water out of the tanks so that the submarine can rise. Study **Figure 5** to learn how ballast tanks work.

✓ Reading Check How do crew members control the density of a submarine?

Figure 5 **Controlling Density Using Ballast Tanks**

When a submarine is floating on the ocean's surface, its ballast tanks are filled mostly with air.

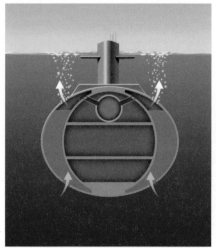

Vent holes on the ballast tanks are opened to allow the submarine to dive. Air escapes as the tanks fill with water.

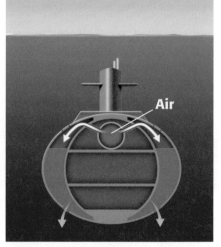

Vent holes are closed, and compressed air is pumped into the ballast tanks to force the water out, so the submarine rises.

Changing Volume

Like a submarine, some fish adjust their overall density to stay at a certain depth in the water. Most bony fishes have an organ called a *swim bladder,* shown in **Figure 6.** This swim bladder is filled with gases produced in a fish's blood. The inflated swim bladder increases the fish's volume and thereby decreases the fish's overall density, which keeps the fish from sinking in the water. The fish's nervous system controls the amount of gas in the bladder. Some fish, such as sharks, do not have a swim bladder. These fish must swim constantly to keep from sinking.

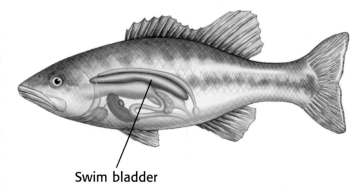

Swim bladder

Figure 6 *Most bony fishes have an organ called a* swim bladder *that allows them to adjust their overall density.*

SECTION Review

Summary

- All fluids exert an upward force called *buoyant force.*
- Buoyant force is caused by differences in fluid pressure.
- Archimedes' principle states that the buoyant force on an object is equal to the weight of the fluid displaced by the object.
- Any object that is more dense than the surrounding fluid will sink. An object that is less dense than the surrounding fluid will float.
- The overall density of an object can be changed by changing the object's shape, mass, or volume.

Using Key Terms

1. Use the following terms in the same sentence: *buoyant force* and *Archimedes' principle.*

Understanding Key Ideas

2. Which of the following changes increases the overall density of the object?

    a. A block of iron is formed into a hollow shape.

    b. A submarine fills its ballast tanks with water.

    c. A submarine fills its ballast tanks with air.

    d. A fish increases the amount of gas in its swim bladder.

3. Explain how differences in fluid pressure create buoyant force on an object.

4. How does an object's density determine whether the object will sink or float in water?

5. Name three methods that can be used to change the overall density of an object.

Math Skills

6. What is the density of an object that has a mass of 184 g and a volume of 50 cm³?

Critical Thinking

7. **Applying Concepts** An object weighs 20 N. It displaces a volume of water that weighs 15 N.

    a. What is the buoyant force on the object?

    b. Will this object float or sink? Explain your answer.

8. **Predicting Consequences** Iron has a density of 7.9 g/cm³. Mercury is a liquid that has a density of 13.5 g/cm³. Will iron float or sink in mercury? Explain your answer.

9. **Evaluating Hypotheses** Imagine that your brother tells you that all heavy objects sink in water. Explain why you agree or disagree with his statement.

Fluids and Motion

Hold two sheets of paper so that the edges are hanging in front of your face about 4 cm apart. The flat faces of the paper should be parallel to each other. Now, blow as hard as you can between the two sheets of paper.

What's going on? You can't separate the sheets by blowing between them. In fact, the sheets move closer together the harder you blow. You may be surprised that the explanation for this unusual occurrence also includes how wings help birds and planes fly and how pitchers throw screwballs.

Fluid Speed and Pressure

The strange reaction of the paper is caused by a property of moving fluids. This property was first described in the 18th century by Daniel Bernoulli (ber NOO lee), a Swiss mathematician. **Bernoulli's principle** states that as the speed of a moving fluid increases, the fluid's pressure decreases. In the case of the paper, air speed between the two sheets increased when you blew air between them. Because air speed increased, the pressure between the sheets decreased. Thus, the higher pressure on the outside of the sheets pushed them together.

Science in a Sink

Bernoulli's principle is at work in **Figure 1.** A table-tennis ball is attached to a string and swung into a stream of water. Instead of being pushed out of the water, the ball is held in the water. Why? The water is moving faster than the air around it, so the water has a lower pressure than the surrounding air. The higher air pressure pushes the ball into the area of lower pressure—the water stream. Try this at home to see for yourself!

What You Will Learn

● Describe the relationship between pressure and fluid speed.
● Analyze the roles of lift, thrust, and wing size in flight.
● Describe drag, and explain how it affects lift.
● Explain Pascal's principle.

Vocabulary

Bernoulli's principle
lift
thrust
drag
Pascal's principle

READING STRATEGY

Reading Organizer As you read this section, create an outline of the section. Use the headings from the section in your outline.

Bernoulli's principle the principle that states that the pressure in a fluid decreases as the fluid's velocity increases

Figure 1 *This ball is pushed by the higher pressure of the air into an area of reduced pressure— the water stream.*

Figure 2 Wing Design and Lift

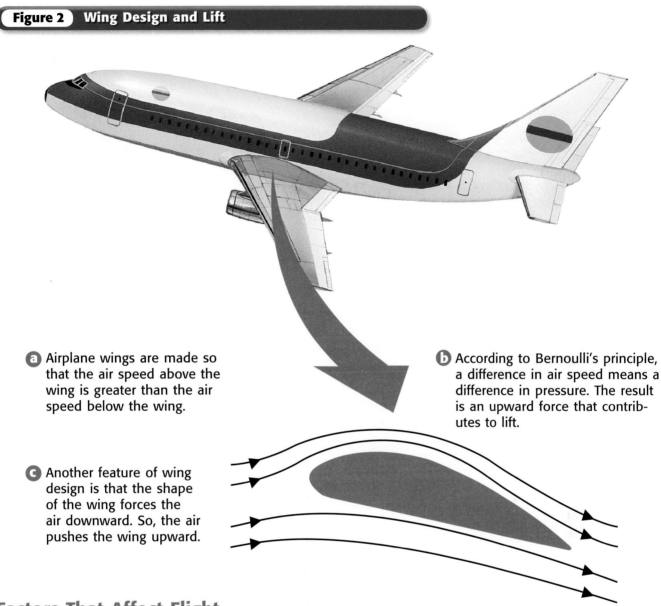

a Airplane wings are made so that the air speed above the wing is greater than the air speed below the wing.

b According to Bernoulli's principle, a difference in air speed means a difference in pressure. The result is an upward force that contributes to lift.

c Another feature of wing design is that the shape of the wing forces the air downward. So, the air pushes the wing upward.

Factors That Affect Flight

A common commercial airplane in the skies today is the Boeing 737 jet. Even without passengers, the plane weighs 350,000 N. How can something so big and heavy get off the ground and fly? Wing shape plays a role in helping these big planes—as well as smaller planes and birds—achieve flight, as shown in **Figure 2.**

According to Bernoulli's principle, the fast-moving air above the wing exerts less pressure than the slow-moving air below the wing. The greater pressure below the wing exerts an upward force. This upward force, known as **lift,** pushes the wings (and the rest of the airplane or bird) upward against the downward pull of gravity.

lift an upward force on an object that moves in a fluid

✔ **Reading Check** **What is lift?** (*See the Appendix for answers to Reading Checks.*)

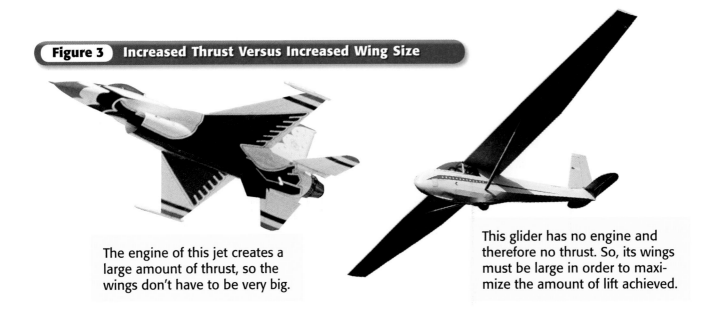

Figure 3 Increased Thrust Versus Increased Wing Size

The engine of this jet creates a large amount of thrust, so the wings don't have to be very big.

This glider has no engine and therefore no thrust. So, its wings must be large in order to maximize the amount of lift achieved.

Thrust and Lift

The amount of lift created by a plane's wing is determined partly by the speed at which air travels around the wing. The speed of a plane is determined mostly by its thrust. **Thrust** is the forward force produced by the plane's engine. In general, a plane with a large amount of thrust moves faster than a plane that has less thrust does. This faster speed means air travels around the wing at a higher speed, which increases lift.

Wing Size, Speed, and Lift

The amount of lift also depends partly on the size of a plane's wings. Look at the jet plane in **Figure 3.** This plane can fly with a relatively small wing size because its engine gives a large amount of thrust. This thrust pushes the plane through the sky at great speeds. So, the jet creates a large amount of lift with small wings by moving quickly through the air. Smaller wings keep a plane's weight low, which also helps it move faster.

Compared with the jet, the glider in **Figure 3** has a large wing area. A glider is an engineless plane. It rides rising air currents to stay in flight. Without engines, gliders produce no thrust and move more slowly than many other kinds of planes. Thus, a glider must have large wings to create the lift it needs to stay in the air.

Bernoulli and Birds

Birds don't have engines, so birds must flap their wings to push themselves through the air. A small bird must flap its wings at a fast pace to stay in the air. But a hawk flaps its wings only occasionally because it has larger wings than the small bird has. A hawk uses its large wings to fly with very little effort. Fully extended, a hawk's wings allow the hawk to glide on wind currents and still have enough lift to stay in the air.

thrust the pushing or pulling force exerted by the engine of an aircraft or rocket

CONNECTION TO
Social Studies

The First Flight The first successful flight of an engine-driven machine that was heavier than air happened in Kitty Hawk, North Carolina, in 1903. Orville Wright was the pilot. The plane flew only 37 m (about the length of a 737 jet) before landing, and the entire flight lasted only 12 s. Research another famous pilot in the history of flight. Make a poster that includes information about the pilot as well as pictures of the pilot and his or her airplane.

ACTIVITY

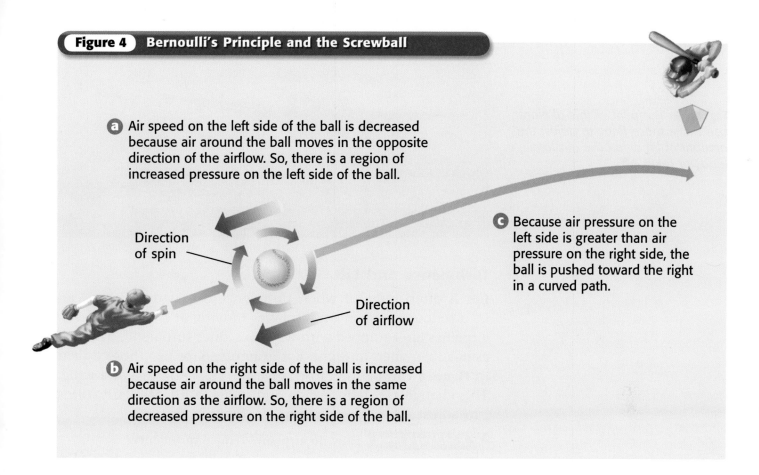

Figure 4 Bernoulli's Principle and the Screwball

a Air speed on the left side of the ball is decreased because air around the ball moves in the opposite direction of the airflow. So, there is a region of increased pressure on the left side of the ball.

Direction of spin

c Because air pressure on the left side is greater than air pressure on the right side, the ball is pushed toward the right in a curved path.

Direction of airflow

b Air speed on the right side of the ball is increased because air around the ball moves in the same direction as the airflow. So, there is a region of decreased pressure on the right side of the ball.

Bernoulli and Baseball

You don't have to look up at a bird or a plane flying through the sky to see Bernoulli's principle in your world. Any time fluids are moving, Bernoulli's principle is at work. **Figure 4** shows how a baseball pitcher can take advantage of Bernoulli's principle to throw a confusing screwball that is difficult for a batter to hit.

Drag and Motion in Fluids

Have you ever walked into a strong wind and noticed that the wind seemed to slow you down? It may have felt like the wind was pushing you backward. Fluids exert a force that opposes the motion of objects moving through the fluids. The force that opposes or restricts motion in a fluid is called **drag.**

In a strong wind, air "drags" on your body and makes it difficult for you to move forward. Drag also works against the forward motion of a plane or bird in flight. Drag is usually caused by an irregular flow of air. An irregular or unpredictable flow of fluids is known as *turbulence.*

drag a force parallel to the velocity of the flow; it opposes the direction of an aircraft and, in combination with thrust, determines the speed of the aircraft

✓ **Reading Check** What is turbulence?

Figure 5 *The pilot of this airplane can move these flaps to adjust the amount of lift when the airplane lands or takes off.*

Turbulence and Lift

Lift is often reduced when turbulence causes drag. Drag can be a serious problem for airplanes moving at high speeds. So, airplanes are equipped with ways to reduce turbulence as much as possible when in flight. For example, flaps like those shown in **Figure 5** can be used to change the shape or area of a wing. This change can reduce drag and increase lift. Similarly, birds can adjust their wing feathers in response to turbulence.

✓ Reading Check How do airplanes reduce turbulence?

Pascal's Principle

Imagine that the water-pumping station in your town increases the water pressure by 20 Pa. Will the water pressure be increased more at a store two blocks away or at a home 2 km away?

Believe it or not, the increase in water pressure will be the same at both locations. This equal change in water pressure is explained by Pascal's principle. **Pascal's principle** states that a change in pressure at any point in an enclosed fluid will be transmitted equally to all parts of that fluid. This principle was discovered by the 17th-century French scientist Blaise Pascal.

Pascal's principle the principle that states that a fluid in equilibrium contained in a vessel exerts a pressure of equal intensity in all directions

Pascal's Principle and Motion

Hydraulic (hie DRAW lik) devices use Pascal's principle to move or lift objects. Liquids are used in hydraulic devices because liquids cannot be easily compressed, or squeezed, into a smaller space. Cranes, forklifts, and bulldozers have hydraulic devices that help them lift heavy objects.

Hydraulic devices can multiply forces. Car brakes are a good example. In **Figure 6,** a driver's foot exerts pressure on a cylinder of liquid. This pressure is transmitted to all parts of the liquid-filled brake system. The liquid moves the brake pads. The pads press against the wheels, and friction stops the car. The force is multiplied because the pistons that push the brake pads are larger than the piston that is pushed by the brake pedal.

Figure 6 *Because of Pascal's principle, the touch of a foot can stop tons of moving metal.*

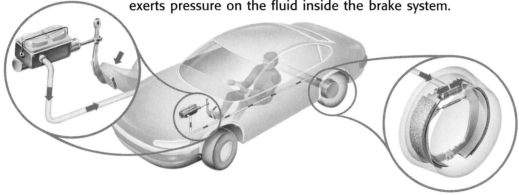

1 When the driver pushes the brake pedal, a small piston exerts pressure on the fluid inside the brake system.

2 The change in pressure is transmitted to the large pistons that push on the brake pads.

SECTION Review

Summary

- Bernoulli's principle states that fluid pressure decreases as the speed of the fluid increases.

- Wing shape allows airplanes to take advantage of Bernoulli's principle to achieve flight.

- Lift on an airplane is determined by wing size and thrust.

- Drag opposes motion through fluids.

- Pascal's principle states that a change in pressure in an enclosed fluid is transmitted equally to all parts of the fluid.

Using Key Terms

For each pair of terms, explain how the meanings of the terms differ.

1. *Bernoulli's principle* and *Pascal's principle*

2. *thrust* and *drag*

Understanding Key Ideas

3. The shape of an airplane's wing helps it gain
   a. drag.
   c. thrust.
   b. lift.
   d. turbulence.

4. What is the relationship between pressure and fluid speed?

5. What is Pascal's principle?

6. What force opposes motion through a fluid? How does this force affect lift?

7. How do thrust and lift help an airplane achieve flight?

Critical Thinking

8. **Applying Concepts** Air moving around a speeding race car can create lift. Upside-down wings, or spoilers, are mounted on the rear of race cars. Use Bernoulli's principle to explain how spoilers reduce the danger of accidents.

9. **Making Inferences** When you squeeze a balloon, where is the pressure inside the balloon increased the most? Explain.

Interpreting Graphics

10. Look at the image below. When the space through which a fluid flows becomes narrow, fluid speed increases. Using this information, explain how the two boats could collide.

SCiLINKS®

NSTA
Developed and maintained by the National Science Teachers Association

For a variety of links related to this chapter, go to www.scilinks.org

Topic: Bernoulli's Principle
SciLinks code: HSM0143

Skills Practice Lab

Fluids, Force, and Floating

Why do some objects sink in fluids but others float? In this lab, you'll get a sinking feeling as you determine that an object floats when its weight equals the buoyant force exerted by the surrounding fluid.

OBJECTIVES

Calculate the buoyant force on an object.

Compare the buoyant force on an object with its weight.

MATERIALS

- balance
- mass set
- pan, rectangular baking
- paper towels
- ruler, metric
- tub, plastic, large rectangular
- water

SAFETY

Procedure

1. Copy the table shown below.

Measurement	Trial 1	Trial 2
Length (l), cm		
Width (w), cm		
Initial height (h_1), cm		
Initial volume (V_1), cm^3 $V_1 = l \times w \times h_1$		
New height (h_2), cm		
New total volume (V_2), cm^3 $V_2 = l \times w \times h_2$	DO NOT WRITE IN BOOK	
Displaced volume (ΔV), cm^3 $\Delta V = V_2 - V_1$		
Mass of displaced water, g $m = \Delta V \times 1$ g/cm^3		
Weight of displaced water, N (buoyant force)		
Weight of pan and masses, N		

2. Fill the tub half full with water. Measure (in centimeters) the length, width, and initial height of the water. Record your measurements in the table.

3. Using the equation given in the table, determine the initial volume of water in the tub. Record your results in the table.

4. Place the pan in the water, and place masses in the pan, as shown on the next page. Keep adding masses until the pan sinks to about three-quarters of its height. Record the new height of the water in the table. Then, use this value to determine and record the new total volume of water plus the volume of water displaced by the pan.

5 Determine the volume of the water that was displaced by the pan and masses, and record this value in the table. The displaced volume is equal to the new total volume minus the initial volume.

6 Determine the mass of the displaced water by multiplying the displaced volume by its density (1 g/cm^3). Record the mass in the table.

7 Divide the mass by 100. The value you get is the weight of the displaced water in newtons (N). This is equal to the buoyant force. Record the weight of the displaced water in the table.

8 Remove the pan and masses, and determine their total mass (in grams) using the balance. Convert the mass to weight (N), as you did in step 7. Record the weight of the masses and pan in the table.

9 Place the empty pan back in the tub. Perform a second trial by repeating steps 4–8. This time, add masses until the pan is just about to sink.

Analyze the Results

1 **Identifying Patterns** Compare the buoyant force (the weight of the displaced water) with the weight of the pan and masses for both trials.

2 **Examining Data** How did the buoyant force differ between the two trials? Explain.

Draw Conclusions

3 **Drawing Conclusions** Based on your observations, what would happen if you were to add even more mass to the pan than you did in the second trial? Explain your answer in terms of the buoyant force.

4 **Making Predictions** What would happen if you put the masses in the water without the pan? What difference does the pan's shape make?

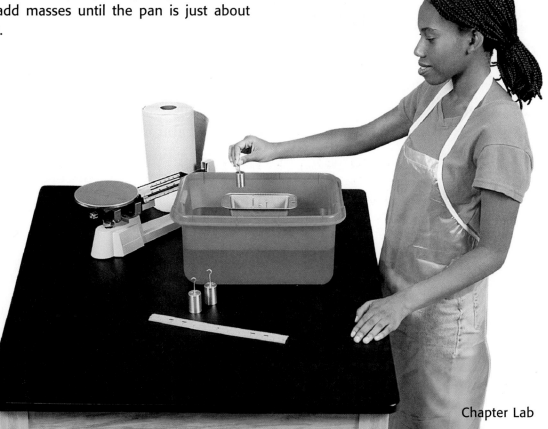

Chapter Review

USING KEY TERMS

In each of the following sentences, replace the incorrect term with the correct term from the word bank.

thrust   pressure
drag   lift
buoyant force   fluid
Pascal's principle
Bernoulli's principle

1 Lift increases with the depth of a fluid.

2 A plane's engines produce drag to push the plane forward.

3 A pascal can be a liquid or a gas.

4 A hydraulic device uses Archimedes' principle to lift or move objects.

5 Atmospheric pressure is the upward force exerted on objects by fluids.

UNDERSTANDING KEY IDEAS

Multiple Choice

6 The design of a wing

  a. causes the air above the wing to travel faster than the air below the wing.

  b. helps create lift.

  c. creates a low-pressure zone above the wing.

  d. All of the above

7 Fluid pressure is always directed

  a. up.   **c.** sideways.

  b. down.   **d.** in all directions.

8 An object surrounded by a fluid will displace a volume of fluid that is

  a. equal to its own volume.

  b. less than its own volume.

  c. greater than its own volume.

  d. denser than itself.

9 If an object weighing 50 N displaces a volume of water that weighs 10 N, what is the buoyant force on the object?

  a. 60 N   **c.** 40 N

  b. 50 N   **d.** 10 N

10 A helium-filled balloon will float in air because

  a. there is more air than helium.

  b. helium is less dense than air.

  c. helium is as dense as air.

  d. helium is more dense than air.

11 Materials that can flow to fit their containers include

  a. gases.

  b. liquids.

  c. both gases and liquids.

  d. gases, liquids, and solids.

Short Answer

12 Where is water pressure greater, at a depth of 1 m in a large lake or at a depth of 2 m in a small pond? Explain your answer.

13 Why are bubbles round?

14 Why are tornadoes like giant vacuum cleaners?

Math Skills

15 Calculate the area of a 1,500 N object that exerts a pressure of 500 Pa (500 N/m^2). Then, calculate the pressure exerted by the same object over twice that area.

CRITICAL THINKING

16 **Concept Mapping** Use the following terms to create a concept map: *fluid, pressure, depth, density,* and *buoyant force.*

17 **Forming Hypotheses** Gases can be easily compressed into smaller spaces. Why would this property of gases make gases less useful than liquids in hydraulic brakes?

18 **Making Comparisons** Will a ship loaded with beach balls float higher or lower in the water than an empty ship? Explain your reasoning.

19 **Applying Concepts** Inside all vacuum cleaners is a high-speed fan. Explain how this fan causes the vacuum cleaner to pick up dirt.

20 **Evaluating Hypotheses** A 600 N girl on stilts says to two 600 N boys sitting on the ground, "I am exerting over twice as much pressure as the two of you are exerting together!" Could this statement be true? Explain your reasoning.

INTERPRETING GRAPHICS

Use the diagram of an iceberg below to answer the questions that follow.

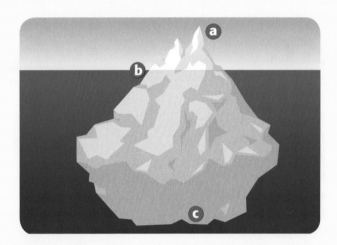

21 At what point (a, b, or c) is water pressure greatest on the iceberg?

22 How much of the iceberg has a weight equal to the buoyant force?

  a. all of it

  b. the section from a to b

  c. the section from b to c

  d. None of the above

23 How does the density of ice compare with the density of water?

24 Why do you think icebergs are dangerous to passing ships?

Standardized Test Preparation

Read each of the passages below. Then, answer the questions that follow each passage.

Passage 1 The Mariana Trench is about 11 km deep—that's deep enough to swallow Mount Everest, the tallest mountain in the world. Fewer than a dozen undersea vessels have ever ventured this deep into the ocean. Why? Water exerts tremendous pressure at this depth. A <u>revolutionary</u> new undersea vessel, *Deep Flight,* has a hull made of an extremely strong ceramic material that can withstand such pressure. Although *Deep Flight* has not made it to the bottom of the Mariana Trench, some scientists think this type of undersea vessel will one day be used routinely to explore the ocean floor.

1. What is the meaning of the word *revolutionary* in this passage?
   A strange
   B overthrowing the government
   C radically different
   D disgusting

2. Based on the name of the undersea vessel described in this passage, what does the vessel look like?
   F a robot
   G a house
   H a car
   I an airplane

3. Based on the passage, which of the following statements is a fact?
   A Scientists hope to fly *Deep Flight* to the top of Mount Everest.
   B *Deep Flight* can withstand very high pressures.
   C Scientists cannot explore the ocean without using *Deep Flight.*
   D *Deep Flight* has gone to the bottom of the Mariana Trench a dozen times.

Passage 2 Buoyancy is an object's ability to float. An object will float if the water it displaces has a mass greater than the object's mass. It will sink if the water it displaces has a mass less than its own mass. But if an object displaces its own mass in water, it will neither float nor sink. Instead, it will remain <u>suspended</u> in the water because of what is called *neutral buoyancy.*

A goldfish has neutral buoyancy. A goldfish has a sac in its body called a *swim bladder.* Gases from blood vessels can diffuse into and out of the swim bladder. When the goldfish needs to rise in the water, for example, gases diffuse into the swim bladder and cause it to inflate. The swim bladder helps the goldfish maintain neutral buoyancy.

1. What is the purpose of this passage?
   A to explain how a goldfish maintains neutral buoyancy
   B to explain how to change the buoyancy of an object
   C to convince people to buy goldfish
   D to describe objects that float and sink

2. What is the meaning of the word *suspended* in this passage?
   F not allowed to attend school
   G stopped for a period of time
   H weighed down
   I supported from sinking

3. What is buoyancy?
   A a sac in a goldfish's body
   B the ability to float
   C the mass of an object
   D an inflated balloon

The graph below shows the water pressure measured by a scientist at different depths in the ocean. Use the graph below to answer the questions that follow.

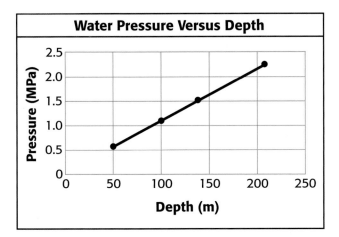

Water Pressure Versus Depth

1. What is the pressure on the object when it is 100 m underwater?

   A 1.0 MPa

   B 1.1 MPa

   C 1.5 MPa

   D 2.0 MPa

2. Based on the data in the graph, which of the following is the best estimate of the pressure at 250 m below the surface of the ocean?

   F 1.7 MPa

   G 2.2 MPa

   H 2.6 MPa

   I 5.0 MPa

3. Which of the following statements best describes the relationship between the water pressure on an object and the depth of the object in the ocean?

   A Water pressure increases as the depth increases.

   B Water pressure decreases as the depth increases.

   C Water pressure does not change as the depth increases.

   D Water pressure has no predictable relationship to the depth.

Read each question below, and choose the best answer.

1. Anna-Marie has a coil of wire. She uses a balance to find that the wire has a mass of 17.8 g. She uses water displacement to find that the volume of the wire is 2.0 cm³. Density is equal to mass divided by volume. What is the density of the wire?

   A 0.11 g/cm³

   B 8.9 g/cm³

   C 19.8 g/cm³

   D 35.6 g/cm³

2. Hussain rode his bike 30 km this weekend. What is this distance expressed in meters?

   F 0.3 m

   G 300 m

   H 30,000 m

   I 300,000 m

3. Olivia purchased 21 tubes of oil paint at $3.95 per tube, which includes tax. What was the total cost of the 21 tubes of paint?

   A $65.15

   B $82.95

   C $89.10

   D $93.50

4. Javi filled a container halfway full with water. The container measures 2 m wide, 3 m long, and 1 m high. How many cubic meters of water are in the container?

   F 2 m³

   G 3 m³

   H 5 m³

   I 6 m³

5. Pressure is equal to force divided by area. Jenny pushes a door with a force of 12 N. The area of her hand is 96 cm². What is the pressure exerted by Jenny's hand on the door?

   A 0.125 N/cm

   B 0.125 N/cm²

   C 8 N/cm

   D 8 N/cm²

Science in Action

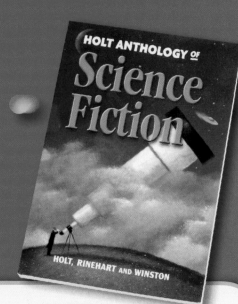

Science, Technology, and Society

Stayin' Aloft—The Story of the Frisbee®

In the late 1800s, a few fun-loving college students invented a game that involved tossing an empty tin pie plate. The pie plate was stamped with the name of a bakery: Frisbie's Pies. So, the game of Frisbie was created. Unfortunately, the metal pie plates tended to develop sharp edges that caused injuries. In 1947, plastic disks were made to replace the metal pie plates. These plastic disks were called Frisbees. How do Frisbees stay in the air? When you throw a Frisbee, you give it thrust. And as it moves through the air, lift is created because of Bernoulli's principle. But you don't have to think about the science behind Frisbees to have fun with them!

Math ACTIVITY

A Frisbee landed 10 m away from where it is thrown. The Frisbee was in the air for 2.5 s. What was the average speed of the Frisbee?

Science Fiction

"Wet Behind the Ears" by Jack C. Haldeman II

Willie Joe Thomas cheated to get a swimming scholarship. Now, he is faced with a major swim meet, and his coach told him that he has to swim or be kicked off the team. Willie Joe could lose his scholarship.

One day, Willie Joe's roommate, Frank, announces that he has developed a new "sliding compound." And Frank also said something about using the compound to make ships go faster. So, Willie Joe thought, if it works for ships, it might work for swimming.

See what happens when Willie Joe tries to save his scholarship by using Frank's compound at the swim meet. Read "Wet Behind the Ears," by Jack C. Haldeman II in the *Holt Anthology of Science Fiction*.

Language Arts ACTIVITY

Analyze the story structure of "Wet Behind the Ears." In your analysis, identify the introduction, the rising action, the climax, and the denouement. Summarize your analysis in a chart.

Alisha Bracken

Scuba Instructor Alisha Bracken first started scuba diving in her freshman year of college. Her first dives were in a saltwater hot spring near Salt Lake City, Utah. "It was awesome," Bracken says. "There were nurse sharks, angelfish, puffer fish and brine shrimp!" Bracken enjoyed her experience so much that she wanted to share it with other people. The best way to do that was to become an instructor and teach other people to dive.

Bracken says one of the biggest challenges of being a scuba instructor is teaching people to adapt and function in a foreign environment. She believes that learning to dive properly is important not only for the safety of the diver but also for the protection of the under-water environment. She relies on science principles to help teach people how to control their movements and protect the natural environment. "Buoyancy is the foundation of teaching people to dive comfortably," she explains. "Without it, we cannot float on the surface or stay off the bottom. Underwater life can be damaged if students do not learn and apply the concepts of buoyancy."

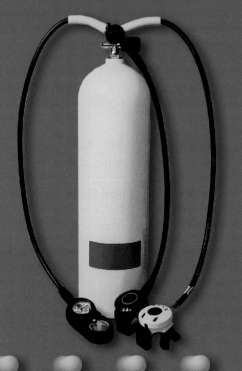

Social Studies ACTIVITY

Scuba divers and other underwater explorers sometimes investigate shipwrecks on the bottom of the ocean. Research the exploration of a specific shipwreck. Make a poster showing what artifacts were retrieved from the shipwreck and what was learned from the exploration.

To learn more about these Science in Action topics, visit go.hrw.com and type in the keyword **HP5FLUF**.

Current Science

Check out Current Science® articles related to this chapter by visiting go.hrw.com. Just type in the keyword **HP5CS07**.

Work and Machines

The Big Idea
Work is the transfer of energy to an object, and power is the rate at which work is done. Machines are devices that help make work easier.

About the PHOTO

"One, two, stroke!" shouts the coach as the team races to the finish line. This paddling team is competing in Hong Kong's annual Dragon Boat Races. The Dragon Boat Festival is a 2,000-year-old Chinese tradition that commemorates Qu Yuan, a national hero. The paddlers that you see here are using the paddles to move the boat forward. Even though they are celebrating by racing their dragon boat, in scientific terms, this team is doing work.

PRE-READING ACTIVITY

FOLDNOTES **Booklet** Before you read the chapter, create the FoldNote entitled "Booklet" described in the **Study Skills** section of the Appendix. Label each page of the booklet with a main idea from the chapter. As you read the chapter, write what you learn about each main idea on the appropriate page of the booklet.

START-UP ACTIVITY

C'mon, Lever a Little!

In this activity, you will use a simple machine, a lever, to make your task a little easier.

Procedure

1. Stack **two books,** one on top of the other, on a **table.**

2. Slide your index finger underneath the edge of the bottom book. Using only the force of your finger, try to lift one side of the books 2 or 3 cm off the table. Is it hard to do so? Write your observations.

3. Slide the end of a **wooden ruler** underneath the edge of the bottom book. Then, slip a **large pencil eraser** or similar object under the ruler.

4. Again, using only your index finger, push down on the edge of the ruler and try to lift the books. Record your observations. **Caution:** Push down slowly to keep the ruler and eraser from flipping.

Analysis

1. Which was easier: lifting the books with your finger or lifting the books with the ruler? Explain your answer.

2. In what way did the direction of the force that your finger applied on the books differ from the direction of the force that your finger applied on the ruler?

Work and Power

Your science teacher has just given you tonight's homework assignment. You have to read an entire chapter by tomorrow! That sounds like a lot of work!

Actually, in the scientific sense, you won't be doing much work at all! How can that be? In science, **work** is done when a force causes an object to move in the direction of the force. In the example above, you may have to put a lot of mental effort into doing your homework, but you won't be using force to move anything. So, in the scientific sense, you will not be doing work—except the work to turn the pages of your book!

What You Will Learn

- Determine when work is being done on an object.
- Calculate the amount of work done on an object.
- Explain the difference between work and power.

Vocabulary

work   power
joule   watt

READING STRATEGY

Reading Organizer As you read this section, make a table comparing work and power.

What Is Work?

The student in **Figure 1** is having a lot of fun, isn't she? But she is doing work, even though she is having fun. She is doing work because she is applying a force to the bowling ball and making the ball move through a distance. However, she is doing work on the ball only as long as she is touching it. The ball will keep moving away from her after she releases it. But she will no longer be doing work on the ball because she will no longer be applying a force to it.

Transfer of Energy

One way you can tell that the bowler in **Figure 1** has done work on the bowling ball is that the ball now has *kinetic energy*. This means that the ball is now moving. The bowler has transferred energy to the ball.

Differences Between Force and Work

Applying a force doesn't always result in work being done. Suppose that you help push a stalled car. You push and push, but the car doesn't budge. The pushing may have made you tired. But you haven't done any work on the car, because the car hasn't moved.

You do work on the car as soon as the car moves. Whenever you apply a force to an object and the object moves in the direction of the force, you have done work on the object.

Figure 1
You might be surprised to find out that bowling is work!

✓ **Reading Check** Is work done every time a force is applied to an object? Explain. (*See the Appendix for answers to Reading Checks.*)

Force and Motion in the Same Direction

Suppose you are in the airport and late for a flight. You have to run through the airport carrying a heavy suitcase. Because you are making the suitcase move, you are doing work on it, right? Wrong! For work to be done on an object, the object must move in the *same direction* as the force. You are applying a force to hold the suitcase up, but the suitcase is moving forward. So, no work is done on the suitcase. But work *is* done on the suitcase when you lift it off the ground.

Work is done on an object if two things happen: (1) the object moves as a force is applied and (2) the direction of the object's motion is the same as the direction of the force. The pictures and arrows in **Figure 2** will help you understand when work is being done on an object.

work the transfer of energy to an object by using a force that causes the object to move in the direction of the force

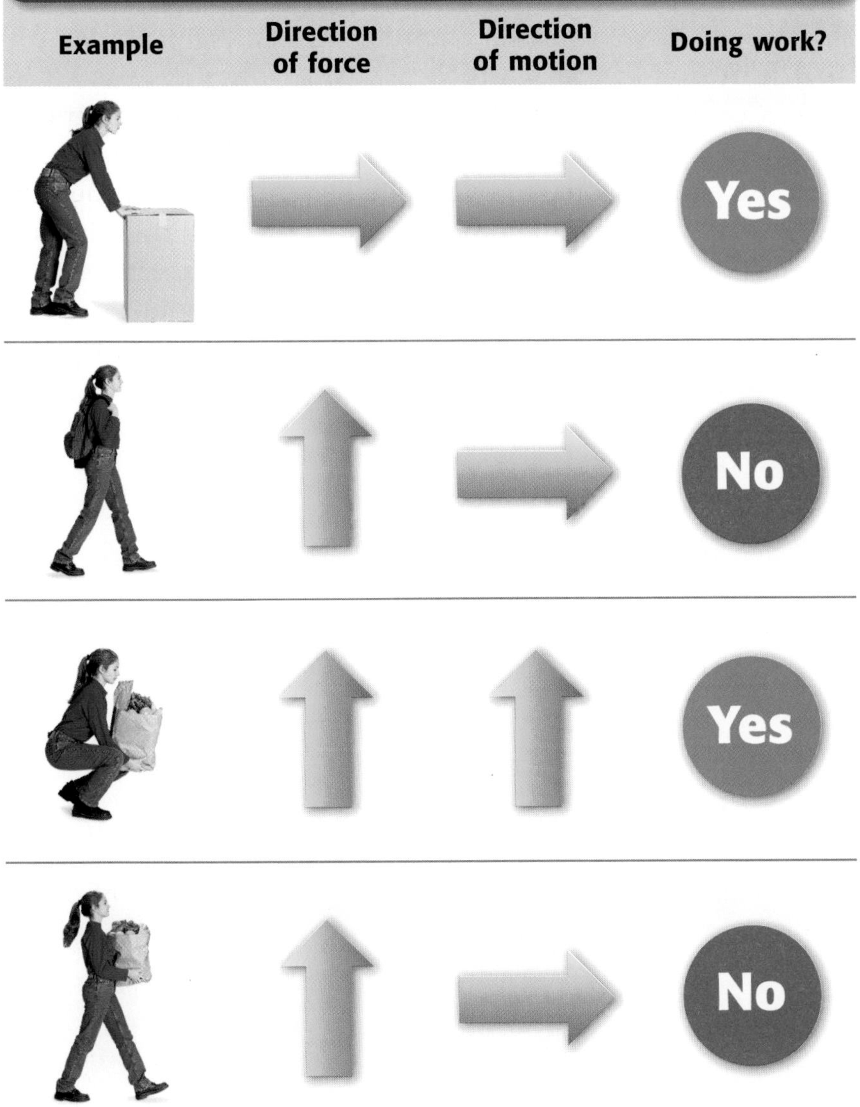

CONNECTION TO Biology

WRITING SKILL **Work in the Human Body**

You may not be doing any work on a suitcase if you are just holding it in your hands, but your body will still get tired from the effort because you are doing work on the muscles inside your body. Your muscles can contract thousands of times in just a few seconds while you try to keep the suitcase from falling. What other situations can you think of that might involve work being done somewhere inside your body? Describe these situations in your **science journal.**

Figure 2 Work or Not Work?

Example	Direction of force	Direction of motion	Doing work?
(person pushing box)	→	→	Yes
(person walking with backpack)	↑	→	No
(person lifting grocery bag)	↑	↑	Yes
(person walking with grocery bag)	↑	→	No

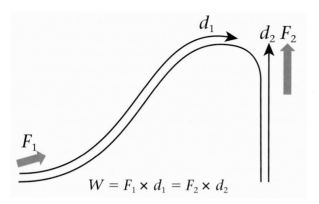

$$W = F_1 \times d_1 = F_2 \times d_2$$

Figure 3 *For each path, the same work is done to move the car to the top of the hill, although distance and force along the two paths differ.*

How Much Work?

Would you do more work on a car by pushing it up a long road to reach the top of a hill or by using a cable to raise the car up the side of a cliff to the top of the same hill? You would certainly need a different amount of force. Common use of the word *work* may make it seem that there would be a difference in the amount of work done in the two cases as well.

Same Work, Different Forces

You may be surprised to learn that the same amount of work is being done to push the car up a road as to raise it up the cliff. Look at **Figure 3.** A certain amount of energy is needed to move the car from the bottom to the top of the hill. Because the car ends up at the same place either way, the work done on the car is the same. However, pushing the car along the road up a hill seems easier than lifting it straight up. Why?

The reason is that work depends on distance as well as force. Consider a mountain climber who reaches the top of a mountain by climbing straight up a cliff, as in **Figure 4.** She must use enough force to overcome her entire weight. But the distance she travels up the cliff is shorter than the distance traveled by hikers who reach the top of the same mountain by walking up a slope. Either way, the same amount of work is done. But the hikers going up a slope don't need to use as much force as if they were going straight up the side of the cliff. This shows how you can use less force to do the same amount of work.

Figure 4 *Climbers going to the top of a mountain do the same amount of work whether they hike up a slope or go straight up a cliff.*

Calculating Work

The amount of work (W) done in moving an object, such as the barbell in **Figure 5,** can be calculated by multiplying the force (F) applied to the object by the distance (d) through which the force is applied, as shown in the following equation:

$$W = F \times d$$

Force is expressed in newtons, and the meter is the basic SI unit for length or distance. Therefore, the unit used to express work is the newton-meter (N × m), which is more simply called the **joule.** Because work is the transfer of energy to an object, the joule (J) is also the unit used to measure energy.

joule the unit used to express energy; equivalent to the amount of work done by a force of 1 N acting through a distance of 1 m in the direction of the force (symbol, J)

✓ **Reading Check** How is work calculated?

Figure 5 **Force Times Distance**

80 N

W = 80 N × 1 m = 80 J
The force needed to lift an object is equal to the gravitational force on the object—in other words, the object's weight.

160 N

W = 160 N × 1 m = 160 J
If you increase the weight, an increased force is needed to lift the object. This increases the amount of work done.

80 N

W = 80 N × 2 m = 160 J
Increasing the distance also increases the amount of work done.

Get to Work!

1. Use a **loop of string** to attach a **spring scale** to a **weight.**
2. Slowly pull the weight across a **table** by dragging the spring scale. Record the amount of force that you exerted on the weight.
3. Use a **metric ruler** to measure the distance that you pulled the weight.

4. Now, use the spring scale to slowly pull the weight up a **ramp.** Pull the weight the same distance that you pulled it across the table.
5. Calculate the work you did on the weight for both trials.
6. How were the amounts of work and force affected by the way you pulled the weight? What other ways of pulling the weight could you test?

Power: How Fast Work Is Done

Like the term *work,* the term *power* is used a lot in everyday language but has a very specific meaning in science. **Power** is the rate at which energy is transferred.

Calculating Power

To calculate power (P), you divide the amount of work done (W) by the time (t) it takes to do that work, as shown in the following equation:

$$P = \frac{W}{t}$$

The unit used to express power is joules per second (J/s), also called the **watt.** One watt (W) is equal to 1 J/s. So if you do 50 J of work in 5 s, your power is 10 J/s, or 10 W.

Power measures how fast work happens, or how quickly energy is transferred. When more work is done in a given amount of time, the power output is greater. Power output is also greater when the time it takes to do a certain amount of work is decreased, as shown in **Figure 6.**

✓ Reading Check How is power calculated?

power the rate at which work is done or energy is transformed

watt the unit used to express power; equivalent to joules per second (symbol, W)

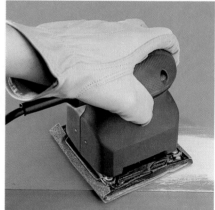

Figure 6 *No matter how fast you can sand by hand, an electric sander can do the same amount of work faster. Therefore, the electric sander has more power.*

MATH FOCUS

More Power to You A stage manager at a play raises the curtain by doing 5,976 J of work on the curtain in 12 s. What is the power output of the stage manager?

Step 1: Write the equation for power.

$$P = \frac{W}{t}$$

Step 2: Replace W and t with work and time.

$$P = \frac{5,976 \text{ J}}{12 \text{ s}} = 498 \text{ W}$$

Now It's Your Turn

1. If it takes you 10 s to do 150 J of work on a box to move it up a ramp, what is your power output?
2. A light bulb is on for 12 s, and during that time it uses 1,200 J of electrical energy. What is the wattage (power) of the light bulb?

Increasing Power

It may take you longer to sand a wooden shelf by hand than by using an electric sander, but the amount of energy needed is the same either way. Only the power output is lower when you sand the shelf by hand (although your hand may get more tired). You could also dry your hair with a fan, but it would take a long time! A hair dryer is more powerful. It can give off energy more quickly than a fan does, so your hair dries faster.

Car engines are usually rated with a certain power output. The more powerful the engine is, the more quickly the engine can move a car. And for a given speed, a more powerful engine can move a heavier car than a less powerful engine can.

SECTION Review

Summary

- In scientific terms, *work* is done when a force causes an object to move in the direction of the force.
- Work is calculated as force times distance. The unit of work is the newton-meter, or joule.
- *Power* is a measure of how fast work is done.
- Power is calculated as work divided by time. The unit of power is the joule per second, or watt.

Using Key Terms

For each pair of terms, explain how the meanings of the terms differ.

1. *work* and *joule*
2. *power* and *watt*

Understanding Key Ideas

3. How is work calculated?
    a. force times distance
    b. force divided by distance
    c. power times distance
    d. power divided by distance

4. What is the difference between work and power?

Math Skills

5. Using a force of 10 N, you push a shopping cart 10 m. How much work did you do?

6. If you did 100 J of work in 5 s, what was your power output?

Critical Thinking

7. **Analyzing Processes** Work is done on a ball when a pitcher throws it. Is the pitcher still doing work on the ball as it flies through the air? Explain.

8. **Applying Concepts** You lift a chair that weighs 50 N to a height of 0.5 m and carry it 10 m across the room. How much work do you do on the chair?

Interpreting Graphics

9. What idea about work and force does the following diagram describe? Explain your answer.

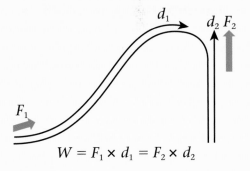

$$W = F_1 \times d_1 = F_2 \times d_2$$

For a variety of links related to this chapter, go to www.scilinks.org

Topic: Work and Power
SciLinks code: HSM1675

What Is a Machine?

You are in the car with your mom on the way to a party when suddenly—KABLOOM hisssss—a tire blows out. "Now I'm going to be late!" you think as your mom pulls over to the side of the road.

You watch as she opens the trunk and gets out a jack and a tire iron. Using the tire iron, she pries the hubcap off and begins to unscrew the lug nuts from the wheel. She then puts the jack under the car and turns the jack's handle several times until the flat tire no longer touches the ground. After exchanging the flat tire with the spare, she lowers the jack and puts the lug nuts and hubcap back on the wheel.

"Wow!" you think, "That wasn't as hard as I thought it would be." As your mom drops you off at the party, you think how lucky it was that she had the right equipment to change the tire.

Machines: Making Work Easier

Now, imagine changing a tire without the jack and the tire iron. Would it have been easy? No, you would have needed several people just to hold up the car! Sometimes, you need the help of machines to do work. A **machine** is a device that makes work easier by changing the size or direction of a force.

When you think of machines, you might think of things such as cars, big construction equipment, or even computers. But not all machines are complicated. In fact, you use many simple machines in your everyday life. **Figure 1** shows some examples of machines.

What You Will Learn

- Explain how a machine makes work easier.
- Describe and give examples of the force-distance trade-off that occurs when a machine is used.
- Calculate mechanical advantage.
- Explain why machines are not 100% efficient.

Vocabulary

machine
work input
work output
mechanical advantage
mechanical efficiency

READING STRATEGY

Prediction Guide Before reading this section, write the title of each heading in this section. Next, under each heading, write what you think you will learn.

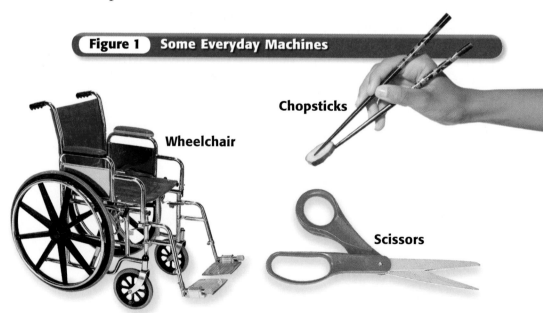

Figure 1 Some Everyday Machines

Chopsticks

Wheelchair

Scissors

Work In, Work Out

Suppose that you need to get the lid off a can of paint. What do you do? One way to pry the lid off is to use a common machine known as a *lever*. **Figure 2** shows a screwdriver being used as a lever. You place the tip of the screwdriver under the edge of the lid and then push down on the screwdriver's handle. The tip of the screwdriver lifts the lid as you push down. In other words, you do work on the screwdriver, and the screwdriver does work on the lid.

Work is done when a force is applied through a distance. Look again at **Figure 2.** The work that you do on a machine is called **work input.** You apply a force, called the *input force,* to the machine through a distance. The work done by the machine on an object is called **work output.** The machine applies a force, called the *output force,* through a distance.

How Machines Help

You might think that machines help you because they increase the amount of work done. But that's not true. If you multiplied the forces by the distances through which the forces are applied in **Figure 2** (remember that $W = F \times d$), you would find that the screwdriver does not do more work on the lid than you do on the screwdriver. Work output can never be greater than work input. Machines allow force to be applied over a greater distance, which means that less force will be needed for the same amount of work.

Reading Check How do machines make work easier? (*See the Appendix for answers to Reading Checks.*)

machine a device that helps do work by either overcoming a force or changing the direction of the applied force

work input the work done on a machine; the product of the input force and the distance through which the force is exerted

work output the work done by a machine; the product of the output force and the distance through which the force is exerted

Output force

Input force

Figure 2 *When you use a machine, you do work on the machine, and the machine does work on something else.*

INTERNET ACTIVITY

For another activity related to this chapter, go to **go.hrw.com** and type in the keyword **HP5WRKW.**

Same Work, Different Force

Machines make work easier by changing the size or direction (or both) of the input force. When a screwdriver is used as a lever to open a paint can, both the size and direction of the input force change. Remember that using a machine does not change the amount of work you will do. As **Figure 3** shows, the same amount of work is done with or without the ramp. The ramp decreases the size of the input force needed to lift the box but increases the distance over which the force is exerted. So, the machine allows a smaller force to be applied over a longer distance.

The Force-Distance Trade-Off

When a machine changes the size of the force, the distance through which the force is exerted must also change. Force or distance can increase, but both cannot increase. When one increases, the other must decrease.

Figure 4 shows how machines change force and distance. Whenever a machine changes the size of a force, the machine also changes the distance through which the force is applied. **Figure 4** also shows that some machines change only the direction of the force, not the size of the force or the distance through which the force is exerted.

✓ Reading Check What are the two things that a machine can change about how work is done?

Figure 3   Input Force and Distance

Lifting this box straight up requires an input force equal to the weight of the box.

$$W = 450 \text{ N} \times 1 \text{ m} = 450 \text{ J}$$

Using a ramp to lift the box requires an input force less than the weight of the box, but the input force must be exerted over a greater distance than if you didn't use a ramp.

$$W = 150 \text{ N} \times 3 \text{ m} = 450 \text{ J}$$

Figure 4 Machines Change the Size and/or Direction of a Force

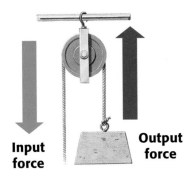

Input force

Output force

A nutcracker *increases* the force but applies it over a *shorter* distance.

A hammer *decreases* the force, but applies it over a *greater* distance.

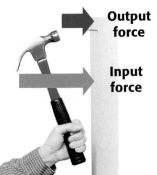

Output force

Input force

A simple pulley changes the *direction* of the input force, but the size of the output force is the same as the input force.

Input force

Output force

When a screwdriver is used as a lever, it *increases* the force and *decreases* the distance over which the force is applied.

Output force

Input force

Mechanical Advantage

Some machines make work easier than others do because they can increase force more than other machines can. A machine's **mechanical advantage** is the number of times the machine multiplies force. In other words, the mechanical advantage compares the input force with the output force.

mechanical advantage a number that tells how many times a machine multiplies force

Calculating Mechanical Advantage

You can find mechanical advantage by using the following equation:

$$mechanical\ advantage\ (MA) = \frac{output\ force}{input\ force}$$

For example, imagine that you had to push a 500 N weight up a ramp and only needed to push with 50 N of force the entire time. The mechanical advantage of the ramp would be calculated as follows:

$$MA = \frac{500\ N}{50\ N} = 10$$

A machine that has a mechanical advantage that is greater than 1 can help move or lift heavy objects because the output force is greater than the input force. A machine that has a mechanical advantage that is less than 1 will reduce the output force but can increase the distance an object moves. **Figure 4** shows an example of such a machine—a hammer.

Finding the Advantage

A grocer uses a handcart to lift a heavy stack of canned food. Suppose that he applies an input force of 40 N to the handcart. The cart applies an output force of 320 N to the stack of canned food. What is the mechanical advantage of the handcart?

Mechanical Efficiency

The work output of a machine can never be greater than the work input. In fact, the work output of a machine is always less than the work input. Why? Some of the work done by the machine is used to overcome the friction created by the use of the machine. But keep in mind that no work is lost. The work output plus the work done to overcome friction is equal to the work input.

The less work a machine has to do to overcome friction, the more efficient the machine is. **Mechanical efficiency** (muh KAN i kuhl e FISH uhn see) is a comparison of a machine's work output with the work input.

Calculating Efficiency

A machine's mechanical efficiency is calculated using the following equation:

$$mechanical\ efficiency = \frac{work\ output}{work\ input} \times 100$$

The 100 in this equation means that mechanical efficiency is expressed as a percentage. Mechanical efficiency tells you what percentage of the work input gets converted into work output.

Figure 5 shows a machine that is used to drill holes in metal. Some of the work input is used to overcome the friction between the metal and the drill. This energy cannot be used to do work on the steel block. Instead, it heats up the steel and the machine itself.

Reading Check How is mechanical efficiency calculated?

Figure 5 *In this machine, some of the work input is converted into sound and heat energy.*

Perfect Efficiency?

An *ideal machine* would be a machine that had 100% mechanical efficiency. An ideal machine's useful work output would equal the work done on the machine. Ideal machines are impossible to build, because every machine has moving parts. Moving parts always use some of the work input to overcome friction. But new technologies help increase efficiency so that more energy is available to do useful work. The train in **Figure 6** is floating on magnets, so there is almost no friction between the train and the tracks. Other machines use lubricants, such as oil or grease, to lower the friction between their moving parts, which makes the machines more efficient.

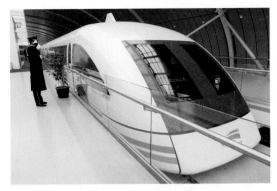

Figure 6 *There is very little friction between this magnetic levitation train and its tracks, so it is highly efficient.*

SECTION Review

Summary

- A machine makes work easier by changing the size or direction (or both) of a force.
- A machine can increase force or distance, but not both.
- Mechanical advantage tells how many times a machine multiplies force.
- Mechanical efficiency is a comparison of a machine's work output with work input.
- Machines are not 100% efficient because some of the work done is used to overcome friction.

Using Key Terms

For each pair of terms, explain how the meanings of the terms differ.

1. *work input* and *work output*

2. *mechanical advantage* and *mechanical efficiency*

Understanding Key Ideas

3. Which of the following is the correct way to calculate mechanical advantage?

   a. input force ÷ output force
   b. output force ÷ input force
   c. work input ÷ work output
   d. work output ÷ work input

4. Explain how using a ramp makes work easier.

5. Give a specific example of a machine, and describe how its mechanical efficiency might be calculated.

6. Why can't a machine be 100% efficient?

Math Skills

7. Suppose that you exert 60 N on a machine and the machine exerts 300 N on another object. What is the machine's mechanical advantage?

8. What is the mechanical efficiency of a machine whose work input is 100 J and work output is 30 J?

Critical Thinking

9. **Making Inferences** For a machine with a mechanical advantage of 3, how does the distance through which the output force is exerted differ from the distance through which the input force is exerted?

10. **Analyzing Processes** Describe the effect that friction has on a machine's mechanical efficiency. How do lubricants increase a machine's mechanical efficiency?

Types of Machines

Imagine that it's a hot summer day. You have a whole ice-cold watermelon in front of you. It would taste cool and delicious— if only you had a machine that could cut it!

The machine you need is a knife. But how is a knife a machine? A knife is actually a very sharp wedge, which is one of the six simple machines. The six simple machines are the lever, the inclined plane, the wedge, the screw, the pulley, and the wheel and axle. All machines are made from one or more of these simple machines.

Levers

Have you ever used the claw end of a hammer to remove a nail from a piece of wood? If so, you were using the hammer as a lever. A **lever** is a simple machine that has a bar that pivots at a fixed point, called a *fulcrum*. Levers are used to apply a force to a load. There are three classes of levers, which are based on the placements of the fulcrum, the load, and the input force.

First-Class Levers

With a first-class lever, the fulcrum is between the input force and the load, as shown in **Figure 1.** First-class levers always change the direction of the input force. And depending on the location of the fulcrum, first-class levers can be used to increase force or to increase distance.

Figure 1 **Examples of First-Class Levers**

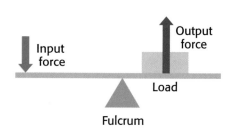
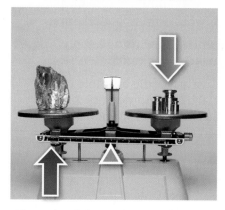
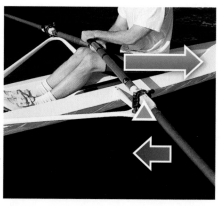

When the fulcrum is closer to the load than to the input force, the lever has a **mechanical advantage of greater than 1.** The output force is increased because it is exerted over a shorter distance.

When the fulcrum is exactly in the middle, the lever has a **mechanical advantage of 1.** The output force is not increased because the input force's distance is not increased.

When the fulcrum is closer to the input force than to the load, the lever has a **mechanical advantage of less than 1.** Although the output force is less than the input force, distance increases.

Figure 2 Examples of Second-Class Levers

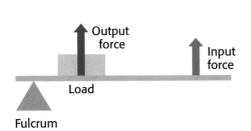

Output force

Input force

Load

Fulcrum

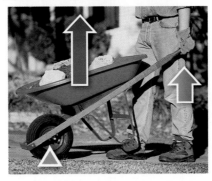

In a **second-class lever,** the output force, or load, is between the input force and the fulcrum.

Using a second-class lever results in a **mechanical advantage of greater than 1.** The closer the load is to the fulcrum, the more the force is increased and the greater the mechanical advantage is.

Second-Class Levers

The load of a second-class lever is between the fulcrum and the input force, as shown in **Figure 2.** Second-class levers do not change the direction of the input force. But they allow you to apply less force than the force exerted by the load. Because the output force is greater than the input force, you must exert the input force over a greater distance.

lever a simple machine that consists of a bar that pivots at a fixed point called a *fulcrum*

Third-Class Levers

The input force in a third-class lever is between the fulcrum and the load, as shown in **Figure 3.** Third-class levers do not change the direction of the input force. In addition, they do not increase the input force. Therefore, the output force is always less than the input force.

✓ Reading Check How do the three types of levers differ from one another? (*See the Appendix for answers to Reading Checks.*)

Figure 3 Examples of Third-Class Levers

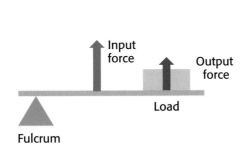

Input force

Output force

Load

Fulcrum

In a **third-class lever,** the input force is between the fulcrum and the load.

Using a third-class lever results in a **mechanical advantage of less than 1** because force is decreased. But third-class levers increase the distance through which the output force is exerted.

pulley a simple machine that consists of a wheel over which a rope, chain, or wire passes

Pulleys

When you open window blinds by pulling on a cord, you're using a pulley. A **pulley** is a simple machine that has a grooved wheel that holds a rope or a cable. A load is attached to one end of the rope, and an input force is applied to the other end. Types of pulleys are shown in **Figure 4.**

Fixed Pulleys

A fixed pulley is attached to something that does not move. By using a fixed pulley, you can pull down on the rope to lift the load up. The pulley changes the direction of the force. Elevators make use of fixed pulleys.

Movable Pulleys

Unlike fixed pulleys, movable pulleys are attached to the object being moved. A movable pulley does not change a force's direction. Movable pulleys do increase force, but they also increase the distance over which the input force must be exerted.

Block and Tackles

When a fixed pulley and a movable pulley are used together, the pulley system is called a *block and tackle*. The mechanical advantage of a block and tackle depends on the number of rope segments.

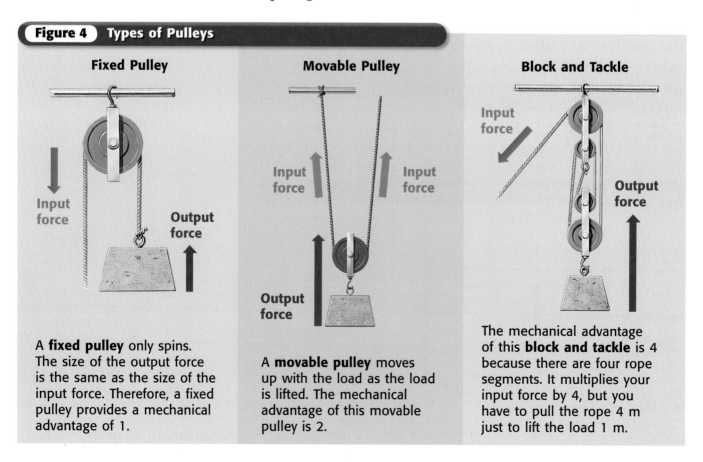

Figure 4 Types of Pulleys

Fixed Pulley

Input force

Output force

A **fixed pulley** only spins. The size of the output force is the same as the size of the input force. Therefore, a fixed pulley provides a mechanical advantage of 1.

Movable Pulley

Input force   Input force

Output force

A **movable pulley** moves up with the load as the load is lifted. The mechanical advantage of this movable pulley is 2.

Block and Tackle

Input force

Output force

The mechanical advantage of this **block and tackle** is 4 because there are four rope segments. It multiplies your input force by 4, but you have to pull the rope 4 m just to lift the load 1 m.

Figure 5 **How a Wheel and Axle Works**

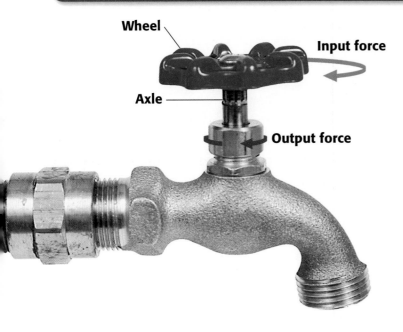

Wheel

Input force

Axle

Output force

ⓐ When a small input force is applied to the wheel, the wheel rotates through a circular distance.

ⓑ As the wheel turns, so does the axle. But because the axle is smaller than the wheel, it rotates through a smaller distance, which makes the output force larger than the input force

Wheel and Axle

Did you know that a faucet is a machine? The faucet shown in **Figure 5** is an example of a **wheel and axle,** a simple machine consisting of two circular objects of different sizes. Doorknobs, wrenches, and steering wheels all use a wheel and axle. **Figure 5** shows how a wheel and axle works.

wheel and axle a simple machine consisting of two circular objects of different sizes; the wheel is the larger of the two circular objects

Mechanical Advantage of a Wheel and Axle

The mechanical advantage of a wheel and axle can be found by dividing the *radius* (the distance from the center to the edge) of the wheel by the radius of the axle, as shown in **Figure 6.** Turning the wheel results in a mechanical advantage of greater than 1 because the radius of the wheel is larger than the radius of the axle.

✓ **Reading Check** How is the mechanical advantage of a wheel and axle calculated?

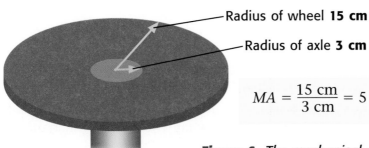

Radius of wheel **15 cm**

Radius of axle **3 cm**

$$MA = \frac{15 \text{ cm}}{3 \text{ cm}} = 5$$

Figure 6 *The mechanical advantage of a wheel and axle is the radius of the wheel divided by the radius of the axle.*

Figure 7 *The work you do on the piano to roll it up the ramp is the same as the work you would do to lift it straight up. An inclined plane simply allows you to apply a smaller force over a greater distance.*

$$MA = \frac{3 \text{ m}}{0.6 \text{ m}} = 5$$

Inclined Planes

Do you remember the story about how the Egyptians built the Great Pyramid? One of the machines they used was the **inclined plane.** An *inclined plane* is a simple machine that is a straight, slanted surface. A ramp is an inclined plane.

Using an inclined plane to load a piano into a truck, as **Figure 7** shows, is easier than lifting the piano into the truck. Rolling the piano along an inclined plane requires a smaller input force than is needed to lift the piano into the truck. The same work is done on the piano, just over a longer distance.

inclined plane a simple machine that is a straight, slanted surface, which facilitates the raising of loads; a ramp

✓ **Reading Check** What is an inclined plane?

Mechanical Advantage of Inclined Planes

The greater the ratio of an inclined plane's length to its height is, the greater the mechanical advantage is. The mechanical advantage (*MA*) of an inclined plane can be calculated by dividing the *length* of the inclined plane by the *height* to which the load is lifted. The inclined plane in **Figure 7** has a mechanical advantage of 3 m/0.6 m = 5.

Mechanical Advantage of an Inclined Plane A heavy box is pushed up a ramp that has an incline of 4.8 m long and 1.2 m high. What is the mechanical advantage of the ramp?

Step 1: Write the equation for the mechanical advantage of an inclined plane.

$$MA = \frac{l}{h}$$

Step 2: Replace *l* and *h* with length and height.

$$MA = \frac{4.8 \text{ m}}{1.2 \text{ m}} = 4$$

Now It's Your Turn

1. A wheelchair ramp is 9 m long and 1.5 m high. What is the mechanical advantage of the ramp?
2. As a pyramid is built, a stone block is dragged up a ramp that is 120 m long and 20 m high. What is the mechanical advantage of the ramp?
3. If an inclined plane were 2 m long and 8 m high, what would be its mechanical advantage?

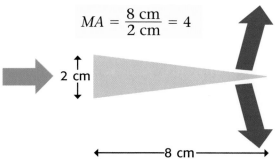

$$MA = \frac{8 \text{ cm}}{2 \text{ cm}} = 4$$

2 cm

←——— 8 cm ———→

Figure 8 *A knife is a common example of a wedge, a simple machine consisting of two inclined planes back to back.*

Wedges

Imagine trying to cut a melon in half with a spoon. It wouldn't be easy, would it? A knife is much more useful for cutting because it is a **wedge.** A *wedge* is a pair of inclined planes that move. A wedge applies an output force that is greater than your input force, but you apply the input force over a greater distance. For example, a knife is a common wedge that can easily cut into a melon and push apart its two halves, as shown in **Figure 8.** Other useful wedges include doorstops, plows, ax heads, and chisels.

Mechanical Advantage of Wedges

The longer and thinner the wedge is, the greater its mechanical advantage is. That's why axes and knives cut better when you sharpen them—you are making the wedge thinner. Therefore, less input force is required. The mechanical advantage of a wedge can be found by dividing the length of the wedge by its greatest thickness, as shown in **Figure 8.**

Screws

A **screw** is an inclined plane that is wrapped in a spiral around a cylinder, as you can see in **Figure 9.** When a screw is turned, a small force is applied over the long distance along the inclined plane of the screw. Meanwhile, the screw applies a large force through the short distance it is pushed. Screws are used most commonly as fasteners.

Mechanical Advantage of Screws

If you could unwind the inclined plane of a screw, you would see that the plane is very long and has a gentle slope. Recall that the longer an inclined plane is compared with its height, the greater its mechanical advantage. Similarly, the longer the spiral on a screw is and the closer together the threads are, the greater the screw's mechanical advantage is. A jar lid is a screw that has a large mechanical advantage.

wedge a simple machine that is made up of two inclined planes and that moves; often used for cutting

screw a simple machine that consists of an inclined plane wrapped around a cylinder

Figure 9 *If you could unwind a screw, you would see that it is actually a very long inclined plane.*

Compound Machines

You are surrounded by machines. You even have machines in your body! But most of the machines in your world are **compound machines,** machines that are made of two or more simple machines. You have already seen one example of a compound machine: a block and tackle. A block and tackle consists of two or more pulleys.

Figure 10 shows a common example of a compound machine. A can opener may seem simple, but it is actually three machines combined. It consists of a second-class lever, a wheel and axle, and a wedge. When you squeeze the handle, you are making use of a second-class lever. The blade of the can opener acts as a wedge as it cuts into the can's top. The knob that you turn to open the can is a wheel and axle.

Mechanical Efficiency of Compound Machines

The mechanical efficiency of most compound machines is low. The efficiency is low because compound machines have more moving parts than simple machines do, thus there is more friction to overcome. Compound machines, such as automobiles and airplanes, can involve many simple machines. It is very important to reduce friction as much as possible, because too much friction can damage the simple machines that make up the compound machine. Friction can be lowered by using lubrication and other techniques.

✓ Reading Check What special disadvantage do compound machines have?

compound machine a machine made of more than one simple machine

Figure 10 *A can opener is a compound machine. The handle is a second-class lever, the knob is a wheel and axle, and a wedge is used to open the can.*

Wheel and axle

Wedge

Second class lever

Summary

- In a first-class lever, the fulcrum is between the force and the load. In a second-class lever, the load is between the force and the fulcrum. In a third-class lever, the force is between the fulcrum and the load.

- The mechanical advantage of an inclined plane is length divided by height. Wedges and screws are types of inclined planes.

- A wedge is a type of inclined plane. Its mechanical advantage is its length divided by its greatest thickness.

- The mechanical advantage of a wheel and axle is the radius of the wheel divided by the radius of the axle.

- Types of pulleys include fixed pulleys, movable pulleys, and block and tackles.

- Compound machines consist of two or more simple machines.

- Compound machines have low mechanical efficiencies because they have more moving parts and therefore more friction to overcome.

Using Key Terms

1. In your own words, write a definition for the term *lever*.

2. Use the following terms in the same sentence: *inclined plane, wedge,* and *screw*.

Understanding Key Ideas

3. Which class of lever always has a mechanical advantage of greater than 1?
   a. first-class
   b. second-class
   c. third-class
   d. None of the above

4. Give an example of each of the following simple machines: first-class lever, second-class lever, third-class lever, inclined plane, wedge, and screw.

Math Skills

5. A ramp is 0.5 m high and has a slope that is 4 m long. What is its mechanical advantage?

6. The radius of the wheel of a wheel and axle is 4 times the radius of the axle. What is the mechanical advantage of the wheel and axle?

Critical Thinking

7. **Applying Concepts** A third-class lever has a mechanical advantage of less than 1. Explain why it is useful for some tasks.

8. **Making Inferences** Which compound machine would you expect to have the lowest mechanical efficiency: a can opener or a pair of scissors? Explain your answer.

Interpreting Graphics

9. Indicate two simple machines being used in the picture below.

For a variety of links related to this chapter, go to www.scilinks.org
Topic: Simple Machines; Compound Machines
SciLinks code: HSM1395; HSM0331

113

Skills Practice Lab

A Powerful Workout

Does the amount of work that you do depend on how fast you do it? No! But the amount of time in which you do work does affect your power—the rate of work done. In this lab, you'll calculate your work and power for climbing a flight of stairs at different speeds. Then you'll compare your power with that of an ordinary household object—a 100 W light bulb.

OBJECTIVES

Calculate the work and power used to climb a flight of stairs.

Compare your work and power with that of a 100 W light bulb.

MATERIALS

- flight of stairs
- ruler, metric
- stopwatch

Ask a Question

1 How does your power in climbing a flight of stairs compare with the power of a 100 W light bulb?

Form a Hypothesis

2 Write a hypothesis that answers the question in step 1. Explain your reasoning.

Data Collection Table				
Height of step (cm)	Number of steps	Height of stairs (m)	Time for slow walk (s)	Time for quick walk (s)

DO NOT WRITE IN BOOK

Test the Hypothesis

3 Copy the Data Collection Table onto a separate sheet of paper.

4 Use a metric ruler to measure the height of one stair step. Record the measurement in your Data Collection Table. Be sure to include units for all measurements.

5 Count the number of stairs, including the top step, and record this number in your Data Collection Table.

6 Calculate the height of the climb by multiplying the number of steps by the height of one step. Record your answer in meters. (You will need to convert your answer from centimeters to meters.)

7 Use a stopwatch to measure how many seconds it takes you to walk slowly up a flight of stairs. Record your measurement in your Data Collection Table.

8 Now measure how many seconds it takes you to walk quickly up a flight of stairs. Be careful not to overexert yourself. This is not a race to see who can get the fastest time!

Analyze the Results

1 **Constructing Tables** Copy the Calculations Table below onto a separate sheet of paper.

Weight (N)	Work (J)	Power for slow walk (W)	Power for quick walk (W)
Calculations Table			
	DO NOT WRITE IN BOOK		

2 **Examining Data** Determine your weight in newtons, and record it in your Calculations Table. Your weight in newtons is your weight in pounds (lb) multiplied by 4.45 N/lb.

3 **Examining Data** Calculate and record your work done in climbing the stairs by using the following equation:

$$work = force \times distance$$

(Hint: If you are having trouble determining the force exerted, remember that force is measured in newtons.)

4 **Examining Data** Calculate and record your power output by using the following equation:

$$power = \frac{work}{time}$$

The unit for power is the watt (1 watt = 1 joule/second).

Draw Conclusions

5 **Evaluating Methods** In step 3 of "Analyze the Results," you were asked to calculate your work done in climbing the stairs. Why weren't you asked to calculate your work for each trial (slow walk and quick walk)?

6 **Drawing Conclusions** Look at your hypothesis. Was your hypothesis correct? Now that you have measured your power, write a statement that describes how your power compares with that of a 100 W light bulb.

7 **Applying Conclusions** The work done to move one electron in a light bulb is very small. Write down two reasons why the power used is large. (Hint: How many electrons are in the filament of a light bulb? How did you use more power in trial 2?)

Communicating Your Data

Your teacher will provide a class data table on the board. Add your average power to the table. Then calculate the average power from the class data. How many students would it take to create power equal to the power of a 100 W bulb?

Chapter Review

USING KEY TERMS

For each pair of terms, explain how the meanings of the terms differ.

1 *work* and *power*

2 *lever* and *inclined plane*

3 *wheel and axle* and *pulley*

UNDERSTANDING KEY IDEAS

Multiple Choice

4 Work is being done when

  a. you apply a force to an object.

  b. an object is moving after you applied a force to it.

  c. you exert a force that moves an object in the direction of the force.

  d. you do something that is difficult.

5 What is the unit for work?

  a. joule

  b. joule per second

  c. newton

  d. watt

6 Which of the following is a simple machine?

  a. a bicycle

  b. a jar lid

  c. a pair of scissors

  d. a can opener

7 A machine can increase

  a. distance by decreasing force.

  b. force by decreasing distance.

  c. neither distance nor force.

  d. Either (a) or (b)

8 What is power?

  a. the strength of someone or something

  b. the force that is used

  c. the work that is done

  d. the rate at which work is done

9 What is the unit for power?

  a. newton

  b. kilogram

  c. watt

  d. joule

Short Answer

10 Identify the two simple machines that make up a pair of scissors.

11 Explain why you do work on a bag of groceries when you pick it up but not when you carry it.

12 Why is the work output of a machine always less than the work input?

13 What does the mechanical advantage of a first-class lever depend upon? Describe how it can be changed.

Math Skills

14 You and a friend together apply a force of 1,000 N to a car, which makes the car roll 10 m in 1 min and 40 s.

  a. How much work did you and your friend do together?

  b. What was the power output?

15 A lever allows a 35 N load to be lifted with a force of 7 N. What is the mechanical advantage of the lever?

CRITICAL THINKING

16 Concept Mapping Use the following terms to create a concept map: *work, force, distance, machine,* and *mechanical advantage.*

17 Analyzing Ideas Explain why levers usually have a greater mechanical efficiency than other simple machines do.

18 Making Inferences The amount of work done on a machine is 300 J, and the machine does 50 J of work. What can you say about the amount of friction that the machine has while operating?

19 Applying Concepts The winding road shown below is a series of inclined planes. Describe how a winding road makes it easier for vehicles to travel up a hill.

20 Predicting Consequences Why wouldn't you want to reduce the friction involved in using a winding road?

21 Making Comparisons How does the way that a wedge's mechanical advantage is determined differ from the way that a screw's mechanical advantage is determined?

22 Identifying Relationships If the mechanical advantage of a certain machine is greater than 1, what does that tell you about the relationship between the input force and distance and output force and distance?

INTERPRETING GRAPHICS

For each of the images below, identify the class of lever used and calculate the mechanical advantage of the lever.

23
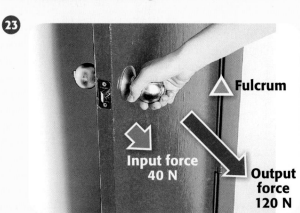

24
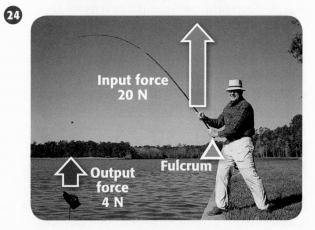

Standardized Test Preparation

Read each of the passages below. Then, answer the questions that follow each passage.

Passage 1 The Great Pyramid, located in Giza, Egypt, covers an area the size of 7 city blocks and rises about 40 stories high. The Great Pyramid was built around 2600 BCE and took less than 30 years to complete. During this time, the Egyptians cut and moved more than 2 million stone blocks, most of which average 2,000 kg. The workers did not have cranes, bulldozers, or any other heavy-duty machines. What they did have were two simple machines—the inclined plane and the lever. Archeologists have found the remains of inclined planes, or ramps, made from mud, stone, and wood. The Egyptians pushed or pulled the blocks along ramps to raise the blocks to the proper height. Notches in many blocks indicate that huge levers were used as giant crowbars to lift and move the heavy blocks.

1. What is the main idea of the passage?
  A Archeologists have found the remains of inclined planes near the pyramids.
  B The Great Pyramid at Giza was built in less than 30 years.
  C The Egyptians cut and moved more than 2 million stone blocks.
  D The Egyptians used simple machines to build the Great Pyramid at Giza.

2. Which of the following is a fact stated in the passage?
  F The Great Pyramid was made using more than 2 million stone blocks.
  G Each of the stone blocks used to build the Great Pyramid was exactly 2,000 kg.
  H Ancient Egyptians used cranes to build the Great Pyramid.
  I The Great Pyramid at Giza has a mass of about 2 million kg.

Passage 2 While riding a bicycle, you have probably experienced vibrations when the wheels of the bicycle hit bumps in the road. The force of the vibrations travels up through the frame to the rider. Slight vibrations can cause discomfort. Large ones can cause you to lose control of the bike and crash. Early bicycle designs made no attempt to dampen the <u>shock</u> of vibrations. Later designs used air-filled rubber tires and softer seats with springs to absorb some of the vibrations. Today's bike designs provide a safer, more comfortable ride. Various new materials—titanium, for example—absorb shock better than traditional steel and aluminum do. More important, designers are putting a variety of shock absorbers—devices that absorb energy—into bike designs.

1. In the passage, what does the term *shock* mean?
  A a medical emergency that can be caused by blood loss
  B a dry material used in early bicycles
  C a feeling of being stunned and surprised
  D a jolt or impact

2. Which of the following is a fact stated in the passage?
  F You have experienced vibrations while bicycle riding.
  G Slight vibrations can cause severe discomfort.
  H Titanium absorbs shock better than aluminum does.
  I Today's bike designs provide a more fashionable ride.

Use the diagram below to answer the questions that follow.

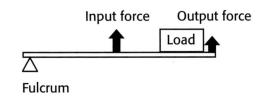

Input force   Output force
Load
Fulcrum

1. How does this lever make work easier?

A by changing the direction of the force

B by increasing both force and distance

C by increasing force and decreasing distance

D by decreasing force and increasing distance

2. What would the mechanical advantage of this lever be?

F less than 1

G 1

H greater than 1

I There is not enough information to determine the answer.

3. What type of lever is the lever in the diagram?

A a first-class lever

B a second-class lever

C a third-class lever

D There is not enough information to determine the answer.

4. Which of the following items is the same type of lever as the lever in the diagram?

F a seesaw

G a wheelbarrow

H a bottle opener

I an arm lifting a barbell

Read each question below, and choose the best answer.

1. For a special musical number during a school choir concert, 6 students stood in the first row, 10 students stood in the second row, and 14 students stood in the third row. If the pattern continued, how many students stood in the fifth row?

A 18

B 22

C 26

D 30

2. Michael baked some bread for his friends. He put 2½ cups of flour in each loaf. He used a total of 12½ cups of flour. How many loaves did he make?

F 2 loaves

G 4 loaves

H 5 loaves

I 15 loaves

3. A force of 15 N is exerted over a distance of 6 m. How much work was done? (Use the equation $W = F \times d$.)

A 21 J

B 21 N

C 90 J

D 90 N

4. If 350 J of work was done in 50 s, what was the power output? (Use the equation $P = W/t$.)

F 7 W

G 70 W

H 1,750 W

I 17,500 W

Standardized Test Preparation

Science in Action

Science, Technology, and Society

Kinetic Sculpture

The collection of tubes, tracks, balls, and blocks of wood shown in the photo is an audio-kinetic sculpture. A conveyor belt lifts the balls to a point high on the track, and the balls wind their way down as they are pulled by the force of gravity and pushed by various other forces. They twist through spirals, drop straight down tubes, and sometimes go up and around loops as if on a roller coaster. All this is made possible by the artist's applications of principles of kinetic energy, the energy of motion.

Math ACTiViTY

A conveyor belt on a kinetic sculpture lifts a ball to a point 0.8 m high. It exerts 0.05 N of force as it does so. How much work does the conveyor belt do on the ball?

Weird Science

Nanomachines

The technology of making things smaller and smaller keeps growing and growing. Powerful computers can now be held in the palm of your hand. But what can motors that are smaller than grains of pepper do? How can gnat-sized robots that can swim through the bloodstream be used? One possible field in which very small machines, *nanomachines*, can be used is in medicine.

Some scientists are looking into the possibility of creating cell-sized machines called *nanobots*. These tiny robots may have many uses in medicine if they can be injected into a person's bloodstream.

Language Arts ACTiViTY

WRITING SKILL Write a short story in which nanobots are used to save someone's life. Describe the machines the nanobots use in destroying deadly bacteria, clearing blood clots, or delivering medicine.

Mike Hensler

The Surf Chair Mike Hensler was a lifeguard at Daytona Beach, Florida, when he realized that it was next to impossible for someone in a wheelchair to come onto the beach. Although he had never invented a machine before, Hensler decided to build a wheelchair that could be driven across sand without getting stuck. He began spending many evenings in his driveway with a pile of lawn-chair parts, designing the chair by trial and error.

The result of Hensler's efforts looks very different from a conventional wheelchair. With huge rubber wheels and a thick frame of white PVC pipe, the Surf Chair not only moves easily over sandy terrain but also is weather resistant and easy to clean. The newest models of the Surf Chair come with optional attachments, such as a variety of umbrellas, detachable armrests and footrests, and even places to attach fishing rods.

Social Studies ACTiViTY

List some simple and compound machines that are used as access devices for people who are disabled. Research how these machines came to be in common use.

To learn more about these Science in Action topics, visit **go.hrw.com** and type in the keyword **HP5WRKF.**

Current Science

Check out Current Science® articles related to this chapter by visiting go.hrw.com. Just type in the keyword HP5CS08.

5

Energy and Energy Resources

The Big Idea

Energy can be changed from one form into another form, but energy cannot be created or destroyed.

About the PHOTO

Imagine that you're a driver in this race. Your car needs a lot of energy to finish. So, it probably needs a lot of gasoline, right? No, it just needs a lot of sunshine! This car runs on solar energy. Solar energy is one of the many forms of energy. Energy is needed to drive a car, turn on a light bulb, play sports, and walk to school. Energy is always being changed into different forms for different uses.

PRE-READING ACTIVITY

FOLDNOTES **Layered Book** Before you read the chapter, create the FoldNote entitled "Layered Book" described in the **Study Skills** section of the Appendix. Label the tabs of the layered book with "Types of energy," "Energy conversions," "Conservation of energy," and "Energy resources." As you read the chapter, write information you learn about each category under the appropriate tab.

START-UP ACTIVITY

Energy Swings!

In this activity, you'll observe a moving pendulum to learn about energy.

Procedure

1. Make a pendulum by tying a **50 cm long string** around the hook of a **100 g hooked mass.**

2. Hold the string with one hand. Pull the mass slightly to the side, and let go of the mass without pushing it. Watch it swing at least 10 times.

3. Record your observations. Note how fast and how high the pendulum swings.

4. Repeat step 2, but pull the mass farther to the side.

5. Record your observations. Note how fast and how high the pendulum swings.

Analysis

1. Does the pendulum have energy? Explain your answer.

2. What causes the pendulum to move?

3. Do you think the pendulum had energy before you let go of the mass? Explain your answer.

What Is Energy?

It's match point. The crowd is silent. The tennis player tosses the ball into the air and then slams it with her racket. The ball flies toward her opponent, who swings her racket at the ball. THWOOSH!! The ball goes into the net, causing it to shake. Game, set, and match!!

The tennis player needs energy to slam the ball with her racket. The ball also must have energy in order to cause the net to shake. Energy is around you all of the time. But what, exactly, is energy?

Energy and Work: Working Together

In science, **energy** is the ability to do work. Work is done when a force causes an object to move in the direction of the force. How do energy and work help you play tennis? The tennis player in **Figure 1** does work on her racket by exerting a force on it. The racket does work on the ball, and the ball does work on the net. When one object does work on another, energy is transferred from the first object to the second object. This energy allows the second object to do work. So, work is a transfer of energy. Like work, energy is expressed in units of joules (J).

✓ **Reading Check** What is energy? (*See the Appendix for answers to Reading Checks.*)

What You Will Learn

- Explain the relationship between energy and work.
- Compare kinetic and potential energy.
- Describe the different forms of energy.

Vocabulary

energy
kinetic energy
potential energy
mechanical energy

energy the capacity to do work

Figure 1 *The tennis player does work and transfers energy to the racket. With this energy, the racket can then do work on the ball.*

Kinetic Energy

In tennis, energy is transferred from the racket to the ball. As it flies over the net, the ball has kinetic (ki NET ik) energy. **Kinetic energy** is the energy of motion. All moving objects have kinetic energy. Like all forms of energy, kinetic energy can be used to do work. For example, kinetic energy allows a hammer to do work on a nail, as shown in **Figure 2.**

kinetic energy the energy of an object that is due to the object's motion

Kinetic Energy Depends on Mass and Speed

An object's kinetic energy can be found by the following equation:

$$kinetic\ energy = \frac{mv^2}{2}$$

The *m* stands for the object's mass in kilograms. The *v* stands for the object's speed. The faster something is moving, the more kinetic energy it has. Also, the greater the mass of a moving object, the greater its kinetic energy is.

A large car has more kinetic energy than a car that has less mass and that is moving at the same speed does. But as you can see from the equation, speed is squared. So speed has a greater effect on kinetic energy than mass does. For this reason, car crashes are much more dangerous at higher speeds than at lower speeds. A moving car has *4 times* the kinetic energy of the same car going half the speed! This is because it's going twice the speed of the slower car, and 2 squared is 4.

Figure 2 *When you swing a hammer, you give it kinetic energy, which does work on the nail.*

MATH FOCUS

Kinetic Energy What is the kinetic energy of a car that has a mass of 1,200 kg and is moving at a speed of 20 m/s?

Step 1: Write the equation for kinetic energy.

$$KE = \frac{mv^2}{2}$$

Step 2: Replace *m* and *v* with the measurements given, and solve.

$$KE = \frac{1{,}200\ kg \times (20\ m/s)^2}{2}$$

$$KE = \frac{1{,}200\ kg \times 400\ m^2/s^2}{2}$$

$$KE = \frac{480{,}000\ kg \bullet m^2/s^2}{2}$$

$$KE = 240{,}000\ kg \bullet m^2/s^2 = 240{,}000\ J$$

Now It's Your Turn

1. What is the kinetic energy of a car that has a mass of 2,400 kg and is moving at 20 m/s? How does this kinetic energy compare to the kinetic energy of the car in the example given at left?
2. What is the kinetic energy of a 4,000 kg elephant that is running at 2 m/s? at 4 m/s? How do the two kinetic energies compare with one another?
3. What is the kinetic energy of a 2,000 kg bus that is moving at 30 m/s?
4. What is the kinetic energy of a 3,000 kg bus that is moving at 20 m/s?

Figure 3 *The stored potential energy of the bow and string allows them to do work on the arrow when the string is released.*

Potential Energy

Not all energy has to do with motion. **Potential energy** is the energy an object has because of its position. For example, the stretched bow shown in **Figure 3** has potential energy. The bow has energy because work has been done to change its shape. The energy of that work is turned into potential energy.

Gravitational Potential Energy

When you lift an object, you do work on it. You use a force that is against the force of gravity. When you do this, you transfer energy to the object and give the object *gravitational potential energy*. Books on a shelf have gravitational potential energy. So does your backpack after you lift it on to your back. The amount of gravitational potential energy that an object has depends on its weight and its height.

Calculating Gravitational Potential Energy

You can find gravitational potential energy by using the following equation:

gravitational potential energy = weight × height

Because weight is expressed in newtons and height in meters, gravitational potential energy is expressed in newton-meters (N•m), or joules (J).

Recall that *work = force × distance*. Weight is the amount of force that you must use on an object to lift it, and height is a distance. So, gravitational potential energy is equal to the amount of work done on the object to lift it to a certain height. Or, you can think of gravitational potential energy as being equal to the work that would be done by the object if it were dropped from that height.

Gravitational Potential Energy What is the gravitational potential energy of a book with a weight of 13 N at a height of 1.5 m off the ground?

Step 1: Write the equation for gravitational potential energy (*GPE*).

GPE = weight × height

Step 2: Replace the weight and height with the measurements given in the problem, and solve.

GPE = 13 N × 1.5 m

GPE = 19.5 N•m = 19.5 J

Now It's Your Turn

1. What is the gravitational potential energy of a cat that weighs 40 N standing on a table that is 0.8 m above the ground?
2. What is the gravitational potential energy of a diver who weighs 500 N standing on a platform that is 10 m off the ground?
3. What is the gravitational potential energy of a diver who weighs 600 N standing on a platform that is 8 m off the ground?

Height Above What?

When you want to find out an object's gravitational potential energy, the "ground" that you measure the object's height from depends on where it is. For example, what if you want to measure the gravitational potential energy of an egg sitting on the kitchen counter? In this case, you would measure the egg's height from the floor. But if you were holding the egg over a balcony several stories from the ground, you would measure the egg's height from the ground! You can see that gravitational potential energy depends on your point of view. So, the height you use in calculating gravitational potential energy is a measure of how far an object has to fall.

Mechanical Energy

How would you describe the energy of the juggler's pins in **Figure 4**? To describe their total energy, you would state their mechanical energy. **Mechanical energy** is the total energy of motion and position of an object. Both potential energy and kinetic energy are kinds of mechanical energy. Mechanical energy can be all potential energy, all kinetic energy, or some of each. You can use the following equation to find mechanical energy:

mechanical energy = potential energy + kinetic energy

Reading Check What two kinds of energy can make up the mechanical energy of an object?

Mechanical Energy in a Juggler's Pin

The mechanical energy of an object remains the same unless it transfers some of its energy to another object. But even if the mechanical energy of an object stays the same, the potential energy or kinetic energy it has can increase or decrease.

Look at **Figure 4.** While the juggler is moving the pin with his hand, he is doing work on the pin to give it kinetic energy. But as soon as the pin leaves his hand, the pin's kinetic energy starts changing into potential energy. How can you tell that the kinetic energy is decreasing? The pin slows down as it moves upwards. Eventually, all of the pin's kinetic energy turns into potential energy, and it stops moving upward.

As the pin starts to fall back down again, its potential energy starts changing back into kinetic energy. More and more of its potential energy turns into kinetic energy. You can tell because the pin speeds up as it falls towards the ground.

potential energy the energy that an object has because of the position, shape, or condition of the object

mechanical energy the amount of work an object can do because of the object's kinetic and potential energies

Figure 4 *As a pin is juggled, its mechanical energy is the sum of its potential energy and its kinetic energy at any point.*

Figure 5 **Thermal Energy in Water**

The particles in an ice cube vibrate in fixed positions and do not have a lot of kinetic energy.

The particles of water in a lake can move more freely and have more kinetic energy than water particles in ice do.

The particles of water in steam move rapidly, so they have more energy than the particles in liquid water do.

Other Forms of Energy

Energy can come in a number of forms besides mechanical energy. These forms of energy include thermal, chemical, electrical, sound, light, and nuclear energy. As you read the next few pages, you will learn what these different forms of energy have to do with kinetic and potential energy.

Thermal Energy

All matter is made of particles that are always in random motion. Because the particles are in motion, they have kinetic energy. *Thermal energy* is all of the kinetic energy due to random motion of the particles that make up an object.

As you can see in **Figure 5,** particles move faster at higher temperatures than at lower temperatures. The faster the particles move, the greater their kinetic energy and the greater the object's thermal energy. Thermal energy also depends on the number of particles. Water in the form of steam has a higher temperature than water in a lake does. But the lake has more thermal energy because the lake has more water particles.

Chemical Energy

Where does the energy in food come from? Food is made of chemical compounds. When compounds such as sugar form, work is done to join the different atoms together. *Chemical energy* is the energy of a compound that changes as its atoms are rearranged. Chemical energy is a form of potential energy because it depends on the position and arrangement of the atoms in a compound.

For another activity related to this chapter, go to **go.hrw.com** and type in the keyword **HP5ENGW.**

Hear That Energy!

1. Make a simple drum by covering the open end of an **empty coffee can** with **wax paper.** Secure the wax paper with a **rubber band.**

2. Using the eraser end of a **pencil,** tap lightly on the wax paper. Describe how the paper responds. What do you hear?

3. Repeat step 2, but tap the paper a bit harder. Compare your results with those of step 2.

4. Cover half of the wax paper with one hand. Now, tap the paper. What happened? How can you describe sound energy as a form of mechanical energy?

Electrical Energy

The electrical outlets in your home allow you to use electrical energy. *Electrical energy* is the energy of moving electrons. Electrons are the negatively charged particles of atoms.

Suppose you plug an electrical device, such as the amplifier shown in **Figure 6,** into an outlet and turn it on. The electrons in the wires will transfer energy to different parts inside the amplifier. The electrical energy of moving electrons is used to do work that makes the sound that you hear from the amplifier.

The electrical energy used in your home comes from power plants. Huge generators turn magnets inside loops of wire. The changing position of a magnet makes electrical energy run through the wire. This electrical energy can be thought of as potential energy that is used when you plug in an electrical appliance and use it.

Figure 6 *The movement of electrons produces the electrical energy that an amplifier and a microphone use to produce sound.*

Sound Energy

Figure 7 shows how a vibrating object transmits energy through the air around it. Sound energy is caused by an object's vibrations. When you stretch a guitar string, the string stores potential energy. When you let the string go, this potential energy is turned into kinetic energy, which makes the string vibrate. The string also transmits some of this kinetic energy to the air around it. The air particles also vibrate, and transmit this energy to your ear. When the sound energy reaches your ear, you hear the sound of the guitar.

Reading Check What does sound energy consist of?

Figure 7 *As the guitar strings vibrate, they cause particles in the air to vibrate. These vibrations transmit sound energy.*

Figure 8 *The energy used to cook food in a microwave is a form of light energy.*

Light Energy

Light allows you to see, but did you know that not all light can be seen? **Figure 8** shows a type of light that we use but can't see. *Light energy* is produced by the vibrations of electrically charged particles. Like sound vibrations, light vibrations cause energy to be transmitted. But the vibrations that transmit light energy don't need to be carried through matter. In fact, light energy can move through a vacuum (an area where there is no matter).

Nuclear Energy

There is a form of energy that comes from a tiny amount of matter. It is used to generate electrical energy, and it gives the sun its energy. It is *nuclear* (NOO klee uhr) *energy*, the energy that comes from changes in the nucleus (NOO klee uhs) of an atom.

Atoms store a lot of potential energy because of the positions of the particles in the nucleus of the atoms. When two or more small nuclei (NOO klee ie) join together, or when the nucleus of a large atom splits apart, energy is given off.

The energy given off by the sun comes from nuclear energy. In the sun, shown in **Figure 9,** hydrogen nuclei join together to make a larger helium nucleus. This reaction, known as *fusion,* gives off a huge amount of energy. The sun's light and heat come from these reactions.

When a nucleus of a heavy element such as uranium is split apart, the potential energy in the nucleus is given off. This kind of nuclear energy is called *fission.* Fission is used to generate electrical energy at nuclear power plants.

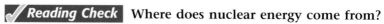 **Reading Check** Where does nuclear energy come from?

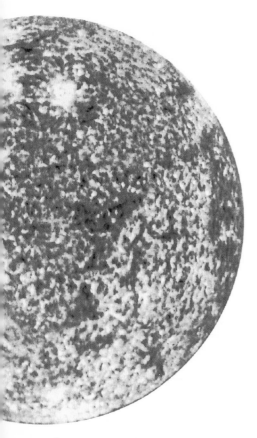

Figure 9 *Without the nuclear energy from the sun, life on Earth would not be possible.*

Summary

- Energy is the ability to do work, and work equals the transfer of energy. Energy and work are expressed in units of joules (J).
- Kinetic energy is energy of motion and depends on speed and mass.
- Potential energy is energy of position. Gravitational potential energy depends on weight and height.
- Mechanical energy is the sum of kinetic energy and potential energy.
- Thermal energy and sound energy can be considered forms of kinetic energy.
- Chemical energy, electrical energy, and nuclear energy can be considered forms of potential energy.

Using Key Terms

1. In your own words, write a definition for the term *energy*.

2. Use the following terms in the same sentence: *kinetic energy, potential energy,* and *mechanical energy.*

Understanding Key Ideas

3. What determines an object's thermal energy?
   a. the motion of its particles
   b. its size
   c. its potential energy
   d. its mechanical energy

4. How are energy and work related?

5. What two factors determine gravitational potential energy?

6. Describe why chemical energy is a form of potential energy.

Critical Thinking

7. **Identifying Relationships** When you hit a nail into a board by using a hammer, the head of the nail gets warm. In terms of kinetic and thermal energy, describe why you think the nail head gets warm.

8. **Applying Concepts** Explain why a high-speed collision may cause more damage to vehicles than a low-speed collision does.

Interpreting Graphics

9. Which part of mechanical energy does the girl in the picture below have the most of?

Developed and maintained by the National Science Teachers Association

For a variety of links related to this chapter, go to www.scilinks.org

Topic: What Is Energy? ; Forms of Energy
SciLinks code: HSM1660; HSM0612

Energy Conversions

Imagine you're finishing a clay mug in art class. You turn around, and your elbow knocks the mug off the table. Luckily, you catch the mug before it hits the ground.

The mug has gravitational potential energy while it is on the table. As the mug falls, its potential energy changes into kinetic energy. This change is an example of an energy conversion. An **energy conversion** is a change from one form of energy to another. Any form of energy can change into any other form of energy. Often, one form of energy changes into more than one other form.

What You Will Learn

- Describe an energy conversion.
- Give examples of energy conversions for the different forms of energy.
- Explain how energy conversions make energy useful.
- Explain the role of machines in energy conversions.

Vocabulary

energy conversion

READING STRATEGY

Brainstorming The key idea of this section is energy conversion. Brainstorm words and phrases related to energy conversion.

energy conversion a change from one form of energy to another

Kinetic Energy and Potential Energy

Look at **Figure 1.** At the instant this picture was taken, the skateboarder on the left side of the picture was hardly moving. How did he get up so high in the air? As you might guess, he was moving at a high speed on his way up the half-pipe. So, he had a lot of kinetic energy. What happened to that energy? His kinetic energy changed into potential energy. Imagine that the picture below is a freeze-frame of a video. What happens once the video starts running again? The skateboarder's potential energy will become kinetic energy once again as he speeds down the side of the half-pipe.

Figure 1 **Potential Energy and Kinetic Energy**

When the skateboarder reaches the top of the half-pipe, his potential energy is at a maximum.

As he speeds down through the bottom of the half-pipe, the skateboarder's kinetic energy is at a maximum.

Elastic Potential Energy

A rubber band can be used to show another example of an energy conversion. Did you know that energy can be stored in a rubber band? Look at **Figure 2.** The wound-up rubber band in the toy airplane has a kind of potential energy called *elastic potential energy*. When the rubber band is let go, the stored energy becomes kinetic energy, spins the propeller, and makes the airplane fly.

You can change the shape of a rubber band by stretching it. Stretching the rubber band takes a little effort. The energy you put into stretching it becomes elastic potential energy. Like the skateboarder at the top of the half-pipe, the stretched rubber band stores potential energy. When you let the rubber band go, it goes back to its original shape. It releases its stored-up potential energy as it does so, as you know if you have ever snapped a rubber band against your skin!

Figure 2 *The wound-up rubber band in this model airplane has potential energy because its shape has been changed.*

Reading Check How is elastic potential energy stored and released? (*See the Appendix for answers to Reading Checks.*)

Conversions Involving Chemical Energy

You may have heard someone say, "Breakfast is the most important meal of the day." Why is eating breakfast so important? As shown in **Figure 3,** chemical energy comes from the food you eat. Your body uses chemical energy to function. Eating breakfast gives your body the energy needed to help you start the day.

Figure 3 Chemical energy of food is converted into kinetic energy when you are active. It is converted into thermal energy to maintain body temperature.

Figure 4 **From Light Energy to Chemical Energy**

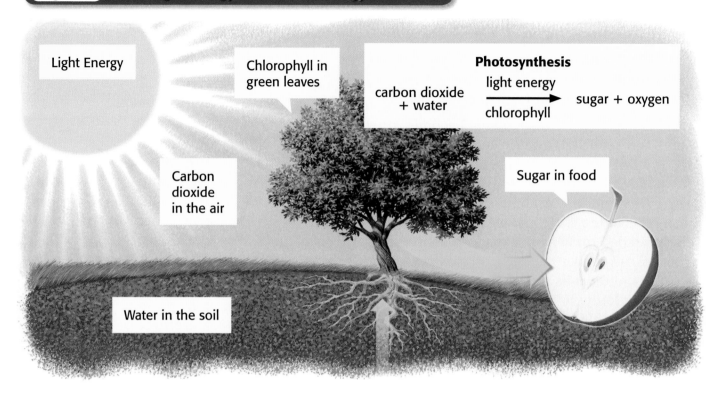

Light Energy

Chlorophyll in green leaves

Photosynthesis

carbon dioxide + water

light energy
→
chlorophyll

sugar + oxygen

Carbon dioxide in the air

Sugar in food

Water in the soil

Energy Conversions in Plants

Did you know that the chemical energy in the food you eat comes from the sun's energy? When you eat fruits, vegetables, or grains, you are taking in chemical energy. This energy comes from a chemical change that was made possible by the sun's energy. When you eat meat from animals that ate plants, you are also taking in energy that first came from the sun.

As shown in **Figure 4,** photosynthesis (FOHT oh SIN thuh sis) uses light energy to make new substances that have chemical energy. In this way, light energy is changed into chemical energy. The chemical energy from a tree can be changed into thermal energy when you burn the tree's wood. So, if you follow the conversion of energy back far enough, the energy from a wood fire actually comes from the sun!

✓ **Reading Check** Where does the energy that plants use to grow come from?

The Process Continues

Let's trace where the energy goes. Plants change light energy into chemical energy. The chemical energy in the food you eat is changed into another kind of chemical energy that your body can use. Your body then uses that energy to give you the kinetic energy that you use in everything you do. It's an endless process—energy is always going somewhere!

Figure 5 Energy Conversions in a Hair Dryer

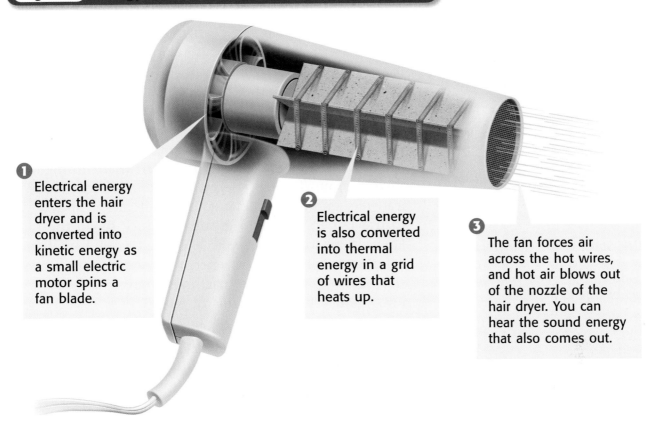

① Electrical energy enters the hair dryer and is converted into kinetic energy as a small electric motor spins a fan blade.

② Electrical energy is also converted into thermal energy in a grid of wires that heats up.

③ The fan forces air across the hot wires, and hot air blows out of the nozzle of the hair dryer. You can hear the sound energy that also comes out.

Why Energy Conversions Are Important

Energy conversions are needed for everything we do. Heating our homes, getting energy from a meal, and many other things use energy conversions. Machines, such as the hair dryer shown in **Figure 5,** help harness energy and make that energy work for you. Electrical energy by itself won't dry your hair. But you can use a hair dryer to change electrical energy into the thermal energy that will help you dry your hair.

Conversions Involving Electrical Energy

You use electrical energy all of the time. When you listen to the radio, when you make toast, and when you take a picture with a camera, you use electrical energy. Electrical energy can easily be changed into other forms of energy. **Table 1** lists some common energy conversions that involve electrical energy.

Table 1 Some Conversions of Electrical Energy	
Alarm clock	electrical energy ⟶ light energy and sound energy
Battery	chemical energy ⟶ electrical energy
Light bulb	electrical energy ⟶ light energy and thermal energy
Blender	electrical energy ⟶ kinetic energy and sound energy

Figure 6 *Some of the energy you transfer to a nutcracker is converted into sound energy as the nutcracker transfers energy to the nut.*

Energy and Machines

You've been learning about energy, its different forms, and the ways that it can change between forms. Another way to learn about energy is to look at how machines use energy. A machine can make work easier by changing the size or direction (or both) of the force needed to do the work.

Suppose you want to crack open a walnut. Using a nutcracker, such as the one shown in **Figure 6,** would be much easier (and less painful) than using your fingers. You transfer energy to the nutcracker, and it transfers energy to the nut. The nutcracker allows you to use less force over a greater distance to do the same amount of work as if you had used your bare hands. Another example of how energy is used by a machine is shown in **Figure 7.** Some machines change the energy put into them into other forms of energy.

Reading Check What are two things that machines can do to force that is put into them?

Figure 7 **Energy Conversions in a Bicycle**

For your bike to start and keep moving, energy must be transferred and converted.

1 Chemical energy in your body is converted into kinetic energy when your muscle fibers contract and relax.

2 Your legs transfer this kinetic energy to the pedals by pushing them around in a circle.

4 The chain moves and transfers energy to the back wheel, which gets you moving!

3 The pedals transfer this kinetic energy to the gear wheel, which transfers kinetic energy to the chain.

Machines as Energy Converters

Machines help you use energy by converting it into the form that you need. **Figure 8** shows a device called a *radiometer*. It was invented to measure energy from the sun. Inside the glass bulb are four small vanes that absorb light energy. The vanes are dark on one side and light on the other. The dark sides absorb light energy better than the light sides do. As gases next to the dark sides of the vanes heat up, the gas molecules move faster, which causes the vanes to turn. The radiometer shows how a machine can convert energy from one form into another. It changes light energy into heat energy into kinetic energy.

Figure 8 *Machines can change energy into different forms. This radiometer converts light energy into kinetic energy.*

SECTION Review

Summary

- An energy conversion is a change from one form of energy to another. Any form of energy can be converted into any other form of energy.
- Kinetic energy is converted to potential energy when an object is moved against gravity.
- Elastic potential energy is another example of potential energy.
- Your body uses the food you eat to convert chemical energy into kinetic energy.
- Plants convert light energy into chemical energy.
- Machines can transfer energy and can convert energy into a more useful form.

Using Key Terms

1. In your own words, write a definition for the term *energy conversion*.

Understanding Key Ideas

2. In plants, energy is transformed from
   a. kinetic to potential.
   b. light to chemical.
   c. chemical to electrical.
   d. chemical to light.

3. Describe a case in which electrical energy is converted into thermal energy.

4. How does your body get the energy that it needs?

5. What is the role of machines in energy conversions?

Critical Thinking

6. **Applying Concepts** Describe the kinetic-potential energy conversions that occur when a basketball bounces.

7. **Applying Concepts** A car that brakes suddenly comes to a screeching halt. Is the sound energy produced in this conversion a useful form of energy? Explain your answer.

Interpreting Graphics

Look at the diagram below, and answer the following questions.

8. What kind of energy does the skier have at the top of the slope?

9. What happens to that energy after the skier races down the slope of the mountain?

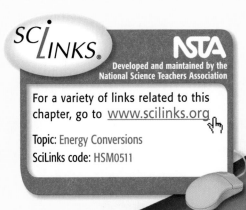

SCiLINKS.

Developed and maintained by the National Science Teachers Association

For a variety of links related to this chapter, go to www.scilinks.org

Topic: Energy Conversions
SciLinks code: HSM0511

137

Conservation of Energy

Many roller coasters have a mechanism that pulls the cars up to the top of the first hill. But the cars are on their own for the rest of the ride.

As the cars go up and down the hills on the track, their potential energy is converted into kinetic energy and back again. But the cars never return to the same height at which they started. Does energy get lost somewhere along the way? No, it is just converted into other forms of energy.

Where Does the Energy Go?

To find out where a roller coaster's original potential energy goes, you have to think about more than just the hills of the roller coaster. Friction plays a part too. **Friction** is a force that opposes motion between two surfaces that are touching. For the roller coaster to move, energy must be used to overcome friction. There is friction between the cars' wheels and the track and between the cars and the air around them. As a result, not all of the potential energy of the cars changes into kinetic energy as the cars go down the first hill. Likewise, as you can see in **Figure 1,** not all of the kinetic energy of the cars changes back into potential energy.

What You Will Learn

- Explain how energy is conserved within a closed system.
- Explain the law of conservation of energy.
- Give examples of how thermal energy is always a result of energy conversion.
- Explain why perpetual motion is impossible.

Vocabulary

friction
law of conservation of energy

READING STRATEGY

Paired Summarizing Read this section silently. In pairs, take turns summarizing the material. Stop to discuss ideas that seem confusing.

Figure 1 Energy Conversions in a Roller Coaster

Not all of the cars' potential energy (*PE*) is converted into kinetic energy (*KE*) as the cars go down the first hill. In addition, not all of the cars' kinetic energy is converted into potential energy as the cars go up the second hill. Some of it is changed into thermal energy because of friction.

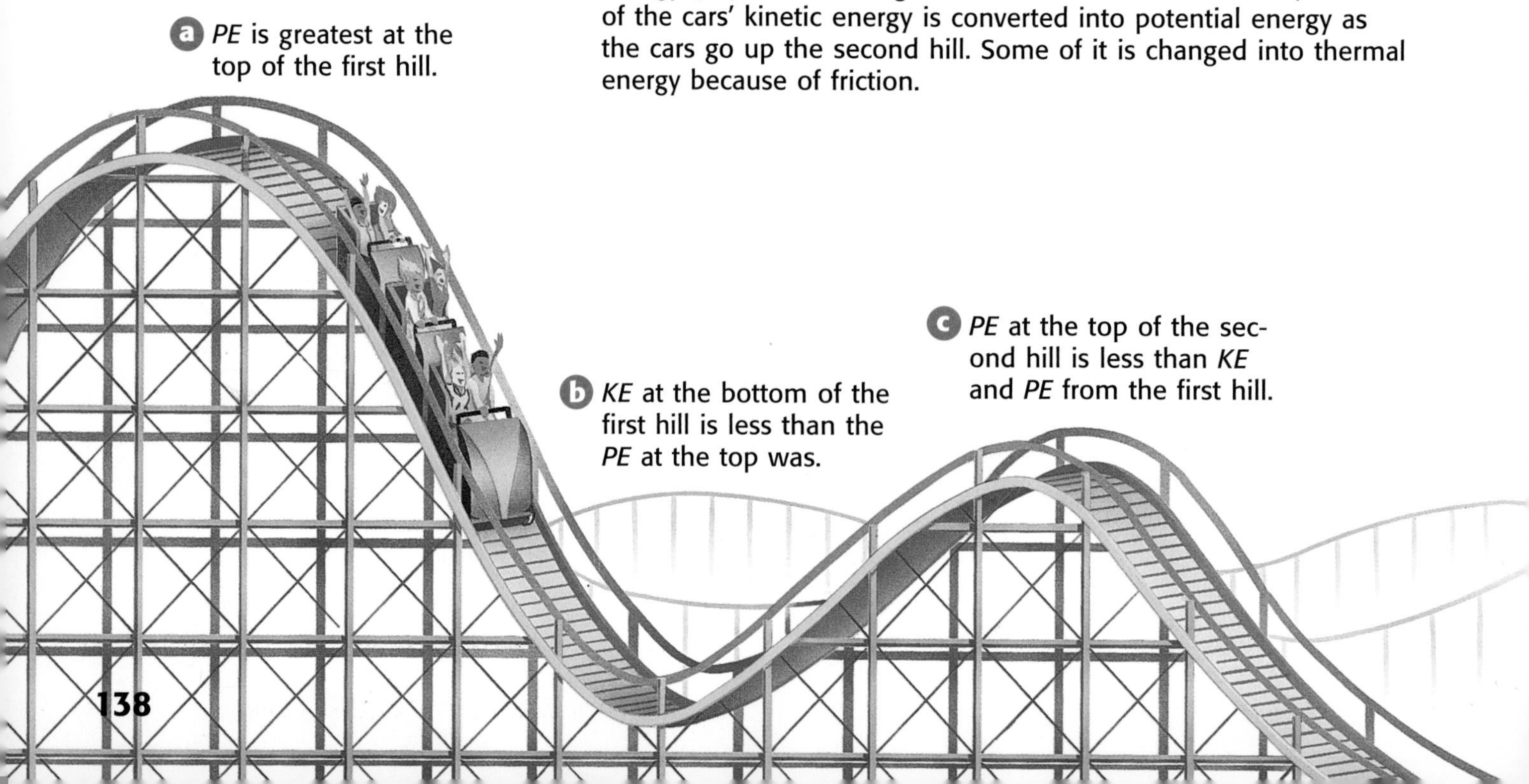

ⓐ *PE* is greatest at the top of the first hill.

ⓑ *KE* at the bottom of the first hill is less than the *PE* at the top was.

ⓒ *PE* at the top of the second hill is less than *KE* and *PE* from the first hill.

Energy Is Conserved Within a Closed System

A *closed system* is a group of objects that transfer energy only to each other. For example, a closed system that involves a roller coaster consists of the track, the cars, and the air around them. On a roller coaster, some mechanical energy (the sum of kinetic and potential energy) is always converted into thermal energy because of friction. Sound energy also comes from the energy conversions in a roller coaster. If you add together the cars' kinetic energy at the bottom of the first hill, the thermal energy due to overcoming friction, and the sound energy made, you end up with the same total amount of energy as the original amount of potential energy. In other words, energy is conserved and not lost.

friction a force that opposes motion between two surfaces that are in contact

law of conservation of energy the law that states that energy cannot be created or destroyed but can be changed from one form to another

Law of Conservation of Energy

Energy is conserved in all cases. Because no exception to this rule has been found, this rule is described as a law. According to the **law of conservation of energy,** energy cannot be created or destroyed. The total amount of energy in a closed system is always the same. As **Figure 2** shows, energy can change from one form to another. But all of the different forms of energy in a system always add up to the same total amount of energy. It does not matter how many energy conversions take place.

Reading Check Why is the conservation of energy considered a scientific law? (*See the Appendix for answers to Reading Checks.*)

Figure 2 **Energy Conservation in a Light Bulb**

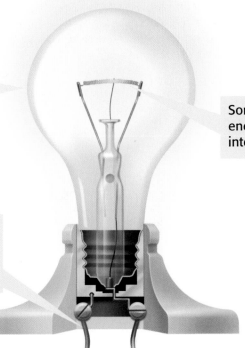

Some energy is converted into thermal energy, which makes the bulb feel warm.

Some electrical energy is converted into light energy.

As electrical energy is carried through the wire, some of it is converted into thermal energy.

No Conversion Without Thermal Energy

Any time one form of energy is converted into another form, some of the original energy always gets converted into thermal energy. The thermal energy due to friction that results from energy conversions is not useful energy. That is, this thermal energy is not used to do work. Think about a car. You put gas into a car. But not all of the gasoline's chemical energy makes the car move. Some wasted thermal energy will always result from the energy conversions. Much of this energy leaves through the radiator and the exhaust pipe.

Perpetual Motion? No Way!

People have sometimes tried to make a machine that would run forever without any additional energy. This perpetual (puhr PECH oo uhl) motion machine would put out exactly as much energy as it takes in. But that's impossible, because some waste thermal energy always results from energy conversions. The only way a machine can keep moving is to have a constant supply of energy. For example, the "drinking bird" shown in **Figure 3** uses thermal energy from the air to evaporate the water from its head. So, it is not a perpetual motion machine.

✓ Reading Check Why is "perpetual motion" impossible?

Energy Conversions

With an adult, find three examples of energy conversions that take place in your home. In your **science journal,** write down the kinds of energy that go into each conversion and the kinds of energy that result. For each type of energy that is output, indicate whether the energy is useful.

ACTIVITY

Figure 3 The "Drinking Bird"

❶ When the bird "drinks," the felt covering its head gets wet.

❷ When the bird is upright, water evaporates from the felt, which decreases the temperature and pressure in the head. Fluid is drawn up from the tail, where pressure is higher, and the bird tips downward.

❸ After the bird "drinks," fluid returns to the tail, the bird flips upright, and the cycle repeats.

Making Conversions Efficient

You may have heard that a car is energy efficient if it gets good gas mileage, and that your home may be energy efficient if it is well insulated. In terms of energy conversions, *energy efficiency* (e FISH uhn see) is a comparison of the amount of energy before a conversion with the amount of useful energy after a conversion. A car with high energy efficiency can go farther than other cars with the same amount of gas.

Energy conversions that are more efficient end up wasting less energy. Look at **Figure 4.** Newer cars tend to be more energy efficient than older cars. One reason is the smooth, aerodynamic (ER oh die NAM ik) shape of newer cars. The smooth shape reduces friction between the car and the surrounding air. Because these cars move through air more easily, they use less energy to overcome friction. So, they are more efficient. Improving the efficiency of machines, such as cars, is important because greater efficiency results in less waste. If less energy is wasted, less energy is needed to operate a machine.

Figure 4 *The shape of newer cars reduces friction between the body of the car and the air.*

More aerodynamic car

Less aerodynamic car

SECTION Review

Summary

- Because of friction, some energy is always converted into thermal energy during an energy conversion.
- Energy is conserved within a closed system. According to the law of conservation of energy, energy cannot be created or destroyed.
- Perpetual motion is impossible because some of the energy put into a machine is converted into thermal energy because of friction.

Using Key Terms

1. Use the following terms in the same sentence: *friction* and *the law of conservation of energy.*

Understanding Key Ideas

2. Perpetual motion is impossible because

   a. things tend to slow down.

   b. energy is lost.

   c. machines are very inefficient.

   d. machines have friction.

3. Describe the energy conversions that take place on a roller coaster, and explain how energy is conserved.

Math Skills

4. A bike is pedaled with 80 J of energy and then coasts. It does 60 J of work in moving forward until it stops. How much of the energy that was put into the bike became thermal energy?

Critical Thinking

5. **Evaluating Conclusions** Imagine that you drop a ball. It bounces a few times and then it stops. Your friend says that the energy that the ball had is gone. Where did the energy go? Evaluate your friend's statement based on energy conservation.

6. **Evaluating Assumptions** If someone says that a car has high energy output, can you conclude that the car is efficient? Explain.

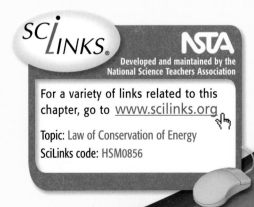

Developed and maintained by the National Science Teachers Association

For a variety of links related to this chapter, go to www.scilinks.org

Topic: Law of Conservation of Energy
SciLinks code: HSM0856

Energy Resources

Energy is used to light and warm our homes. It is used to make food, clothing, and other things. It is also used to transport people and products from place to place. Where does all of this energy come from?

An *energy resource* is a natural resource that can be converted into other forms of energy in order to do useful work. In this section, you will learn about several energy resources, including the one that most other energy resources come from—the sun.

Nonrenewable Resources

Some energy resources, called **nonrenewable resources,** cannot be replaced or are replaced much more slowly than they are used. Fossil fuels are the most important nonrenewable resources.

Oil and natural gas, shown in **Figure 1,** as well as coal, are the most common fossil fuels. **Fossil fuels** are energy resources that formed from the buried remains of plants and animals that lived millions of years ago. These plants stored energy from the sun by photosynthesis. Animals used and stored this energy by eating the plants. So, fossil fuels are concentrated forms of the sun's energy. Now, millions of years later, energy from the sun is released when these fossil fuels are burned.

✓ Reading Check Why are fossil fuels considered nonrenewable resources? *(See the Appendix for answers to Reading Checks.)*

What You Will Learn

- Name several energy resources.
- Explain how the sun is the source of most energy on Earth.
- Evaluate the advantages and disadvantages of using various energy resources.

Vocabulary

nonrenewable resource
fossil fuel
renewable resource

READING STRATEGY

Reading Organizer As you read this section, make a table comparing nonrenewable resources and renewable resources.

nonrenewable resource a resource that forms at a rate that is much slower than the rate at which it is consumed

fossil fuel a nonrenewable energy resource formed from the remains of organisms that lived long ago

| Figure 1 | Formation of Fossil Fuels |

Crushed by sediment and heated by Earth, remains of organisms that lived millions of years ago slowly turned into oil or petroleum.

Formed in much the same way that petroleum formed, natural gas is often found with petroleum deposits.

Uses of Fossil Fuels

All fossil fuels contain stored energy from the sun, which can be converted into other kinds of energy. **Figure 2** shows some different ways that fossil fuels are used in our society.

People have been getting energy from the burning of coal, a fossil fuel, for hundreds of years. Today, burning coal is still a very common way to generate electrical energy. Many products, such as gasoline, wax, and plastics, are made from petroleum, another fossil fuel. A third kind of fossil fuel, natural gas, is often used in home heating.

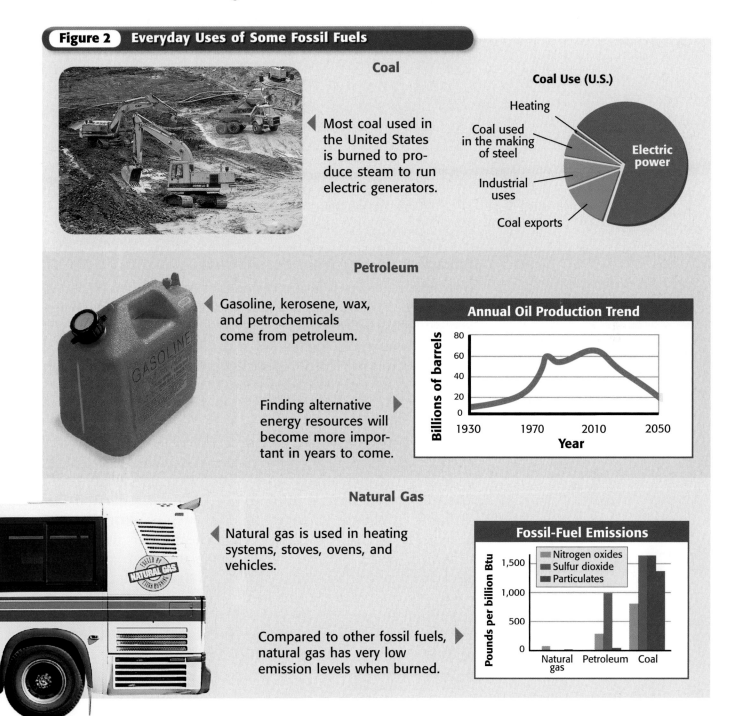

Figure 2 **Everyday Uses of Some Fossil Fuels**

Coal

Most coal used in the United States is burned to produce steam to run electric generators.

Coal Use (U.S.)
- Heating
- Coal used in the making of steel
- Industrial uses
- Coal exports
- Electric power

Petroleum

Gasoline, kerosene, wax, and petrochemicals come from petroleum.

Finding alternative energy resources will become more important in years to come.

Annual Oil Production Trend

Natural Gas

Natural gas is used in heating systems, stoves, ovens, and vehicles.

Compared to other fossil fuels, natural gas has very low emission levels when burned.

Fossil-Fuel Emissions
- Nitrogen oxides
- Sulfur dioxide
- Particulates

Figure 3 Converting Fossil Fuels into Electrical Energy

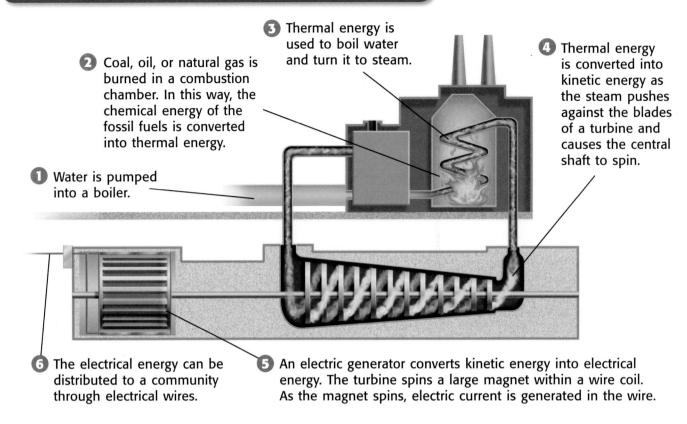

3 Thermal energy is used to boil water and turn it to steam.

2 Coal, oil, or natural gas is burned in a combustion chamber. In this way, the chemical energy of the fossil fuels is converted into thermal energy.

4 Thermal energy is converted into kinetic energy as the steam pushes against the blades of a turbine and causes the central shaft to spin.

1 Water is pumped into a boiler.

6 The electrical energy can be distributed to a community through electrical wires.

5 An electric generator converts kinetic energy into electrical energy. The turbine spins a large magnet within a wire coil. As the magnet spins, electric current is generated in the wire.

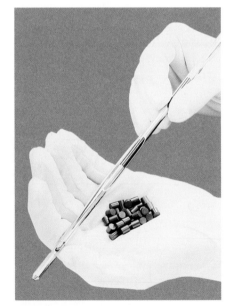

Figure 4 *A single uranium fuel pellet contains the energy equivalent of about 1 metric ton of coal.*

Electrical Energy from Fossil Fuels

One way to generate electrical energy is to burn fossil fuels. In fact, fossil fuels are the main source of electrical energy generated in the United States. *Electric generators* convert the chemical energy in fossil fuels into electrical energy by the process shown in **Figure 3.** The chemical energy in fossil fuels is changed into the electrical energy that you use every day.

Nuclear Energy

Another way to generate electrical energy is to use nuclear energy. Like fossil-fuel power plants, a nuclear power plant generates thermal energy that boils water to make steam. The steam then turns a turbine, which runs a generator. The spinning generator changes kinetic energy into electrical energy. However, the fuels used in nuclear power plants differ from fossil fuels. Nuclear energy is generated from radioactive elements, such as uranium, shown in **Figure 4.** In a process called *nuclear fission* (NOO klee uhr FISH uhn), the nucleus of a uranium atom is split into two smaller nuclei, which releases nuclear energy. Because the supply of these elements is limited, nuclear energy is a nonrenewable resource.

✓ Reading Check Where does nuclear energy come from?

Renewable Resources

Some energy resources, called **renewable resources,** are naturally replaced more quickly than they are used. Some renewable resources, such as solar energy and wind energy, are considered practically limitless.

renewable resource a natural resource that can be replaced at the same rate at which the resource is consumed

Solar Energy

Sunlight can be changed into electrical energy through solar cells. These cells can be used in devices such as calculators. Solar cells can also be placed on the roof of a house to provide electrical energy. Some houses can use solar energy by allowing sunlight into the house through large windows. The sun's energy can then be used to heat the house.

Energy from Water

The sun causes water to evaporate and fall again as rain that flows through rivers. The potential energy of water in a reservoir can be changed into kinetic energy as the water flows through a dam. **Figure 5** shows a hydroelectric dam. Falling water turns turbines in a dam. The turbines are connected to a generator that changes kinetic energy into electrical energy.

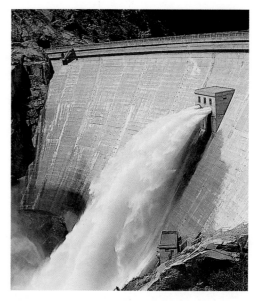

Figure 5 *This dam converts the energy from water going downstream into electrical energy.*

Wind Energy

Wind is caused by the sun's heating of Earth's surface. Because Earth's surface is not heated evenly, wind is created. The kinetic energy of wind can turn the blades of a windmill. Wind turbines are shown in **Figure 6.** A wind turbine changes the kinetic energy of the air into electrical energy by turning a generator.

Figure 6 *These wind turbines are converting wind energy into electrical energy.*

Geothermal Energy

Thermal energy caused by the heating of Earth's crust is called *geothermal energy*. Some geothermal power plants pump water underground next to hot rock. The water returns to the surface as steam, which can then turn the turbine of a generator.

✓ Reading Check Where does geothermal energy come from?

Biomass

Plants use and store energy from the sun. Organic matter, such as plants, wood, and waste, that can be burned to release energy is called *biomass*. **Figure 7** shows an example. Some countries depend on biomass for energy.

The Two Sides to Energy Resources

All energy resources have advantages and disadvantages. How can you decide which energy resource to use? **Table 1** compares several energy resources. Depending on where you live, what you need energy for, and how much energy you need, one energy resource may be a better choice than another.

Figure 7 *Plants capture the sun's energy. When wood is burned, it releases the energy it got from the sun, which can be used to generate electrical energy.*

Table 1 Advantages and Disadvantages of Energy Resources		
Energy Resource	**Advantages**	**Disadvantages**
Fossil fuels	• provide a large amount of thermal energy per unit of mass • are easy to get and transport • can be used to generate electricity and to make products such as plastic	• are nonrenewable • produce smog • release substances that can cause acid precipitation • create a risk of oil spills
Nuclear	• is a very concentrated form of energy • does not produce air pollution	• produces radioactive waste • is nonrenewable
Solar	• is an almost limitless source of energy • does not produce pollution	• is expensive to use for large-scale energy production • is practical only in sunny areas
Water	• is renewable • does not produce air pollution	• requires dams, which disrupt a river's ecosystem • is available only where there are rivers
Wind	• is renewable • is relatively inexpensive to generate • does not produce air pollution	• is practical only in windy areas
Geothermal	• is an almost limitless source of energy • power plants require little land	• is practical only in areas near hot spots • produces wastewater, which can damage soil
Biomass	• is renewable • is inexpensive	• requires large areas of farmland • produces smoke

Choosing the Right Energy Resource

As **Table 1** shows, each source of energy that we know about on Earth has advantages and disadvantages. For example, you have probably heard that fossil fuels pollute the air. They will also run out after they are used up. Even renewable resources have their drawbacks. Generating lots of energy from solar energy is difficult. So it cannot be used to meet the energy needs of large cities. Geothermal energy is limited to the "hot spots" in the world where it is available. Hydroelectric energy requires large dams, which can affect the ecology of river life. Energy planning in all parts of the world requires careful consideration of energy needs and the availability and responsible use of resources.

CONNECTION TO Social Studies

WRITING SKILL **Earth's Energy Resources** Find examples of places in the world where the various energy resources mentioned in this chapter are used. List them in your **science journal.** Discuss any patterns that you notice, such as which regions of the world use certain energy resources.

SECTION Review

Summary

- An energy resource is a natural resource that can be converted into other forms of energy in order to do useful work.

- Nonrenewable resources cannot be replaced after they are used or can be replaced only after long periods of time. They include fossil fuels and nuclear energy.

- Renewable resources can be replaced in nature over a relatively short period of time. They include energy from the sun, wind, and water; geothermal energy; and biomass.

- The sun is the source of most energy on Earth.

- Choices about energy resources depend on where you live and what you need energy for.

Using Key Terms

1. In your own words, write a definition for the term *fossil fuel.*

Complete each of the following sentences by choosing the correct term from the word bank.

nonrenewable resources
renewable resources

2. There is a practically limitless supply of ___.

3. ___ are used up more quickly than they are being replaced.

Understanding Key Ideas

4. Which of the following is a renewable resource?
   a. wind
   b. coal
   c. nuclear energy
   d. petroleum

5. Compare fossil fuels and biomass as energy resources.

6. Trace electrical energy back to the sun.

Critical Thinking

7. **Making Comparisons** Describe the similarities and differences between transforming energy in a hydroelectric dam and a wind turbine.

8. **Analyzing Ideas** Name an energy resource that does NOT depend on the sun.

Interpreting Graphics

9. Use the pie chart below to explain why renewable resources are becoming more important to the United States.

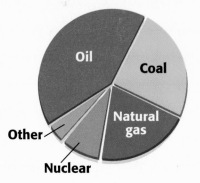

U.S. Energy Sources

Oil
Coal
Natural gas
Other
Nuclear

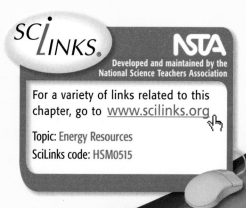

SCI LINKS

NSTA Developed and maintained by the National Science Teachers Association

For a variety of links related to this chapter, go to www.scilinks.org

Topic: Energy Resources
SciLinks code: HSM0515

Skills Practice Lab

Finding Energy

OBJECTIVES

Form a hypothesis about where kinetic energy comes from.

Test your hypothesis by collecting and analyzing data.

MATERIALS

- books (2 or 3)
- masking tape
- meterstick
- metric balance
- rolling cart
- stopwatch
- wooden board

When you coast down a hill on a bike or skateboard, you may notice that you pick up speed, or go faster and faster. Because you are moving, you have kinetic energy—the energy of motion. Where does that energy come from? When you pedal the bike or push the skateboard, you are the source of the kinetic energy. But where does the kinetic energy come from when you roll down a hill without making any effort? In this lab, you will find out where such kinetic energy comes from.

Ask a Question

1 Where does the kinetic energy come from when you roll down a hill?

Form a Hypothesis

2 Write a hypothesis that is a possible answer to the question above. Explain your reasoning.

Test the Hypothesis

3 Copy the Data Collection Table below.

Data Collection Table							
Height of ramp (m)	**Length of ramp (m)**	**Mass of cart (kg)**	**Weight of cart (N)**	**Time of trial (s)**			**Average time (s)**
				1	**2**	**3**	

DO NOT WRITE IN BOOK

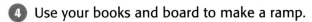

④ Use your books and board to make a ramp.

⑤ Use masking tape to mark a starting line at the top of the ramp. Be sure the starting line is far enough down from the top of the ramp to allow the cart to be placed behind the line.

⑥ Use masking tape to mark a finish line at the bottom of the ramp.

⑦ Find the height of the ramp by measuring the height of the starting line and subtracting the height of the finish line. Record the height of the ramp in your Data Collection Table.

⑧ Measure the distance in meters between the starting line and the finish line. In the Data Collection Table, record this distance as the length of the ramp.

⑨ Use the balance to find the mass of the cart in grams. Convert this measurement to kilograms by dividing it by 1,000. In your Data Collection Table, record the mass in kilograms.

⑩ Multiply the mass by 10 to get the weight of the cart in newtons. Record this weight in your Data Collection Table.

⑪ Set the cart behind the starting line, and release it. Use a stopwatch to time how long the cart takes to reach the finish line. Record the time in your Data Collection Table.

⑫ Repeat step 11 twice more, and average the results. Record the average time in your Data Collection Table.

Analyze the Results

① **Organizing Data** Copy the Calculations Table shown at right onto a separate sheet of paper.

② **Analyzing Data** Calculate and record the quantities for the cart in the Calculations Table by using your data and the four equations that follow.

Calculations Table			
Average speed (m/s)	Final speed (m/s)	Kinetic energy at bottom (J)	Gravitational potential energy at top (J)
DO NOT WRITE IN BOOK			

$$average\ speed = \frac{length\ of\ ramp}{average\ time}$$

Final speed = 2 × average speed
(This equation works because the cart accelerates smoothly from 0 m/s.)

$$kinetic\ energy = \frac{mass \times (final\ speed)^2}{2}$$

(Remember that $1\ kg \cdot m^2/s^2 = 1\ J$, the unit used to express energy.)

Gravitational potential energy =
weight × height
(Remember that $1\ N = 1\ kg \cdot m/s^2$, so $1\ N \times 1\ m = 1\ kg \cdot m^2/s^2 = 1\ J$)

Draw Conclusions

③ **Drawing Conclusions** How does the cart's gravitational potential energy at the top of the ramp compare with its kinetic energy at the bottom? Does this support your hypothesis? Explain your answer.

④ **Evaluating Data** You probably found that the gravitational potential energy of the cart at the top of the ramp was almost, but not exactly, equal to the kinetic energy of the cart at the bottom of the ramp. Explain this finding.

⑤ **Applying Conclusions** Suppose that while riding your bike, you coast down both a small hill and a large hill. Compare your final speed at the bottom of the small hill with your final speed at the bottom of the large hill. Explain your answer.

Chapter Review

USING KEY TERMS

For each pair of terms, explain how the meanings of the terms differ.

1 *potential energy* and *kinetic energy*

2 *mechanical energy* and *energy conversion*

3 *friction* and *the law of conservation of energy*

4 *renewable resources* and *nonrenewable resources*

5 *energy resources* and *fossil fuels*

UNDERSTANDING KEY IDEAS

Multiple Choice

6 Kinetic energy depends on
- **a.** mass and volume.
- **b.** velocity and weight.
- **c.** weight and height.
- **d.** velocity and mass.

7 Gravitational potential energy depends on
- **a.** mass and velocity.
- **b.** weight and height.
- **c.** mass and weight.
- **d.** height and distance.

8 Which of the following types of energy is not a renewable resource?
- **a.** wind energy
- **b.** nuclear energy
- **c.** solar energy
- **d.** geothermal energy

9 Which of the following sentences describes a conversion from chemical energy to thermal energy?
- **a.** Food is digested and used to regulate body temperature.
- **b.** Charcoal is burned in a barbecue pit.
- **c.** Coal is burned to produce steam.
- **d.** All of the above

10 When energy changes from one form to another, some of the energy always changes into
- **a.** kinetic energy.
- **b.** potential energy.
- **c.** thermal energy.
- **d.** mechanical energy.

Short Answer

11 Name two forms of energy, and relate them to kinetic or potential energy.

12 Give three examples of one form of energy being converted into another form.

13 Explain what a closed system is, and how energy is conserved within it.

14 How are fossil fuels formed?

Math Skills

15 A box has 400 J of gravitational potential energy.
- **a.** How much work had to be done to give the box that energy?
- **b.** If the box weighs 100 N, how far above the ground is it?

16 Concept Mapping Use the following terms to create a concept map: *energy, machines, sound energy, hair dryer, electrical energy, energy conversions, thermal energy,* and *kinetic energy*.

17 Applying Concepts Describe what happens in terms of energy when you blow up a balloon and release it.

18 Identifying Relationships After you coast down a hill on your bike, you will eventually come to a complete stop. Use this fact to explain why perpetual motion is impossible.

19 Predicting Consequences Imagine that the sun ran out of energy. What would happen to our energy resources on Earth?

20 Analyzing Processes Look at the photo below. Beginning with the pole vaulter's breakfast, trace the energy conversions necessary for the event shown to take place.

21 Forming Hypotheses Imagine two cars, one of which is more efficient than the other. Suggest two possible reasons one car is more efficient.

22 Evaluating Hypotheses Describe how you would test the two hypotheses you proposed in item 21. How would you determine whether one, both, or neither hypothesis is a factor in the car's efficiency?

Use the graphic below to answer the questions that follow.

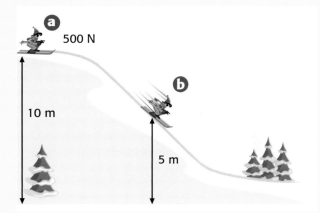

23 What is the skier's gravitational potential energy at point *a*?

24 What is the skier's gravitational potential energy at point *b*?

25 What is the skier's kinetic energy at point *b*? (Hint: mechanical energy = potential energy + kinetic energy)

READING

Read each of the passages below. Then, answer the questions that follow each passage.

Passage 1 Gas hydrates are icy formations of water and methane. Methane is the main component of natural gas. The methane in gas hydrates is made by bacteria in the ocean. Large areas of hydrates have been found off the coasts of North Carolina and South Carolina in marine sediments. In just two areas that are each about the size of Rhode Island, scientists think there may be 70 times the amount of natural gas used by the United States in 1 year. The energy from gas hydrates could be used to drive machinery or generate electrical energy.

1. How large are each of the two gas hydrate deposits mentioned in this article?
- **A** about the size of the United States
- **B** about the size of South Carolina
- **C** about the size of North Carolina
- **D** about the size of Rhode Island

2. What are gas hydrates mainly made of?
- **F** bacteria and sediments
- **G** water and methane
- **H** natural gas and water
- **I** ice and sediments

3. How long could U.S. natural gas needs be met by all the gas in both deposits mentioned?
- **A** 1 year
- **B** 2 years
- **C** 70 years
- **D** 140 years

4. Where do methane gas hydrates come from?
- **F** ocean water
- **G** bacteria
- **H** sediments
- **I** ice

Passage 2 Two new technologies may reduce the price of electric cars. One is called a *hybrid electric vehicle*. This vehicle has a small gasoline engine that provides extra power and recharges the batteries. The other technology uses hydrogen fuel cells instead of batteries. These cells use the hydrogen present in more-conventional fuels, such as gasoline or ethanol, to produce an electric current that powers the car.

1. In this passage, what does *vehicle* mean?
- **A** electric
- **B** hybrid
- **C** car
- **D** current

2. Which of the following are conventional fuels?
- **F** gasoline and ethanol
- **G** hydrogen and ethanol
- **H** gasoline and hydrogen
- **I** only hydrogen

3. Which of the following is a fact in this passage?
- **A** A hybrid electric vehicle runs partly on gasoline.
- **B** All electric cars are hybrid.
- **C** All electric cars use hydrogen fuel cells.
- **D** Hydrogen fuel cells use conventional fuel.

4. What do the two new technologies described in the passage have in common?
- **F** They do not use conventional fuels.
- **G** They may reduce the price of electric cars.
- **H** They use hybrid engines.
- **I** They use hydrogen to produce an electric current.

The pie chart below shows U.S. energy use by source of energy. Use the chart below to answer the questions that follow.

U.S. Energy Sources

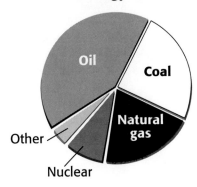

1. According to the graph, the United States relies on fossil fuels for about what percentage of its energy?
   A 30%
   B 45%
   C 60%
   D 80%

2. Nuclear energy represents about what percentage of U.S. energy sources?
   F 15%
   G 30%
   H 50%
   I 70%

3. Which energy source accounts for about 25% of U.S. energy?
   A oil
   B coal
   C natural gas
   D nuclear energy

Read each question below, and choose the best answer.

1. Gerald bought 2.5 kg of apples. How many grams of apples did he buy?
   A 0.0025 g
   B 0.25 g
   C 25 g
   D 2,500 g

2. Which group contains ratios that are equivalent to 3/8?
   F 6/16, 9/24, 12/32
   G 6/16, 12/24, 12/32
   H 6/24, 12/32, 15/40
   I 6/9, 9/24, 15/40

3. Carmen went to a bookstore. She bought three books for $7.99 each and four books for $3.35 each. Which number sentence can be used to find *c*, the total cost of the books?
   A $c = 3 + (7.99 \times 1) + (4 \times 3.35)$
   B $c = (1 \times 7.99) + (3 \times 3.35)$
   C $c = (3 \times 7.99) + (4 \times 3.35)$
   D $c = (3 \times 7.99) \times (4 \times 3.35)$

4. Rhonda's Mobile Car Washing charges $15 to wash a customer's car. Vacuuming the car costs an extra $10. Rhonda wants to know how much money she earned last week. When she looks at her appointment book, Rhonda finds that she washed a total of 50 cars. Only 20 of these cars were vacuumed after being washed. How much money did Rhonda earn last week?
   F $500
   G $750
   H $950
   I $1050

Science in Action

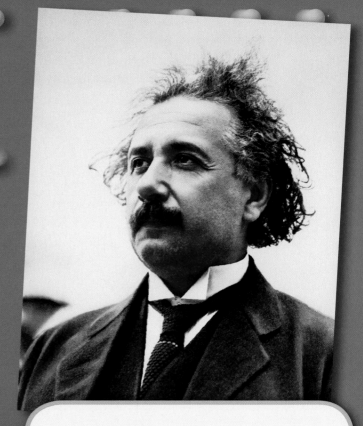

Science, Technology, and Society

Underwater Jet Engines

Almost all boats that have engines use propellers. But in 2002, a British company announced that it had developed an underwater jet engine.

The underwater jet engine works by producing steam in a gasoline-powered boiler. When the steam hits the water, it condenses to a very small volume, which creates a vacuum. This vacuum causes thrust by sucking in water from the front of the tube. The underwater jet engine is extremely energy-efficient, produces a great amount of thrust, and creates very little pollution.

Social Studies ACTiViTY

Research the kinds of water propulsion people have used throughout history. Note which kinds were improvements on previous technology and which were completely new.

Scientific Discoveries

$E = mc^2$

The famous 20th-century scientist Albert Einstein discovered an equation that is almost as famous as he is. That equation is $E = mc^2$. You may have heard of it before. But what does it mean?

The equation represents a relationship between mass and energy. E represents energy, m represents mass, and c represents the speed of light. So, $E = mc^2$ means that a small amount of mass has a very large amount of energy! Nuclear reactors harness this energy, which is given off when radioactive atoms split.

Math ACTiViTY

The speed of light is approximately 300,000,000 m/s. How much energy is equivalent to the mass of 0.00000002 g of hydrogen?

Cheryl Mele

Power-Plant Manager Cheryl Mele is the manager of the Decker Power Plant in Austin, Texas, where she is in charge of almost 1 billion watts of electric power generation. Most of the electric power is generated by a steam-driven turbine system that uses natural gas fuel. Gas turbines are also used. Together, the systems make enough electrical energy for many homes and businesses.

Cheryl Mele says her job as plant manager is to do "anything that needs doing." Her training as a mechanical engineer allows her to run tests and to find problems in the plant. Previously, Mele had a job helping to design more-efficient gas turbines. That job helped prepare her for the job of plant manager.

Mele believes that engineering and power-plant management are interesting jobs because they allow you to work with many new technologies. Mele thinks young people should pursue what interests them. "Be sure to connect the math you learn to the science you are doing," she says. "This will help you to understand both."

Language Arts ACTIVITY

Look up the word *energy* in a dictionary. Compare the different definitions you find to the definition given in this chapter.

To learn more about these Science in Action topics, visit go.hrw.com and type in the keyword **HP5ENGF.**

Current Science

Check out Current Science® articles related to this chapter by visiting go.hrw.com. Just type in the keyword **HP5CS09.**

6

Heat and Heat Technology

The Big Idea

Heat is energy that moves from an object at a higher temperature to an object at a lower temperature.

About the PHOTO

This ice climber is using a lot of special equipment. This equipment includes a rope, a safety helmet, an ice pick, and warm clothing. The climber's clothing, which includes insulating layers inside a protective outer layer, keeps his body heat from escaping into the cold air. If he weren't wearing enough protective clothing, he would be feeling very cold, because thermal energy always moves into areas of lower temperature.

PRE-READING ACTIVITY

FOLDNOTES **Two-Panel Flip Chart**
Before you read the chapter, create the FoldNote entitled "Two-Panel Flip Chart" described in the **Study Skills** section of the Appendix. Label the flaps of the two-panel flip chart with "Heat" and "Temperature." As you read the chapter, write information you learn about each category under the appropriate flap.

START-UP ACTIVITY

Some Like It Hot

Sometimes, you can estimate an object's temperature by touching the object. In this activity, you will find out how well your hand works as a thermometer!

Procedure

1. Gather small pieces of the following materials: **metal, wood, plastic foam, rock, plastic,** and **cardboard.** Allow the materials to sit untouched on a table for a few minutes.

2. Put the palms of your hands on each of the materials. List the materials in order from coolest to warmest.

3. Place a **thermometer strip** on the surface of each material. Record the temperature of each material.

Analysis

1. Which material felt the warmest to your hands?

2. Which material had the highest temperature? Was it the same material that felt the warmest?

3. Why do you think some materials felt warmer than others?

4. Was your hand a good thermometer? Explain why or why not.

Temperature

You probably put on a sweater or a jacket when it's cold. Likewise, you probably wear shorts in the summer when it gets hot. But how hot is hot, and how cold is cold?

Think about the knobs on a water faucet: they are labeled "H" for hot and "C" for cold. But does only hot water come out when the hot-water knob is on? You may have noticed that when you first turn on the hot water, the water is warm or even cool. Is the label on the knob wrong? The terms *hot* and *cold* are not scientific terms. If you really want to specify how hot or cold something is, you must use temperature.

What Is Temperature?

You probably think of temperature as a measure of how hot or cold something is. But using the terms *hot* and *cold* can be confusing. Imagine that you are outside on a hot day. You step onto a shady porch where a fan is blowing. You think it feels cool there. Then, your friend comes out onto the porch from an air-conditioned house. She thinks it feels warm! Using the word *temperature* instead of words such as *cool* or *warm* avoids confusion. Scientifically, **temperature** is a measure of the average kinetic energy of the particles in an object.

Temperature and Kinetic Energy

All matter is made of atoms or molecules that are always moving, even if it doesn't look like they are. Because the particles are in motion, they have kinetic energy. The faster the particles are moving, the more kinetic energy they have. Look at **Figure 1.** The more kinetic energy the particles of an object have, the higher the temperature of the object is.

What You Will Learn

● Describe how temperature relates to kinetic energy.
● Compare temperatures on different temperature scales.
● Give examples of thermal expansion.

Vocabulary

temperature
thermal expansion
absolute zero

READING STRATEGY

Prediction Guide Before reading this section, write the title of each heading in this section. Next, under each heading, write what you think you will learn.

temperature a measure of how hot (or cold) something is; specifically, a measure of the average kinetic energy of the particles in an object

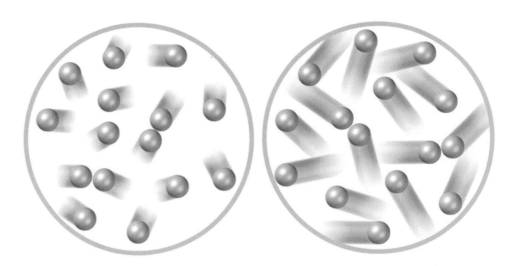

Figure 1 *The gas particles on the right have a higher average kinetic energy than those on the left. So, the gas on the right is at a higher temperature.*

Quick Lab

Hot or Cold?

1. Put both your hands into a **bucket of warm water,** and note how the water feels.

2. Now, put one hand into a **bucket of cold water** and the other into a **bucket of hot water.**

3. After a minute, take your hands out of the hot and cold water and put them back in the warm water. Note how the water feels to each hand.

4. Can you rely on your hands to determine temperature? Explain your observations.

Average Kinetic Energy of Particles

Particles of matter are always moving. But they move in different directions and at different speeds. The motion of particles is random. Because particles are moving at different speeds, individual particles have different amounts of kinetic energy. But the *average* kinetic energy of all the particles in an object can be measured. When you measure an object's temperature, you measure the average kinetic energy of all the particles in the object.

The temperature of a substance depends on the average kinetic energy of all its particles. Its temperature does not depend on how much of it you have. Look at **Figure 2.** A pot of tea and a cup of tea each have a different amount of tea. But their atoms have the same average kinetic energy. So, the pot of tea and the cup of tea are at the same temperature.

✓ Reading Check How is temperature related to kinetic energy? (*See the Appendix for answers to Reading Checks.*)

INTERNET ACTIVITY

For another activity related to this chapter, go to **go.hrw.com** and type in the keyword **HP5HOTW.**

Figure 2 *There is more tea in the teapot than in the mug. But the temperature of the tea in the mug is the same as the temperature of the tea in the teapot.*

Measuring Temperature

How would you measure the temperature of a steaming cup of hot chocolate? Would you take a sip of it or stick your finger in it? You probably would not. You would use a thermometer.

Using a Thermometer

Many thermometers are thin glass tubes filled with a liquid. Mercury and alcohol are often used in thermometers because they remain in liquid form over a large temperature range.

Thermometers can measure temperature because of a property called thermal expansion. **Thermal expansion** is the increase in volume of a substance because of an increase in temperature. As a substance's temperature increases, its particles move faster and spread out. So, there is more space between them, and the substance expands. Mercury and alcohol expand by constant amounts for a given change in temperature.

Look at the thermometers in **Figure 3.** They are all at the same temperature. So, the alcohol in each thermometer has expanded the same amount. But the number for each thermometer is different because a different temperature scale is marked on each one.

Reading Check What property makes thermometers work?

thermal expansion an increase in the size of a substance in response to an increase in the temperature of the substance

absolute zero the temperature at which molecular energy is at a minimum (0 K on the Kelvin scale or −273.16°C on the Celsius scale)

Figure 3 Three Temperature Scales

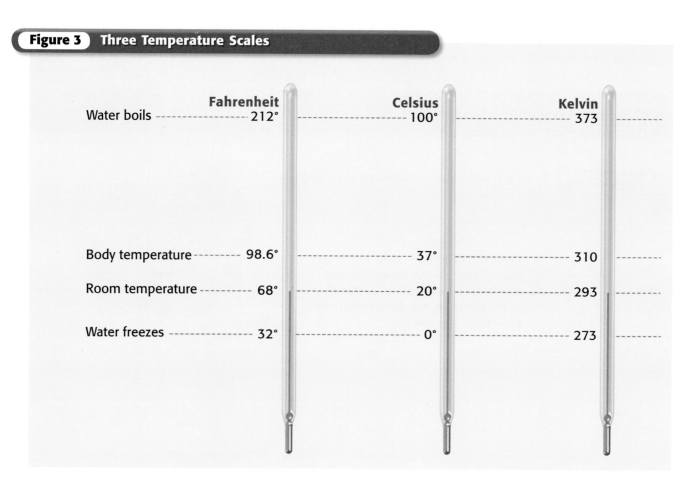

	Fahrenheit	Celsius	Kelvin
Water boils	212°	100°	373
Body temperature	98.6°	37°	310
Room temperature	68°	20°	293
Water freezes	32°	0°	273

Temperature Scales

Look at **Figure 4.** When a weather report is given, you will probably hear the temperature given in degrees Fahrenheit (°F). Scientists, however, often use the Celsius scale. In the Celsius scale, the temperature range between the freezing point and boiling point of water is divided into 100 equal parts, called degrees Celsius (°C). A third scale, the Kelvin (or absolute) scale, is the official SI temperature scale. The Kelvin scale is divided into units called kelvins (K)—not degrees kelvin.

The lowest temperature on the Kelvin scale is 0 K, which is called **absolute zero.** Absolute zero (about –459°F) is the temperature at which all molecular motion stops. It is not possible to actually reach absolute zero, although temperatures very close to 0 K have been reached in laboratories.

Temperature Conversion

As shown by the thermometers on the previous page, a given temperature is represented by different numbers on the three temperature scales. For example, the freezing point of water is 32°F, 0°C, or 273 K.

The temperature 0°C is actually much higher than 0 K. But a *change* of one kelvin is equal to a change of one Celsius degree. The temperature 0°C is higher than 0°F, but a change of one Fahrenheit degree is *not* equal to a change of one Celsius degree. You can convert from one scale to another using the equations shown in **Table 1** below.

Converting Temperatures

Use the equations in **Table 1** to answer the following questions:

1. What temperature on the Celsius scale is equivalent to 373 K?
2. Absolute zero is 0 K. What is the equivalent temperature on the Celsius scale? on the Fahrenheit scale?
3. Which temperature is colder, 0°F or 200 K?

Table 1 Converting Between Temperature Units

To convert	Use the equation	Example
Celsius to Fahrenheit °C ⟶ °F	$°F = \left(\frac{9}{5} \times °C\right) + 32$	Convert 45°C to degrees Fahrenheit. $°F = \left(\frac{9}{5} \times 45°C\right) + 32 = 113°F$
Fahrenheit to Celsius °F ⟶ °C	$°C = \frac{5}{9} \times (°F - 32)$	Convert 68°F to degrees Celsius. $°C = \frac{5}{9} \times (68°F - 32) = 20°C$
Celsius to Kelvin °C ⟶ K	$K = °C + 273$	Convert 45°C to Kelvins. $K = 45°C + 273 = 318 K$
Kelvin to Celsius K ⟶ °C	$°C = K - 273$	Convert 32 K to degrees Celsius. $°C = 32 K - 273 = -241°C$

Figure 4 *Weather reports that you see on the news usually give temperatures in degrees Fahrenheit (°F).*

More About Thermal Expansion

You have learned about how thermal expansion works in the liquids that fill thermometers. Thermal expansion has many other applications. Below, you will read about a case in which thermal expansion can be dangerous, one in which it can be useful, and one in which it can carry you into the air!

Expansion Joints on Highways

Have you ever gone across a highway bridge in a car? You probably heard and felt a "thuh-thunk" every couple of seconds as you went over the bridge. That sound is made when the car goes over small gaps called *expansion joints,* shown in **Figure 5.**

If the weather is very hot, the bridge can heat up enough to expand. As it expands, there is a danger of the bridge breaking. Expansion joints keep segments of the bridge apart so that they have room to expand without the bridge breaking.

✓ **Reading Check** What is the purpose of expansion joints in a bridge?

Bimetallic Strips in Thermostats

Thermal expansion also occurs in a thermostat, the device that controls the heater in your home. Some thermostats have a bimetallic strip inside. A *bimetallic strip* is made of two different metals stacked in a thin strip. Because different materials expand at different rates, one of the metals expands more than the other when the strip gets hot. This makes the strip coil and uncoil in response to changes in temperature. This coiling and uncoiling closes and opens an electric circuit that turns the heater on and off in your home, as shown in **Figure 6.**

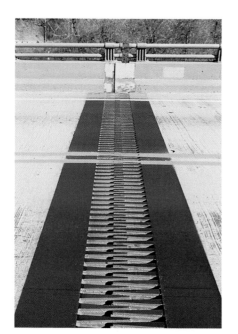

Figure 5 *This gap in the bridge allows the concrete to expand and contract without breaking.*

Figure 6 **How a Thermostat Works**

Electrical contacts   **Bimetallic strip**

a As the room temperature drops below the desired level, the bimetallic strip coils more tightly, and the glass tube tilts. A drop of mercury closes an electric circuit that turns the heater on.

b As the room temperature rises above the desired level, the bimetallic strip uncoils slightly, becoming larger. The drop of mercury rolls back in the tube, opening the electric circuit, and the heater turns off.

Thermal Expansion in Hot-Air Balloons

You may have heard the expression "Hot air rises." If you have ever seen hot-air balloons peacefully gliding through the sky, you have seen this principle at work. But why does hot air rise?

When a gas is heated, as shown in **Figure 7,** its particles have more kinetic energy. They move around more quickly, so there is more space between them. The gas is then able to expand if it is not kept at the same volume by its container. When air (which is a mixture of gases) inside a hot-air balloon is heated, the air expands. As it expands, it becomes less dense than the air outside the balloon. So, the balloon goes up, up, and away!

Figure 7 *Thermal expansion helps get these hot-air balloons off the ground.*

SECTION Review

Summary

- Temperature is a measure of the average kinetic energy of the particles of a substance.
- Fahrenheit, Celsius, and Kelvin are three temperature scales.
- Thermal expansion is the increase in volume of a substance due to an increase in temperature.
- Absolute zero (0 K, or −273°C) is the lowest possible temperature.
- A thermostat works because of the thermal expansion of a bimetallic strip.

Using Key Terms

1. In your own words, write a definition for the term *temperature.*

2. Use each of the following terms in a separate sentence: *thermal expansion* and *absolute zero.*

Understanding Key Ideas

3. Which of the following is the coldest temperature possible?
   a. 0 K
   b. 0°C
   c. 0°F
   d. −273°F

4. Does temperature depend on the amount of the substance? Explain.

5. Describe the process of thermal expansion.

Math Skills

6. Convert 35°C to degrees Fahrenheit.

7. Convert 34°F to degrees Celsius.

8. Convert 0°C to kelvins.

9. Convert 100 K to degrees Celsius.

Critical Thinking

10. **Predicting Consequences** Why do you think heating a full pot of soup on the stove could cause the soup to overflow?

11. **Analyzing Processes** During thermal expansion, what happens to the density of a substance?

12. **Forming Hypotheses** A glass of cold water whose particles had a low average kinetic energy was placed on a table. The average kinetic energy in the cold water increased, while the average kinetic energy of the part of the table under the glass decreased. What do you think happened?

SCLINKS®

NSTA
Developed and maintained by the
National Science Teachers Association

For a variety of links related to this chapter, go to www.scilinks.org

Topic: What Is Temperature?
SciLinks code: HSM1664

What Is Heat?

It's time for your annual physical. The doctor comes in and begins her exam by placing a metal stethoscope on your back. You jump a little and say, "Whoa! That's cold!"

What is it about the stethoscope that made it feel cold? The answer has to do with how energy moves between the metal and your skin. In this section, you'll learn about this kind of energy transfer.

Transferred Thermal Energy

You might think of the word *heat* as having to do with things that feel hot. But heat also has to do with things that feel cold—such as the stethoscope. In fact, heat is what causes objects to feel hot or cold or to get hot or cold under the right conditions. You probably use the word *heat* every day to mean different things. However, in this chapter, you will use only one specific meaning for *heat*. **Heat** is the energy transferred between objects that are at different temperatures.

Why do some things feel hot, while others feel cold? When two objects at different temperatures come into contact, energy is always transferred from the object that has the higher temperature to the object that has the lower temperature. Look at **Figure 1.** The doctor's stethoscope touches your back. Energy is transferred from your back to the stethoscope because your back has a higher temperature (about 37°C) than the stethoscope (probably room temperature, about 20°C) has. This energy is transferred quickly, so the stethoscope feels cold to you.

What You Will Learn

● Define *heat* as thermal energy transferred between objects at different temperatures.

● Compare conduction, convection, and radiation.

● Use specific heat capacity to calculate heat.

Vocabulary

heat	convection
thermal energy	radiation
thermal conduction	specific
thermal conductor	heat
thermal insulator	

READING STRATEGY

Paired Summarizing Read this section silently. In pairs, take turns summarizing the material. Stop to discuss ideas that seem confusing.

heat the energy transferred between objects that are at different temperatures

Figure 1 *The metal stethoscope feels cold because of heat!*

Heat and Thermal Energy

If heat is transferred energy, what form of energy is being transferred? The answer is thermal energy. **Thermal energy** is the total kinetic energy of the particles that make up a substance. Thermal energy, which is measured in joules (J), depends partly on temperature. Something at a high temperature has more thermal energy than it would have at a lower temperature. Thermal energy also depends on how much of a substance there is. Look at **Figure 2.** The more particles there are in a substance at a given temperature, the greater the thermal energy of the substance is.

Figure 2 *Although both soups are at the same temperature, there is more soup in the pan. So, the soup in the pan has more thermal energy than the soup in the bowl.*

Reaching the Same Temperature

Look at **Figure 3.** When objects that have different temperatures come into contact, energy will always be transferred. Energy will pass from the warmer object to the cooler object until both have the same temperature. When objects that are touching each other have the same temperature, there is no net change in the thermal energy of either one. Although one object may have more thermal energy than the other object, both objects will be at the same temperature.

thermal energy the kinetic energy of a substance's atoms

✓ **Reading Check** What will happen if two objects at different temperatures come into contact? (*See the Appendix for answers to Reading Checks.*)

Figure 3 Transfer of Thermal Energy

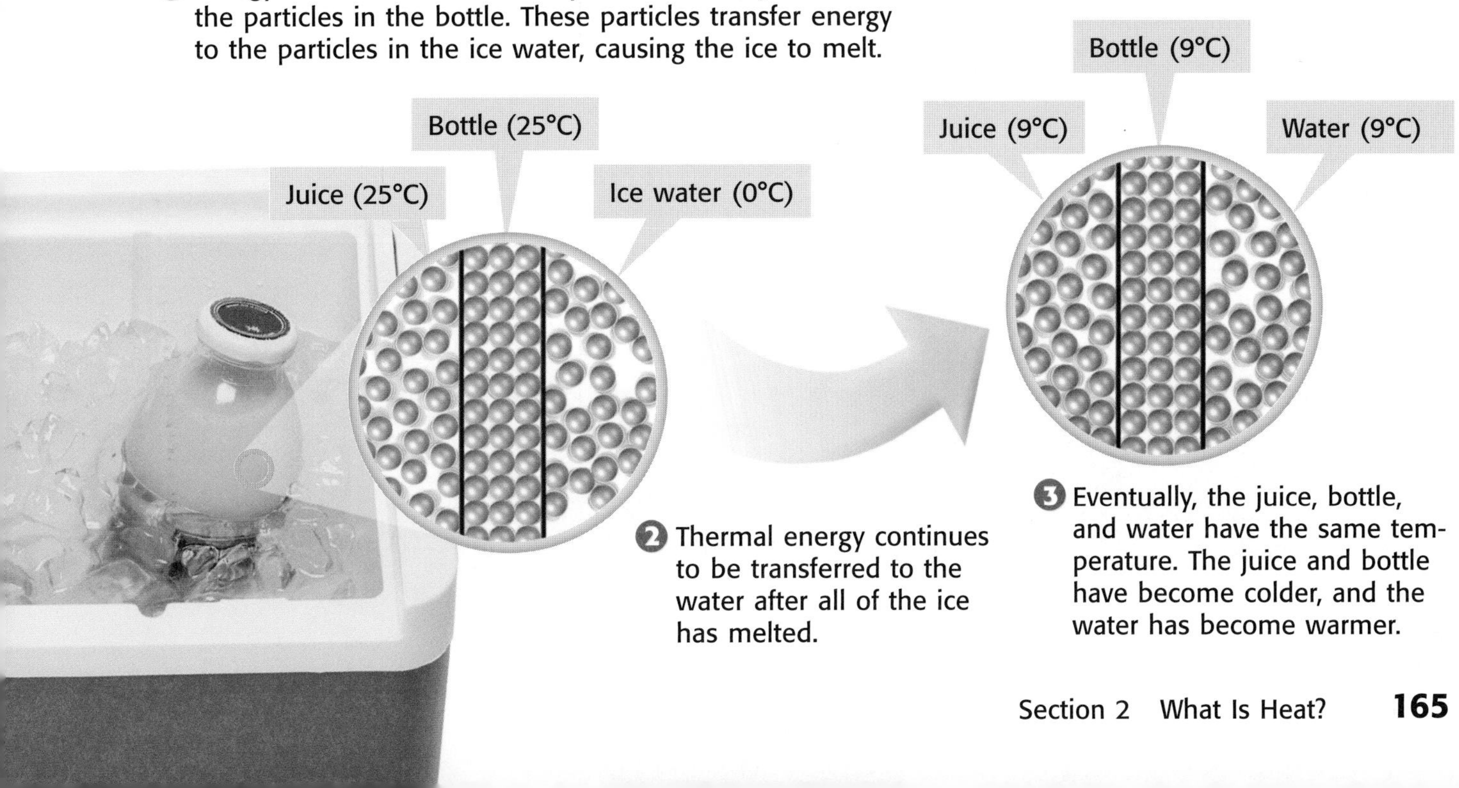

❶ Energy is transferred from the particles in the juice to the particles in the bottle. These particles transfer energy to the particles in the ice water, causing the ice to melt.

Bottle (25°C)

Juice (25°C)   Ice water (0°C)

Bottle (9°C)

Juice (9°C)   Water (9°C)

❷ Thermal energy continues to be transferred to the water after all of the ice has melted.

❸ Eventually, the juice, bottle, and water have the same temperature. The juice and bottle have become colder, and the water has become warmer.

Quick Lab

Heat Exchange

1. Fill a **film canister** with **hot water.** Insert the **thermometer apparatus** prepared by your teacher. Record the temperature.

2. Fill a **250 mL beaker** two-thirds full with **cool water.** Insert **another thermometer** into the cool water, and record its temperature.

3. Place the canister in the cool water. Record the temperature measured by each thermometer every 30 s.

4. When the thermometers read nearly the same temperature, stop and graph your data. Plot temperature (*y*-axis) versus time (*x*-axis).

5. Describe what happens to the rate of energy transfer as the two temperatures get closer.

thermal conduction the transfer of energy as heat through a material

Conduction, Convection, and Radiation

You already know several examples of energy transfer. You know that stoves transfer energy to soup in a pot. You adjust the temperature of your bath water by adding cold or hot water to the tub. And the sun warms your skin. In the next few pages, you'll learn about three ways to transfer thermal energy: *conduction, convection,* and *radiation.*

Conduction

Imagine that you have put a cold metal spoon in a bowl of hot soup, as shown in **Figure 4.** Soon, the handle of the spoon warms up—even though it is not in the soup! The entire spoon gets warm because of conduction. **Thermal conduction** is the transfer of thermal energy from one substance to another through direct contact. Conduction can also occur within a substance, such as the spoon in **Figure 4.**

How does conduction work? When objects touch each other, their particles collide. Thermal energy is transferred from the higher-temperature substance to the lower-temperature substance. Remember that particles of substances at different temperatures have different average kinetic energies. So, when particles collide, particles with higher kinetic energy transfer energy to those with lower kinetic energy. This transfer makes some particles slow down and other particles speed up until all particles have the same average kinetic energy. As a result, the substances have the same temperature.

Figure 4 *The end of this spoon will warm up because conduction, the transfer of energy through direct contact, occurs all the way up the handle.*

Conductors and Insulators

Substances that conduct thermal energy very well are called **thermal conductors.** For example, the metal in a doctor's stethoscope is a conductor. Energy is transferred rapidly from your warm skin to the cool stethoscope. That's why the stethoscope feels cold. Substances that do not conduct thermal energy very well are called **thermal insulators.** For example, a doctor's wooden tongue depressor is an insulator. It is at the same temperature as the stethoscope. But the tongue depressor doesn't feel cold. The reason is that thermal energy is transferred very slowly from your tongue to the wood. Some typical conductors and insulators are shown in **Table 1** at right.

✓ Reading Check How can two objects that are the same temperature feel as if they are at different temperatures?

Table 1 Conductors and Insulators	
Conductors	**Insulators**
Curling iron	Flannel shirt
Cookie sheet	Oven mitt
Iron skillet	Plastic spatula
Copper pipe	Fiberglass insulation
Stove coil	Ceramic bowl

Convection

A second way thermal energy is transferred is **convection,** the transfer of thermal energy by the movement of a liquid or a gas. Look at **Figure 5.** When you boil water in a pot, the water moves in roughly circular patterns because of convection. The water at the bottom of a pot on a stove burner gets hot because it is touching the pot (conduction). As it heats, the water becomes less dense because its higher-energy particles spread apart. The warmer water rises through the denser, cooler water above it. At the surface, the warm water begins to cool. The particles move closer together, making the water denser. The cooler water then sinks back to the bottom. It is heated again, and the cycle begins again. This circular motion of liquids or gases due to density differences that result from temperature differences is called a *convection current.*

thermal conductor a material through which energy can be transferred as heat

thermal insulator a material that reduces or prevents the transfer of heat

convection the transfer of thermal energy by the circulation or movement of a liquid or gas

Figure 5 *The repeated rising and sinking of water during boiling are due to convection.*

Radiation

A third way thermal energy is transferred is **radiation,** the transfer of energy by electromagnetic waves, such as visible light and infrared waves. Unlike conduction and convection, radiation can involve either an energy transfer between particles of matter or an energy transfer across empty space.

All objects, including the heater in **Figure 6,** radiate electromagnetic waves. The sun emits visible light, which you can see, and waves of other frequencies, such as infrared and ultraviolet waves, which you cannot see. When your body absorbs infrared waves, you feel warmer.

Radiation and the Greenhouse Effect

Earth's atmosphere acts like the windows of a greenhouse. It allows the sun's visible light to pass through it. A greenhouse also traps heat energy, keeping the inside warm. The atmosphere traps some energy, too. This process, called the *greenhouse effect,* is illustrated in **Figure 7.** If our atmosphere did not trap the sun's energy in this way, most of the sun's energy that reached Earth would be radiated immediately back into space. Earth would be a cold, lifeless planet.

The atmosphere traps the sun's energy because of *greenhouse gases,* such as water vapor, carbon dioxide, and methane, which trap energy especially well. Some scientists are concerned that high levels of greenhouse gases in the atmosphere may trap too much energy and make Earth too warm.

Reading Check What is the greenhouse effect?

Figure 6 *The coils of this portable heater warm a room partly by radiating visible light and infrared waves.*

Figure 7 The Greenhouse Effect

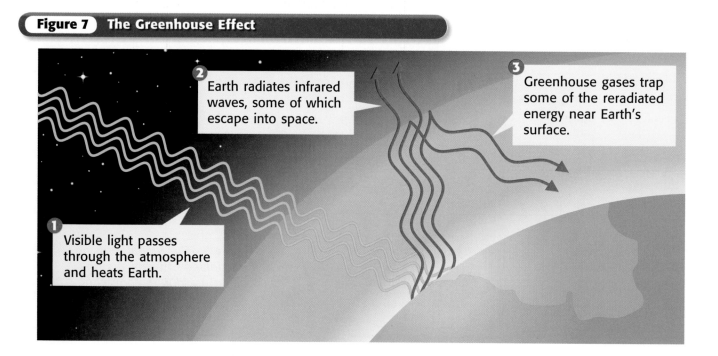

2. Earth radiates infrared waves, some of which escape into space.

3. Greenhouse gases trap some of the reradiated energy near Earth's surface.

1. Visible light passes through the atmosphere and heats Earth.

Heat and Temperature Change

Have you ever fastened your seat belt on a hot summer day? If so, you may have noticed that the metal buckle felt hotter than the cloth belt did. Why?

Thermal Conductivity

Different substances have different thermal conductivities. *Thermal conductivity* is the rate at which a substance conducts thermal energy. The metal buckle of a seat belt, such as the one shown in **Figure 8,** has a higher thermal conductivity than the cloth belt has. Because of its higher thermal conductivity, the metal transfers energy more rapidly to your hand when you touch it than the cloth does. So, even if the cloth and metal are at the same temperature, the metal feels hotter.

Figure 8 *The cloth part of a seat belt does not feel as hot as the metal part.*

Specific Heat

Another difference between the metal and the cloth is how easily each changes temperature when it absorbs or loses energy. When equal amounts of energy are transferred to or from equal masses of different substances, the change in temperature for each substance will differ. **Specific heat** is the amount of energy needed to change the temperature of 1 kg of a substance by 1°C.

Look at **Table 2.** The specific heat of the cloth of a seat belt is more than twice that of the metal buckle. So, for equal masses of metal and cloth, the same thermal energy will increase the temperature of the metal twice as much as the cloth. The higher the specific heat of something is, the more energy it takes to increase its temperature. **Table 2** shows that most metals have very low specific heats. On the other hand, the specific heat of water is very high. This is why swimming-pool water usually feels cool, even on a hot day. The same energy heats up the air more than it heats up the water.

specific heat the quantity of heat required to raise a unit mass of homogeneous material 1 K or 1°C in a specified way given constant pressure and volume

CONNECTION TO Social Studies

WRITING SKILL **Living near Coastlines** Water has a higher specific heat than land does. Because of water's high specific heat, the ocean has a moderating effect on the weather of coastal areas. The mild weather of coastal areas is one reason they tend to be heavily populated. Find out what the weather is like in various coastal areas in the world. Research the various reasons why coastal areas tend to be heavily populated, and write a brief report in your **science journal.**

Table 2 Specific Heat of Some Common Substances			
Substance	**Specific heat (J/kg•°C)**	**Substance**	**Specific heat (J/kg•°C)**
Lead	128	Glass	837
Gold	129	Aluminum	899
Copper	387	Cloth of seat belt	1,340
Iron	448	Ice	2,090
Metal of seat belt	500	Water	4,184

Heat, Temperature, and Amount

Unlike temperature, energy transferred between objects can not be measured directly. Instead, it must be calculated. When calculating energy transferred between objects, you can use the definition of *heat* as the amount of energy that is transferred between two objects that are at different temperatures. Heat can then be expressed in joules (J).

How much energy is needed to heat a cup of water to make tea? To answer this question, you have to consider the water's mass, its change in temperature, and its specific heat. These are all listed in **Figure 9.** In general, if you know an object's mass, its change in temperature, and its specific heat, you can use the equation below to calculate heat.

Mass of water = 0.2 kg
Temperature (before) = 25°C
Temperature (after) = 80°C
Specific heat of
    water = 4,184 J/kg•°C

Figure 9 *Information used to calculate heat, the amount of energy transferred to the water, is shown above.*

$$heat \text{ (J)} = specific\ heat \text{ (J/kg•°C)} \times mass \text{ (kg)} \times change\ in\ temperature \text{ (°C)}$$

Calculating Heat

Using the equation above, you can calculate the heat transferred to the water. Because the water's temperature increases, the value of heat is positive. You can also use this equation to calculate the heat transferred from an object when it cools down. The value for heat would then be negative because the temperature decreases.

✓ Reading Check What are the three pieces of information needed to calculate heat?

Calculating Heat Calculate the heat transferred to a mass of 0.2 kg of water to change the temperature of the water from 25°C to 80°C. (The specific heat of water is 4,184 J/kg•°C.)

Step 1: Write the equation for calculating heat.

$$heat = specific\ heat \times mass \times change\ in\ temperature$$

Step 2: Replace the specific heat, mass, and temperature change with the values given in the problem, and solve.

$$heat = 4{,}184 \text{ J/kg•°C} \times 0.2 \text{ kg} \times (80°C - 25°C)$$
$$heat = 46{,}024 \text{ J}$$

Now It's Your Turn

1. Imagine that you heat 2.0 kg of water to make pasta. The temperature of the water before you heat it is 40°C, and the temperature after is 100°C. How much heat was transferred to the water?

Summary

- Heat is energy transferred between objects that are at different temperatures.
- Thermal energy is the total kinetic energy of the particles that make up a substance.
- Thermal energy will always be transferred from higher to lower temperature.
- Transfer of thermal energy ends when two objects that are in contact are at the same temperature.
- Conduction, convection, and radiation are three ways thermal energy is transferred.

- Specific heat is the amount of energy needed to change the temperature of 1 kg of a substance by 1°C.
- Energy transferred by heat cannot be measured directly. It must be calculated using specific heat, mass, and change in temperature.
- Energy transferred by heat is expressed in joules (J) and is calculated as follows: *heat* (J) = *specific heat* (J/kg•°C) × *mass* (kg) × *change in temperature* (°C).

Using Key Terms

For each pair of terms, explain how the meanings of the terms differ.

1. *thermal conductor* and *thermal insulator*
2. *convection* and *radiation*

Understanding Key Ideas

3. Two objects at different temperatures are in contact. Which of the following happens to their thermal energy?
   a. Their thermal energies remain the same.
   b. Thermal energy passes from the cooler object to the warmer object.
   c. Thermal energy passes from the warmer object to the cooler object.
   d. Thermal energy passes back and forth equally between the two objects.

4. What is heat?

Math Skills

5. The specific heat of lead is 128 J/kg•°C. How much heat is needed to raise the temperature of a 0.015 kg sample of lead by 10°C?

Critical Thinking

6. **Making Inferences** Two objects have the same total thermal energy. They are different sizes. Are they at the same temperature? Explain.

7. **Applying Concepts** Why do many metal cooking utensils have wooden handles?

Interpreting Graphics

8. Look at the photo below. It shows examples of heat transfer by conduction, convection, and radiation. Indicate which type of heat transfer is happening next to each letter.

For a variety of links related to this chapter, go to www.scilinks.org

Topic: What Is Heat?
SciLinks code: HSM1661

Matter and Heat

Have you ever eaten a frozen juice bar outside on a hot summer day? It's pretty hard to finish the entire thing before it starts to drip and make a big mess!

The juice bar melts because the sun radiates energy to the frozen juice bar. The energy absorbed by the juice bar increases the kinetic energy of the molecules in the juice bar, which starts to change to a liquid.

States of Matter

The matter that makes up a frozen juice bar has the same identity whether the juice bar is frozen or has melted. The matter is just in a different form, or state. The **states of matter** are the physical forms in which a substance can exist. Matter consists of particles that can move around at different speeds. The state a substance is in depends on the speed of its particles, the attraction between them, and the pressure around them. Three familiar states of matter are solid, liquid, and gas, shown in **Figure 1.**

Thermal energy is the total energy of all the particles that make up a substance. Suppose that you have equal masses of a substance in its three states, each at a different temperature. The substance will have the most thermal energy as a gas and the least thermal energy as a solid. The reason is that the particles of a gas move around fastest.

What You Will Learn

● Identify three states of matter.
● Explain how heat affects matter during a change of state.
● Describe how heat affects matter during a chemical change.
● Explain what a *calorimeter* is used for.

Vocabulary

states of matter
change of state

READING STRATEGY

Brainstorming The key idea of this section is the relationship between matter and heat. Brainstorm words and phrases related to matter and heat.

Figure 1   Particles of a Solid, a Liquid, and a Gas

Particles of a gas, such as carbon dioxide, move fast enough to overcome nearly all of the attraction between them. The particles move independently of one another.

Particles of a liquid move fast enough to overcome some of the attraction between them. The particles are able to slide past one another.

Particles of a solid, such as ice, do not move fast enough to overcome the strong attraction between them, so they are held tightly together. The particles vibrate in place.

Changes of State

When you melt cheese to make a cheese dip, such as that shown in **Figure 2,** the cheese changes from a solid to a thick, gooey liquid. A **change of state** is a change of a substance from one state of matter to another. A change of state is a *physical change* that affects one or more physical properties of a substance without changing the identity of the substance. Changes of state include *freezing* (liquid to solid), *melting* (solid to liquid), *boiling* (liquid to gas), and *condensing* (gas to liquid).

Energy and Changes of State

Suppose that you put an ice cube in a pan and set the pan on a stove burner. Soon, the ice will turn to water and then to steam. If you made a graph of the temperature of the ice versus the energy involved during this process, it would look something like the graph in **Figure 3.**

As the ice is heated, its temperature increases from –25°C to 0°C. As the ice melts, its temperature remains at 0°C even as more energy is added. This added energy changes the arrangement of the molecules in the ice. The temperature of the ice remains the same until all of the ice has become liquid water. At that point, the water's temperature starts to increase from 0°C to 100°C. At 100°C, the water begins to change to steam. Even as more energy is added, the water's temperature stays at 100°C as long as there is liquid water present. When all of the water has become steam, the temperature again increases.

✓ **Reading Check** What happens to the temperature of a substance while it is undergoing a change of state? (*See the Appendix for answers to Reading Checks.*)

Figure 2 *When you melt cheese, you change the state of the cheese but not its identity.*

states of matter the physical forms of matter, which include solid, liquid, and gas

change of state the change of a substance from one physical state to another

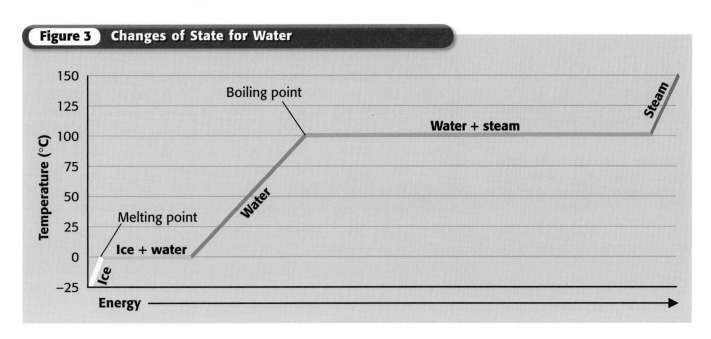

Figure 3 Changes of State for Water

Temperature (°C)

Melting point

Boiling point

Ice

Ice + water

Water

Water + steam

Steam

Energy

Figure 4 *In a natural-gas fireplace, the methane in natural gas and the oxygen in air change into carbon dioxide and water. As a result of the change, energy is given off, making a room feel warmer.*

Heat and Chemical Changes

Heat is involved not only in changes of state, which are physical changes, but also in *chemical changes*—changes that occur when one or more substances are changed into entirely new substances that have different properties. During a chemical change, new substances are formed.

For a new substance to form, old bonds between particles must be broken, and new bonds must be formed. The breaking and creating of bonds between particles involves energy. Sometimes, a chemical change requires that thermal energy be put into substances for a reaction to occur. Other times, a chemical change, such as the one shown in **Figure 4,** will result in a release of energy.

Food and Chemical Energy

Food contains substances from which your body gets energy. Energy that your body can use is released when chemical compounds such as carbohydrates are broken down in your body. The energy is released in chemical reactions.

You have probably seen Nutrition Facts labels, such as the one shown in **Figure 5** on the left. Among other information, such labels show how much chemical energy is in a certain amount of the food. The Calorie is the unit of energy that is often used to measure chemical energy in food. One Calorie is equivalent to 4,184 J.

How do you measure how many Calories of energy are in a certain amount of food? Because the Calorie is a measure of energy, it is also a measure of heat. The amount of energy in food can therefore be measured by a device that measures heat.

Figure 5 *A serving of this fruit contains 120 Cal (502,080 J) of energy, which becomes available when the fruit is eaten.*

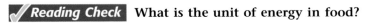 **Reading Check** What is the unit of energy in food?

Calorimeters

A *calorimeter* (KAL uh RIM uht uhr) is a device that measures heat. When one object transfers thermal energy to another object, the energy lost by one object is gained by the other object. This is the key to how a calorimeter works. Inside a calorimeter, shown in **Figure 6,** thermal energy is transferred from a known mass of a test substance to a known mass of another substance, usually water.

The energy of food, in Calories, is found in this way. In a special kind of calorimeter called a *bomb calorimeter,* a food sample is burned. The energy that is released is transferred to the water. By measuring the temperature change of the water and using water's specific heat, you can determine the exact amount of energy transferred by the food sample to the water. This amount of energy (heat) equals the energy content of the food.

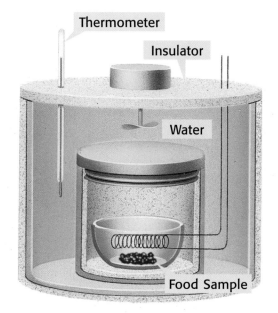

Figure 6 *A bomb calorimeter can measure energy content in food by measuring how much heat is given off by a food sample when it is burned.*

SECTION Review

Summary

- States of matter include solid, liquid, and gas.
- Thermal energy transferred during a change of state does not change a substance's temperature. Rather, it causes a substance's particles to be rearranged.
- Chemical changes can cause thermal energy to be released or absorbed.
- A calorimeter can measure energy changes by measuring heat.

Using Key Terms

1. Use each of the following terms in a separate sentence: *states of matter* and *change of state*.

Understanding Key Ideas

2. What determines a substance's state?
   a. the size of its particles
   b. the amount of the substance
   c. the speed of its particles and the attraction between them
   d. the chemical energy that the substance has

3. During a change of state, why doesn't the temperature of the substance change?

Math Skills

4. When burned in a calorimeter, a sample of popcorn released 627,600 J. How much energy, in Calories, did the popcorn have?

Critical Thinking

5. **Applying Concepts** Many cold packs used for sports injuries are activated by bending the package, causing the substances inside to chemically react. How is heat involved in this process?

6. **Analyzing Processes** When water evaporates (changes from a liquid to a gas), the air near the water's surface becomes cooler. Explain why.

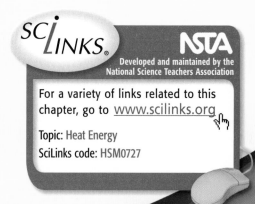

Developed and maintained by the National Science Teachers Association

For a variety of links related to this chapter, go to www.scilinks.org

Topic: Heat Energy
SciLinks code: HSM0727

Heat Technology

You probably wouldn't be surprised to learn that the heater in your home is an example of heat technology. But did you know that automobiles, refrigerators, and air conditioners are also examples of heat technology?

It's true! You can travel long distances, you can keep your food cold, and you can feel comfortable indoors during the summer—all because of heat technology.

Heating Systems

Many homes and buildings have a central heating system that controls the temperature in every room. On the next few pages, you will see some different central heating systems.

Hot-Water Heating

The high specific heat of water makes it useful for heating systems. A hot-water heating system is shown in **Figure 1.** A hot-water heater raises the temperature of water, which is pumped through pipes that lead to radiators in each room. The radiators then heat the colder air surrounding them. The water returns to the hot-water heater to be heated again.

What You Will Learn

● Analyze several kinds of heating systems.
● Describe how a heat engine works.
● Explain how a refrigerator keeps food cold.
● List some effects of heat technology on the environment.

Vocabulary

insulation
heat engine
thermal pollution

READING STRATEGY

Reading Organizer As you read this section, create an outline of the section. Use the headings from the section in your outline.

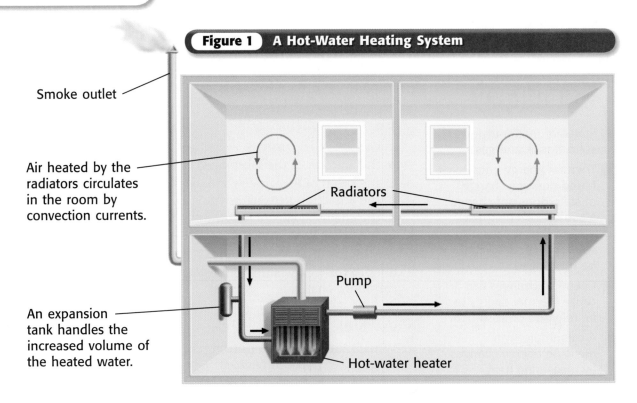

Figure 1 A Hot-Water Heating System

Smoke outlet

Air heated by the radiators circulates in the room by convection currents.

Radiators

Pump

An expansion tank handles the increased volume of the heated water.

Hot-water heater

Figure 2 A Warm-Air Heating System

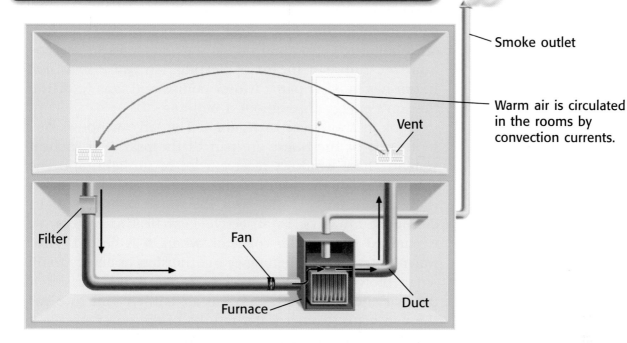

Smoke outlet

Warm air is circulated in the rooms by convection currents.

Vent

Filter

Fan

Furnace

Duct

Warm-Air Heating

Air cannot hold as much thermal energy as water can. But warm-air heating systems are used in many homes and offices in the United States. In a warm-air heating system, shown in **Figure 2,** air is heated by burning fuel (usually natural gas) in a furnace. The warm air travels through ducts to different rooms. The warm air heats air in the rooms. Cooler air sinks below the warm air and enters a vent near the floor. Then, a fan forces the cooler air into the furnace. The air is heated and returned to the ducts. An air filter cleans the air as it moves through the system.

insulation a substance that reduces the transfer of electricity, heat, or sound

Heating and Insulation

Heat may quickly escape out of a house during cold weather, and during hot weather a house may heat up. To keep the house comfortable, a heating system must run much of the time during the winter. Air conditioners often must run most of the time in the summer to keep a house cool. This can be wasteful. Insulation can help reduce the energy needed to heat and cool buildings. Fiberglass insulation is shown in **Figure 3.** **Insulation** is a material that reduces the transfer of thermal energy. When insulation is used in walls, ceilings, and floors, less heat passes into or out of the building. Insulation helps a house stay warm in the winter and cool in the summer.

Figure 3 Millions of tiny air pockets in this insulation help prevent thermal energy from flowing into or out of a building.

✓ **Reading Check** How does insulation help reduce energy costs? (*See the Appendix for answers to Reading Checks.*)

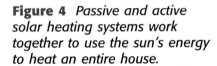

WRITING SKILL **Home Heating and Cooling**

Find out from an adult what kinds of systems are used in your home for heating and cooling. In your **science journal**, describe how these systems work. Also, describe any energy-saving methods used in your home.

Solar Heating

The sun gives off a huge amount of energy. Solar heating systems use this energy to heat houses and buildings. A *passive solar heating system* does not have moving parts. It relies on a building's structural design and materials to use energy from the sun as a means of heating. An *active solar heating system* has moving parts. It uses pumps and fans to distribute the sun's energy throughout a building.

Look at the house in **Figure 4.** The large windows on the south side of the house are part of the passive solar heating system. These windows receive a lot of sunlight, and energy enters through the windows into the rooms. Thick concrete walls absorb energy and keep the house warm at night or during cloudy days. In an active solar heating system, water is pumped to the solar collector, where it is heated. The hot water is pumped through pipes and transfers its energy to them. A fan blowing over the pipes helps the pipes transfer their thermal energy to the air. Warm air is then sent into rooms through vents. Cooler water returns to the water storage tank to be pumped back through the solar collector.

Figure 4 *Passive and active solar heating systems work together to use the sun's energy to heat an entire house.*

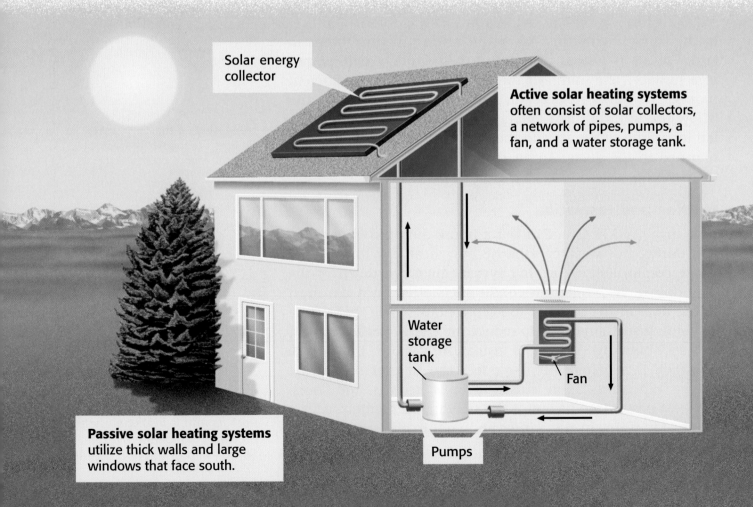

Solar energy collector

Active solar heating systems often consist of solar collectors, a network of pipes, pumps, a fan, and a water storage tank.

Water storage tank

Fan

Pumps

Passive solar heating systems utilize thick walls and large windows that face south.

Heat Engines

Did you know that automobiles work because of heat? A car has a **heat engine,** a machine that uses heat to do work. In a heat engine, fuel combines with oxygen in a chemical change that releases thermal energy. Heat engines burn fuel through this process, called *combustion.* Heat engines that burn fuel outside the engine are called *external combustion engines.* Heat engines that burn fuel inside the engine are called *internal combustion engines.* In both types of engines, fuel is burned to release thermal energy that can be used to do work.

☑ **Reading Check** What kind of energy do combustion engines use?

External Combustion Engines

A simple steam engine, shown in **Figure 5,** is an example of an external combustion engine. Coal is burned to heat water in a boiler and change the water to steam. The steam expands, which pushes a piston. The piston can be attached to other parts of the machine that do work.

Modern steam engines, such as those used to generate electrical energy at a power plant, drive turbines instead of pistons. In the case of generators that use steam to do work, thermal energy is converted into electrical energy.

heat engine a machine that transforms heat into mechanical energy, or work

CONNECTION TO Oceanography

Energy from the Ocean
Ocean engineers are developing a new technology called *Ocean Thermal Energy Conversion,* or OTEC. OTEC uses temperature differences between surface water and deep water in the ocean to generate electrical energy. Research more information about OTEC, and make a model or a poster demonstrating how it works.

ACTIVITY

Figure 5 An External Combustion Engine

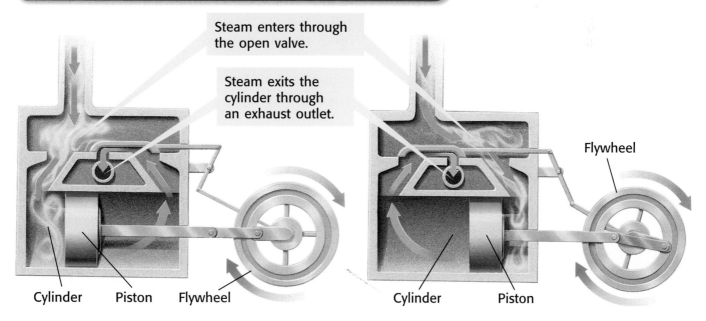

Steam enters through the open valve.

Steam exits the cylinder through an exhaust outlet.

Flywheel

Cylinder   Piston   Flywheel

Cylinder   Piston

❶ The expanding steam enters the cylinder from one side. The steam does work on the piston, forcing the piston to move.

❷ As the piston moves to the other side, a second valve opens, and steam enters. The steam does work on the piston and moves it back. The motion of the piston turns a flywheel.

Wire to spark plug

Cylinder

Piston

Crankshaft

Figure 6 *The continuous cycling of the four strokes in the cylinders converts thermal energy into the kinetic energy needed to make a car move.*

Figure 7 *This air-conditioning unit keeps a building cool by moving thermal energy from inside the building to the outside.*

Internal Combustion Engines

The six-cylinder car engine shown in **Figure 6** is an internal combustion engine. Fuel is burned inside the engine. The fuel used is gasoline, which is burned inside the cylinders. The cylinders go through a series of steps in burning the fuel.

First, a mixture of gasoline and air enters each cylinder as the piston moves down. This step is called the *intake stroke.* Next, the crankshaft turns and pushes the piston up, compressing the fuel mixture. This step is called the *compression stroke.* Next comes the *power stroke,* in which the spark plug uses electrical energy to ignite the compressed fuel mixture. As the mixture of fuel and air burns, it expands and forces the piston down. Finally, during the *exhaust stroke,* the crankshaft turns, and the piston is forced back up, pushing exhaust gases out of the cylinder.

Cooling Systems

When the summer gets hot, an air-conditioned room can feel very refreshing. Cooling systems are used to transfer thermal energy out of a particular area so that it feels cooler. An air conditioner, shown in **Figure 7,** is a cooling system that transfers thermal energy from a warm area inside a building or car to an area outside. Thermal energy naturally tends to go from areas of higher temperature to areas of lower temperature. So, to transfer thermal energy outside where it is warmer, the air-conditioning system must do work. It's like walking uphill: if you are going against gravity, you must do work.

Figure 8 How a Refrigerator Works

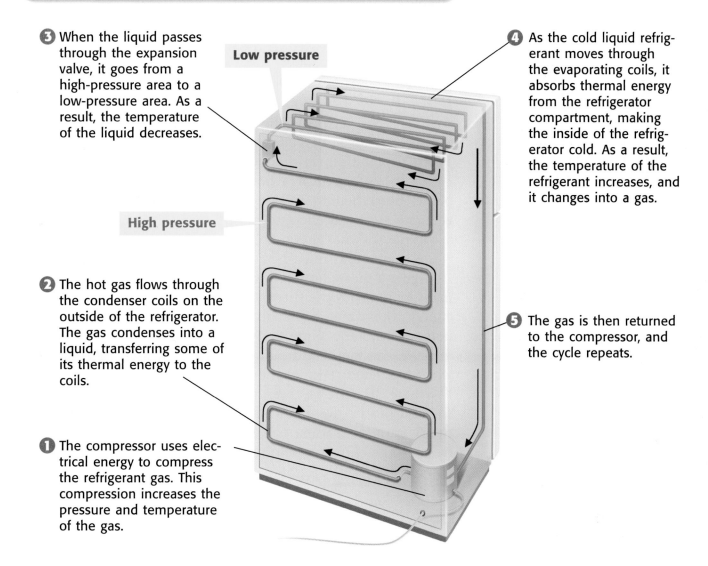

3 When the liquid passes through the expansion valve, it goes from a high-pressure area to a low-pressure area. As a result, the temperature of the liquid decreases.

Low pressure

High pressure

2 The hot gas flows through the condenser coils on the outside of the refrigerator. The gas condenses into a liquid, transferring some of its thermal energy to the coils.

1 The compressor uses electrical energy to compress the refrigerant gas. This compression increases the pressure and temperature of the gas.

4 As the cold liquid refrigerant moves through the evaporating coils, it absorbs thermal energy from the refrigerator compartment, making the inside of the refrigerator cold. As a result, the temperature of the refrigerant increases, and it changes into a gas.

5 The gas is then returned to the compressor, and the cycle repeats.

Cooling and Energy

Most cooling systems require electrical energy to do the work of cooling. The electrical energy is used by a device called a compressor. The *compressor* does the work of compressing the refrigerant. The *refrigerant* is a gas that has a boiling point below room temperature, which allows it to condense easily.

To keep many foods fresh, you store them in a refrigerator. A refrigerator is another example of a cooling system. **Figure 8** shows how a refrigerator continuously transfers thermal energy from inside the refrigerator to the condenser coils on the outside of the refrigerator. That's why the area near the back of a refrigerator feels warm.

✓ **Reading Check** How does the inside of a refrigerator stay at a temperature that is cooler than the temperature outside the refrigerator?

Heat Technology and Thermal Pollution

Heating systems, car engines, and cooling systems all transfer thermal energy to the environment. Unfortunately, too much thermal energy released to the environment can have a negative effect.

Thermal Pollution

thermal pollution a temperature increase in a body of water that is caused by human activity and that has a harmful effect on water quality and on the ability of that body of water to support life

One of the negative effects of excess thermal energy is **thermal pollution,** the excessive heating of a body of water. Thermal pollution can happen near large power plants, which are often located near a body of water. Many electric-power plants burn fuel to release thermal energy that is used to generate electrical energy. Unfortunately, it is not possible for all of that thermal energy to do work. So, some thermal energy waste results and must be released to the environment.

Figure 9 shows how cool water is circulated through a power plant to absorb waste thermal energy. As the cool water absorbs energy, the water heats up. Sometimes the heated water is dumped into the same body of water that it came from. As a result, the temperature of the water can increase. Increased water temperature in lakes and streams can harm animals that live there. In extreme cases, the increase in temperature downstream from a power plant can adversely affect the ecosystem of the river or lake. Some power plants reduce thermal pollution by cooling the water before it is returned to the river.

Reading Check Give an example of thermal pollution.

Figure 9 *Thermal pollution from power plants can result if the plant raises the water temperature of lakes and streams.*

Cool water

Warm water

Summary

- Central heating systems include hot-water heating systems and warm-air heating systems.

- Solar heating systems can be passive or active. In passive solar heating, a building takes advantage of the sun's energy without the use of moving parts. Active solar heating uses moving parts to aid the flow of solar energy throughout a building.

- Heat engines use heat to do work.

- The two kinds of heat engines are external combustion engines, which burn fuel outside the engine, and internal combustion engines, which burn fuel inside the engine.

- A cooling system transfers thermal energy from cooler temperatures to warmer temperatures by doing work.

- Transferring excess thermal energy to lakes and rivers can result in thermal pollution.

Using Key Terms

1. Use each of the following terms in a separate sentence: *insulation*, *heat engine*, and *thermal pollution*.

Understanding Key Ideas

2. Which of the following describes how cooling systems transfer thermal energy?

   a. Thermal energy naturally flows from cooler areas to warmer areas.

   b. Thermal energy naturally flows from warmer areas to cooler areas.

   c. Work is done to transfer thermal energy from warmer areas to cooler areas.

   d. Work is done to transfer thermal energy from cooler areas to warmer areas.

3. Compare a hot-water heating system with a warm-air heating system.

4. What is the difference between an external combustion engine and an internal combustion engine?

Critical Thinking

5. **Identifying Relationships** How are changes of state important in how a refrigerator works?

6. **Expressing Opinions** Compare the advantages and disadvantages of solar heating systems. What do you think their overall benefits are, compared with those of other heating systems?

Interpreting Graphics

7. Look at the graph below. It shows the cost of heating a certain house month by month over the course of a year. During which times of the year is the most energy used for heating? Explain your answer.

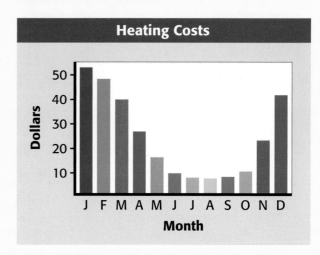

Heating Costs

Dollars (y-axis): 10, 20, 30, 40, 50

Month (x-axis): J F M A M J J A S O N D

Skills Practice Lab

Feel the Heat

OBJECTIVES

Measure the temperature change when hot and cold objects come into contact.

Compare materials for their ability to hold thermal energy.

MATERIALS

- balance, metric
- cups, plastic-foam, 9 oz (2)
- cylinder, graduated, 100 mL
- nails (10 to 12)
- string, 30 cm length
- paper towels
- rubber band
- thermometer
- water, cold
- water, hot

SAFETY

Heat is the energy transferred between objects at different temperatures. Energy moves from objects at higher temperatures to objects at lower temperatures. If two objects are left in contact for a while, the warmer object will cool down and the cooler object will warm up until they eventually reach the same temperature. In this activity, you will combine equal masses of water and nails at different temperatures to determine which has a greater effect on the final temperature.

Ask a Question

1. When you combine substances at two different temperatures, will the final temperature be closer to the initial temperature of the warmer substance or of the colder substance, or halfway in between?

Form a Hypothesis

2. Write a prediction that answers the question in item 1.

Test the Hypothesis

3. Copy the table below onto a separate sheet of paper.

4. Use the rubber band to bundle the nails together. Find and record the mass of the bundle. Tie a length of string around the bundle, leaving one end of the string 15 cm long.

5. Put the bundle of nails into one of the cups, letting the string dangle outside the cup. Fill the cup with enough hot water to cover the nails, and set it aside for at least 5 min.

Data Collection Table					
Trial	Mass of nails (g)	Volume of water that equals mass of nails (mL)	Initial temp. of water and nails (°C)	Initial temp. of water to which nails will be transferred (°C)	Final temp. of water and nails combined (°C)
1					
2					

DO NOT WRITE IN BOOK

6. Use the graduated cylinder to measure enough cold water to exactly equal the mass of the nails (1 mL of water = 1 g). Record this volume in the table.

7. Measure and record the temperature of the hot water with the nails and the temperature of the cold water.

8. Use the string to transfer the bundle of nails to the cup of cold water. Use the thermometer to monitor the temperature of the water-nail mixture. When the temperature stops changing, record this final temperature in the table.

9. Empty the cups, and dry the nails.

10. For Trial 2, repeat steps 4 through 9, but switch the hot and cold water. Record all of your measurements.

Analyze the Results

1. **Analyzing Results** In Trial 1, you used equal masses of cold water and nails. Did the final temperature support your initial prediction? Explain.

2. **Analyzing Results** In Trial 2, you used equal masses of hot water and nails. Did the final temperature support your initial prediction? Explain.

3. **Explaining Events** In Trial 1, which material—the water or the nails—changed temperature the most after you transferred the nails? What about in Trial 2? Explain your answers.

Draw Conclusions

4. **Drawing Conclusions** The cold water in Trial 1 gained energy. Where did the energy come from?

5. **Evaluating Results** How does the energy gained by the nails in Trial 2 compare with the energy lost by the hot water in Trial 2? Explain.

6. **Applying Conclusions** Which material seems to be able to hold energy better? Explain your answer.

7. **Interpreting Information** Specific heat is a property of matter that indicates how much energy is required to change the temperature of 1 kg of a material by 1°C. Which material in this activity has a higher specific heat (changes temperature less for the same amount of energy)?

8. **Making Predictions** Would it be better to have pots and pans made from a material with a high specific heat or a low specific heat? Explain your answer.

Communicating Your Data

Share your results with your classmates. Discuss how you would change your prediction to include your knowledge of specific heat.

Chapter Review

USING KEY TERMS

For each pair of terms, explain how the meanings of the terms differ.

1 *temperature* and *thermal energy*

2 *conduction* and *heat*

3 *conductor* and *insulator*

4 *states of matter* and *change of state*

5 *heat engine* and *thermal pollution*

UNDERSTANDING KEY IDEAS

Multiple Choice

6 Which of the following temperatures is the lowest?

a. 100°C

b. 100°F

c. 100 K

d. They are all the same.

7 Which of the following materials would NOT be a good insulator?

a. wood

b. cloth

c. metal

d. rubber

8 In an air conditioner, thermal energy is

a. transferred from areas of higher temperatures to areas of lower temperatures.

b. transferred from areas of lower temperatures to areas of higher temperatures.

c. used to do work.

d. transferred into the building.

9 The units of energy that you read on a food label are

a. Newtons.

b. Calories.

c. Joules.

d. Both (b) and (c)

10 Compared wih the Pacific Ocean, a cup of hot chocolate has

a. more thermal energy and a higher temperature.

b. less thermal energy and a higher temperature.

c. more thermal energy and a lower temperature.

d. less thermal energy and a lower temperature.

Short Answer

11 How does temperature relate to kinetic energy?

12 What are the differences between conduction, convection, and radiation?

13 Explain how heat affects matter during a change of state.

Math Skills

14 The weather forecast calls for a temperature of 84°F. What is the corresponding temperature in degrees Celsius? in kelvins?

15 Suppose 1.3 kg of water is heated from 20°C to 100°C. How much energy was transferred to the water? (Water's specific heat is 4,184 J/kg•°C.)

CRITICAL THINKING

16 Concept Mapping Create a concept map using the following terms: *thermal energy, temperature, radiation, heat, conduction,* and *convection.*

17 Applying Concepts The metal lid is stuck on a glass jar of jelly. Explain why running hot water over the lid will help you get the lid off.

18 Applying Concepts How does a down jacket keep you warm? (Hint: Think about what insulation does.)

19 Predicting Consequences Would opening the refrigerator cool a room in a house? Explain your answer.

20 Evaluating Assumptions Someone claims that a large bowl of soup has more thermal energy than a small bowl of soup. Is this always true? Explain.

21 Analyzing Processes In a hot-air balloon, air is heated by a flame. Explain how this enables the balloon to float in the air.

22 Analyzing Processes What is different about the two kinds of metal on the bimetallic strip of a thermostat coil?

23 Making Comparisons How is radiation different from both conduction and convection?

INTERPRETING GRAPHICS

Examine the graph below, and then answer the questions that follow.

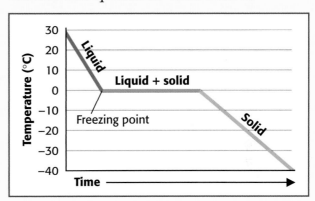

24 What physical change does this graph illustrate?

25 What is the freezing point of this liquid?

26 What is happening at the point where the line is horizontal?

Standardized Test Preparation

Read each of the passages below. Then, answer the questions that follow each passage.

Passage 1 All matter is made up of particles. Temperature is a measure of the average kinetic energy of these particles. The colder a substance gets, the less kinetic energy its particles have, and the slower the particles move. In theory, at absolute zero (–273°C), all movement of particles should stop. Scientists are working in laboratories to cool matter so much that the temperature approaches absolute zero.

1. What is the purpose of this text?
  A to entertain
  B to influence
  C to express
  D to inform

2. What does information in the passage suggest?
  F Matter at absolute zero no longer exists.
  G No one knows what would happen to matter at absolute zero.
  H It is currently not possible to cool matter to absolute zero.
  I Scientists have cooled matter to absolute zero.

3. What information does the passage give about the relationship between kinetic energy and temperature?
  A The higher the temperature, the more kinetic energy a substance has.
  B There is no relationship between temperature and kinetic energy.
  C The higher the temperature, the less kinetic energy a substance has.
  D No one knows what the relationship between kinetic energy and temperature is.

Passage 2 Birds and mammals burn fuel to maintain body temperatures that are usually greater than the air temperature of their surroundings. A lot of energy is necessary to maintain a high body temperature. Tiny animals such as shrews and hummingbirds maintain high body temperatures only during the day. At night or when the air temperature falls significantly, these tiny creatures go into a state called torpor. When an animal is in torpor, its respiration and heart rate are slow. Circulation continues primarily to major organs. Body temperature drops. Because their body processes are slowed, animals in torpor use much less energy than they usually need.

1. Which of the following would be the **best** summary of this passage?
  A Some animals use less energy than other animals.
  B Some animals use more energy than other animals.
  C Some animals maintain high body temperatures only during the day, going into torpor at night.
  D Going into torpor at night is necessary for some animals to maintain high body temperatures.

2. What happens when an animal goes into torpor?
  F Respiration and heart rate slow, and body temperature drops.
  G Normal respiration and heart rate are maintained, and body temperature drops.
  H Respiration and heart rate increase, and body temperature drops.
  I Respiration and heart rate increase, and body temperature rises.

The figure below shows a thermometer in each of two graduated cylinders holding water. Use the figure below to answer the questions that follow.

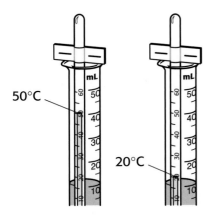

50°C

20°C

1. Which graduated cylinder contains more water?

   A The cylinder on the left contains more.

   B The cylinder on the right contains more.

   C The cylinders contain equal amounts.

   D There is not enough information to determine the answer.

2. If the two cylinders are touching each other, what will happen to the thermal energy in the cylinders?

   F It will pass from the left cylinder to the right cylinder.

   G It will pass from the right cylinder to the left cylinder.

   H It will pass equally between the two cylinders.

   I Nothing will happen.

3. If the water in the graduated cylinders is mixed together, which of the following will most likely be the temperature of the mixture?

   A 25°C

   B 35°C

   C 50°C

   D 70°C

Read each question below, and choose the best answer.

1. Elena has a bag containing 4 blue marbles, 6 red marbles, and 3 green marbles. She picks 1 marble at random. What is the probability of her picking a blue marble?

   A 1 in 13

   B 1 in 4

   C 4 in 13

   D 9 in 13

2. If $8 - 2n = -30$, what is the value of n?

   F 7

   G 19

   H 68

   I 120

3. A rectangle has sides of 4 cm and 10 cm. If the lengths of each of its sides are reduced by half, what will the change in the area of the rectangle be?

   A 1/4 as much area

   B 1/2 as much area

   C 2 times as much area

   D 4 times as much area

4. The specific heat of copper is 387 J/kg•°C. If the temperature of 0.05 kg of copper is raised from 25°C to 30°C, how much heat was put into the copper?

   F 96.8 J

   G 484 J

   H 581 J

   I 96,800 J

5. A change in temperature of 1°C is equal to a change in temperature of 1 K. The temperature 0°C is equal to the temperature 273 K. If the temperature is 300 K, what is the temperature in degrees Celsius?

   A –27°C

   B 27°C

   C 54°C

   D 73°C

Standardized Test Preparation

Science in Action

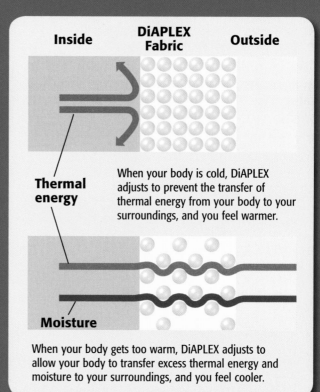

Inside	DiAPLEX Fabric	Outside

Thermal energy

When your body is cold, DiAPLEX adjusts to prevent the transfer of thermal energy from your body to your surroundings, and you feel warmer.

Moisture

When your body gets too warm, DiAPLEX adjusts to allow your body to transfer excess thermal energy and moisture to your surroundings, and you feel cooler.

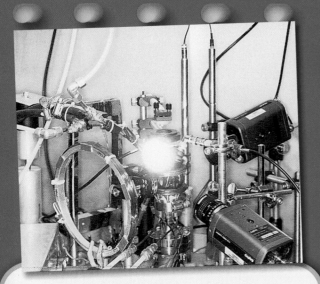

Scientific Discoveries

The Deep Freeze

All matter is made up of tiny, constantly vibrating particles. Temperature is a measure of the average kinetic energy of particles. The colder a substance gets, the slower its particles move. Scientists are interested in how matter behaves when it is cooled to almost absolute zero, the absence of all thermal energy, which is about −273°C. In one method, scientists aim lasers at gas particles, holding them so still that their temperature is less than one-millionth of a degree from absolute zero. It's like turning on several garden hoses and pointing each from a different angle at a soccer ball so that the ball won't move in any direction.

Math ACTIVITY

Think of the coldest weather you have ever been in. What was the temperature? Convert this temperature to kelvins. Compare this temperature with absolute zero.

Science, Technology, and Society

DiAPLEX®: The Intelligent Fabric

Wouldn't it be great if you had a winter coat that could automatically adjust to keep you cozy regardless of the outside temperature? Well, scientists have developed a new fabric called DiAPLEX that can be used to make such a coat!

Like most winter coats, DiAPLEX is made from nylon. But whereas most nylon fabrics have thousands of tiny pores, or openings, DiAPLEX doesn't have pores. It is a solid film. This film makes DiAPLEX even more waterproof than other nylon fabrics.

Language Arts ACTIVITY

WRITING SKILL Think of two different items of clothing that you wear when the weather is cool or cold. Write a paragraph explaining how you think each of them works in keeping you warm when it is cold outside. Does one keep you warmer than the other? How does it do so?

Michael Reynolds

Earthship Architect Would you want to live in a house without a heating system? You could if you lived in an Earthship! Earthships are the brainchild of Michael Reynolds, an architect in Taos, New Mexico. These houses are designed to make the most of our planet's most abundant source of energy, the sun.

Each Earthship takes full advantage of passive solar heating. For example, large windows face south in order to maximize the amount of energy the house receives from the sun. Each home is partially buried in the ground. The soil helps keep the energy that comes in through the windows inside the house.

To absorb the sun's energy, the outer walls of Earthships are massive and thick. The walls may be made with crushed aluminum cans or stacks of old automobile tires filled with dirt. These materials absorb the sun's energy and naturally heat the house. Because an Earthship maintains a temperature around 15°C (about 60°F), it can keep its occupants comfortable through all but the coldest winter nights.

Social Studies ACTIVITY

Find out more about Michael Reynolds and other architects who have invented unique ways of building houses that are energy-efficient. Present your findings.

go.hrw.com

To learn more about these Science in Action topics, visit go.hrw.com and type in the keyword **HP5HOTF.**

Current Science

Check out Current Science® articles related to this chapter by visiting go.hrw.com. Just type in the keyword **HP5CS10.**

Skills Practice Lab

Built for Speed

Imagine that you are an engineer at GoCarCo, a toy-vehicle company. GoCarCo is trying to beat the competition by building a new toy vehicle. Several new designs are being tested. Your boss has given you one of the new toy vehicles and instructed you to measure its speed as accurately as possible with the tools you have. Other engineers (your classmates) are testing the other designs. Your results could decide the fate of the company!

Procedure

1 How will you accomplish your goal? Write a paragraph to describe your goal and your procedure for this experiment. Be sure that your procedure includes several trials.

2 Show your plan to your boss (teacher). Get his or her approval to carry out your procedure.

3 Perform your stated procedure. Record all data. Be sure to express all data in the correct units.

Analyze the Results

1 What was the average speed of your vehicle? How does your result compare with the results of the other engineers?

2 Compare your technique for determining the speed of your vehicle with the techniques of the other engineers. Which technique do you think is the most effective?

3 Was your toy vehicle the fastest? Explain why or why not.

Applying Your Data

Think of several conditions that could affect your vehicle's speed. Design an experiment to test your vehicle under one of those conditions. Write a paragraph to explain your procedure. Be sure to include an explanation of how that condition changes your vehicle's speed.

Skills Practice Lab

Relating Mass and Weight

Why do objects with more mass weigh more than objects with less mass? All objects have weight on Earth because their mass is affected by Earth's gravitational force. Because the mass of an object on Earth is constant, the relationship between the mass of an object and its weight is also constant. You will measure the mass and weight of several objects to verify the relationship between mass and weight on the surface of Earth.

MATERIALS

- balance, metric
- classroom objects, small
- paper, graph
- scissors
- spring scale (force meter)
- string

SAFETY

Procedure

1 Copy the table below.

Mass and Weight Measurements		
Object	Mass (g)	Weight (N)
	DO NOT WRITE IN BOOK	

2 Using the metric balance, find the mass of five or six small classroom objects designated by your teacher. Record the masses.

3 Using the spring scale, find the weight of each object. Record the weights. (You may need to use the string to create a hook with which to hang some objects from the spring scale, as shown at right.)

Analyze the Results

1 Using your data, construct a graph of weight (y-axis) versus mass (x-axis). Draw a line that best fits all your data points.

2 Does the graph confirm the relationship between mass and weight on Earth? Explain your answer.

Skills Practice Lab

Science Friction

In this experiment, you will investigate three types of friction—static, sliding, and rolling—to determine which is the largest force and which is the smallest force.

Ask a Question

1 Which type of friction is the largest force—static, sliding, or rolling? Which is the smallest?

Form a Hypothesis

2 Write a statement or statements that answer the questions above. Explain your reasoning.

Test the Hypothesis

3 Cut a piece of string, and tie it in a loop that fits in the textbook, as shown on the next page. Hook the string to the spring scale.

4 Practice the next three steps several times before you collect data.

5 To measure the static friction between the book and the table, pull the spring scale very slowly. Record the largest force on the scale before the book starts to move.

6 After the book begins to move, you can determine the sliding friction. Record the force required to keep the book sliding at a slow, constant speed.

7 Place two or three rods under the book to act as rollers. Make sure the rollers are evenly spaced. Place another roller in front of the book so that the book will roll onto it. Pull the force meter slowly. Measure the force needed to keep the book rolling at a constant speed.

MATERIALS

- rods, wood or metal (3–4)
- scissors
- spring scale (force meter)
- string
- textbook (covered)

SAFETY

Analyze the Results

1 Which type of friction was the largest? Which was the smallest?

2 Do the results support your hypothesis? If not, how would you revise or retest your hypothesis?

Draw Conclusions

3 Compare your results with those of another group. Are there any differences? Working together, design a way to improve the experiment and resolve possible differences.

Skills Practice Lab

A Marshmallow Catapult

Catapults use projectile motion to launch objects. In this lab, you will build a simple catapult and determine the angle at which the catapult will launch an object the farthest.

MATERIALS

- marshmallows, miniature (2)
- meterstick
- protractor
- spoon, plastic
- tape, duct
- wood block, 3.5 cm × 3.5 cm × 1 cm

SAFETY

Ask a Question

1 At what angle, from 10° to 90°, will a catapult launch a marshmallow the farthest?

Form a Hypothesis

2 Write a hypothesis that is a possible answer to your question.

Angle	Distance 1 (cm)	Distance 2 (cm)	Average distance	Data Collection
10°	DO NOT WRITE IN BOOK			

Test the Hypothesis

3 Copy the table above. In your table, add one row each for 20°, 30°, 40°, 50°, 60°, 70°, 80°, and 90° angles.

4 Using duct tape, attach the plastic spoon to the 1 cm side of the block. Use enough tape to attach the spoon securely.

5 Place one marshmallow in the center of the spoon, and tape it to the spoon. This marshmallow serves as a ledge to hold the marshmallow that will be launched.

6 Line up the bottom corner of the block with the bottom center of the protractor, as shown in the photograph. Start with the block at 10°.

7 Place a marshmallow in the spoon, on top of the taped marshmallow. Pull the spoon back lightly, and let go. Measure and record the distance from the catapult that the marshmallow lands. Repeat the measurement, and calculate an average.

8 Repeat step 7 for each angle up to 90°.

Analyze the Results

1 At what angle did the catapult launch the marshmallow the farthest? Explain any differences from your hypothesis.

Draw Conclusions

2 At what angle should you throw a ball or shoot an arrow so that it will fly the farthest? Why? Support your answer with your data.

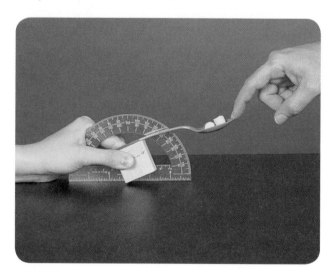

Model-Making Lab

Blast Off!

You have been hired as a rocket scientist for NASA. Your job is to design a rocket that will have a controlled flight while carrying a payload. Keep in mind that Newton's laws will have a powerful influence on your rocket.

MATERIALS

- balloon, long, thin
- cup, paper, small
- fishing line, 3 m
- meterstick
- pencil
- pennies
- straw, straight plastic
- string, 15 cm (2)
- tape, masking
- twist tie

SAFETY

Procedure

1. When you begin your experiment, your teacher will tape one end of the fishing line to the ceiling.

2. Use a pencil to poke a small hole in each side of the cup near the top. Place a 15 cm piece of string through each hole, and tape down the ends inside.

3. Inflate the balloon, and use the twist tie to hold it closed.

4. Tape the free ends of the strings to the sides of the balloon near the bottom. The cup should hang below the balloon. Your model rocket should look like a hot-air balloon.

5. Thread the fishing line that is hanging from the ceiling through the straw. Tape the balloon securely to the straw. Tape the loose end of the fishing line to the floor.

6. Untie the twist tie while holding the end of the balloon closed. When you are ready, release the end of the balloon. Mark and record the maximum height of the rocket.

7. Repeat the procedure, adding a penny to the cup each time until your rocket cannot lift any more pennies.

Analyze the Results

1. In a paragraph, describe how all three of Newton's laws influenced the flight of your rocket.

Draw Conclusions

2. Draw a diagram of your rocket. Label the action and reaction forces.

Applying Your Data

Brainstorm ways to modify your rocket so that it will carry the most pennies to the maximum height. Select the best design. When your teacher has approved all the designs, build and launch your rocket. Which variable did you modify? How did this variable affect your rocket's flight?

Quite a Reaction

Catapults have been used for centuries to throw objects great distances. According to Newton's third law of motion (whenever one object exerts a force on a second object, the second object exerts an equal and opposite force on the first), when an object is launched, something must also happen to the catapult. In this activity, you will build a kind of catapult that will allow you to observe the effects of Newton's third law of motion and the law of conservation of momentum.

Procedure

1 Glue the cardboard rectangles together to make a stack of three.

2 Push two of the pushpins into the cardboard stack near the corners at one end, as shown below. These pushpins will be the anchors for the rubber band.

3 Make a small loop of string.

4 Put the rubber band through the loop of string, and then place the rubber band over the two pushpin anchors. The rubber band should be stretched between the two anchors with the string loop in the middle.

5 Pull the string loop toward the end of the cardboard stack opposite the end with the anchors, and fasten the loop in place with the third pushpin.

6 Place the six straws about 1 cm apart on a tabletop or on the floor. Then, carefully center the catapult on top of the straws.

7 Put the marble in the closed end of the V formed by the rubber band.

8 Use scissors to cut the string holding the rubber band, and observe what happens. (Be careful not to let the scissors touch the cardboard catapult when you cut the string.)

MATERIALS

- cardboard rectangles, 10 cm × 15 cm (3)
- glue
- marble
- meterstick
- pushpins (3)
- rubber band
- scissors
- straws, plastic (6)
- string

SAFETY

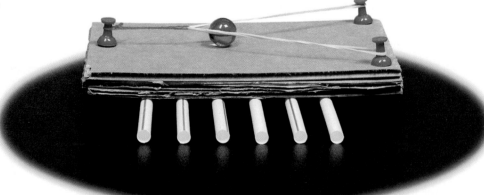

9. Reset the catapult with a new piece of string. Try launching the marble several times to be sure that you have observed everything that happens during a launch. Record all your observations.

Analyze the Results

1. Which has more mass, the marble or the catapult?

2. What happened to the catapult when the marble was launched?

3. How far did the marble fly before it landed?

4. Did the catapult move as far as the marble did?

Draw Conclusions

5. Explain why the catapult moved backward.

6. If the forces that made the marble and the catapult move apart are equal, why didn't the marble and the catapult move apart the same distance? (Hint: The fact that the marble can roll after it lands is not the answer.)

7. The momentum of an object depends on the mass and velocity of the object. What is the momentum of the marble before it is launched? What is the momentum of the catapult? Explain your answers.

8. Using the law of conservation of momentum, explain why the marble and the catapult move in opposite directions after the launch.

Applying Your Data

How would you modify the catapult if you wanted to keep it from moving backward as far as it did? (It still has to rest on the straws.) Using items that you can find in the classroom, design a catapult that will move backward less than the one originally designed.

Skills Practice Lab

Density Diver

Crew members of a submarine can control the submarine's density underwater by allowing water to flow into and out of special tanks. These changes in density affect the submarine's position in the water. In this lab, you'll control a "density diver" to learn for yourself how the density of an object affects its position in a fluid.

MATERIALS

- bottle, plastic, with screw-on cap, 2 L
- dropper, medicine
- water

SAFETY

Ask a Question

1 How does the density of an object determine whether the object floats, sinks, or maintains its position in a fluid?

Form a Hypothesis

2 Write a possible answer to the question above.

Test the Hypothesis

3 Completely fill the 2 L plastic bottle with water.

4 Fill the diver (medicine dropper) approximately halfway with water, and place it in the bottle. The diver should float with only part of the rubber bulb above the surface of the water. If the diver floats too high, carefully remove it from the bottle, and add a small amount of water to the diver. Place the diver back in the bottle. If you add too much water and the diver sinks, empty out the bottle and diver, and go back to step 3.

5 Put the cap on the bottle tightly so that no water leaks out.

6 Apply various pressures to the bottle. Carefully watch the water level inside the diver as you squeeze and release the bottle. Record what happens.

7 Try to make the diver rise, sink, or stop at any level. Record your technique and your results.

Analyze the Results

1 How do the changes inside the diver affect its position in the surrounding fluid?

2 What relationship did you observe between the diver's density and the diver's position in the fluid?

Draw Conclusions

3 Explain how your density diver is like a submarine.

4 Explain how pressure on the bottle is related to the diver's density. Be sure to include Pascal's principle in your explanation.

Skills Practice Lab

Inclined to Move

In this lab, you will examine a simple machine—an inclined plane. Your task is to compare the work done with and without the inclined plane and to analyze the effects of friction.

Ask a Question

1 Write a question that you can test regarding inclined planes.

Form a Hypothesis

2 Write a possible answer to the question you wrote.

Test the Hypothesis

3 Copy the table at right.

4 Tie a piece of string around a book. Attach the spring scale to the string. Use the spring scale to slowly lift the book to a height of 50 cm. Record the output force (the force needed to lift the book). The output force is constant throughout the lab.

5 Use the board and blocks to make a ramp 10 cm high at the highest point. Measure and record the ramp length.

6 Keeping the spring scale parallel to the ramp, as shown, slowly raise the book. Record the input force (the force needed to pull the book up the ramp).

7 Increase the height of the ramp by 10 cm. Repeat step 6. Repeat this step for each ramp height up to 50 cm.

Analyze the Results

1 The real work done includes the work done to overcome friction. Calculate the real work at each height by multiplying the ramp length (converted to meters) by the input force. Graph your results, plotting work (*y*-axis) versus height (*x*-axis).

MATERIALS

- board, wooden
- blocks
- book, small
- meterstick
- paper, graph
- spring scale
- string

SAFETY

Force Versus Height

Ramp height (cm)	Output force (N)	Ramp length (cm)	Input force (N)
10			
20			
30	DO NOT WRITE IN BOOK		
40			
50			

2 The ideal work is the work you would do if there were no friction. Calculate the ideal work at each height by multiplying the ramp height (cm) by the output force. Plot the data on your graph.

Draw Conclusions

3 Does it require more or less force and work to raise the book by using the ramp? Explain, using your calculations.

4 What is the relationship between the height of the inclined plane and the input force?

Skills Practice Lab

Wheeling and Dealing

A crank handle, such as that used in pencil sharpeners, ice-cream makers, and water wells, is one kind of wheel and axle. In this lab, you will use a crank handle to find out how a wheel and axle helps you do work. You will also determine what effect the length of the handle has on the operation of the machine.

MATERIALS

- C-clamps (2)
- handles (4)
- mass, large
- meterstick
- spring scale
- string, 0.5 m
- wheel-and-axle assembly

SAFETY

Ask a Question

1 What effect does the length of a handle have on the operation of a crank?

Form a Hypothesis

2 Write a possible answer to the question above.

Test the Hypothesis

3 Copy Table 1.

4 Measure the radius (in meters) of the large dowel in the wheel-and-axle assembly. Record this in Table 1 as the axle radius, which remains constant throughout the lab. (Hint: Measure the diameter, and divide by 2.)

5 Using the spring scale, measure the weight of the large mass. Record this in Table 1 as the output force, which remains constant throughout the lab.

6 Use two C-clamps to secure the wheel-and-axle assembly to the table, as shown.

7 Measure the length (in meters) of handle 1. Record this length as a wheel radius in Table 1.

8 Insert the handle into the hole in the axle. Attach one end of the string to the large mass and the other end to the screw in the axle. The mass should hang down, and the handle should turn freely.

9 Turn the handle to lift the mass off the floor. Hold the spring scale upside down, and attach it to the end of the handle. Measure the force (in newtons) as the handle pulls up on the spring scale. Record this as the input force.

Table 1	Data Collection			
Handle	Axle radius (m)	Output force (N)	Wheel radius (m)	Input force (N)
1				
2				
3		*DO NOT WRITE IN BOOK*		
4				

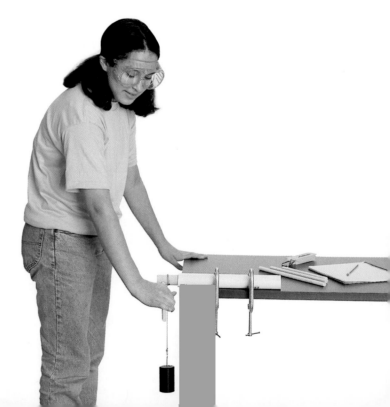

10 Remove the spring scale, and lower the mass to the floor. Remove the handle.

11 Repeat steps 7 through 10 with the other three handles. Record all data in Table 1.

Analyze the Results

1 Copy Table 2.

Table 2 Calculations						
Handle	Axle distance (m)	Wheel distance (m)	Work input (J)	Work output (J)	Mechanical efficiency (%)	Mechanical advantage
1						
2			DO NOT WRITE IN BOOK			
3						
4						

2 Calculate the following for each handle, using the equations given. Record your answers in Table 2.

a. *Distance axle rotates =*
   $2 \times \pi \times$ *axle radius*

   Distance wheel rotates =
   $2 \times \pi \times$ *wheel radius*

   (Use 3.14 for the value of π.)

b. *Work input =*
   input force × wheel distance

   Work output =
   output force × axle distance

c. *Mechanical efficiency =*
   $\dfrac{work\ output}{work\ input} \times 100$

d. *Mechanical advantage =*
   $\dfrac{wheel\ radius}{axle\ radius}$

Draw Conclusions

3 What happens to work output and work input as the handle length increases? Why?

4 What happens to mechanical efficiency as the handle length increases? Why?

5 What happens to mechanical advantage as the handle length increases? Why?

6 What will happen to mechanical advantage if the handle length is kept constant and the axle radius gets larger?

7 What factors were controlled in this experiment? What was the variable?

Inquiry Lab

Building Machines

You are surrounded by machines. Some are simple machines, such as ramps for wheelchair access to a building. Others are compound machines, such as elevators and escalators, that are made of two or more simple machines. In this lab, you will design and build several simple machines and a compound machine.

Ask a Question

1 How can simple machines be combined to make compound machines?

Form a Hypothesis

2 Write a possible answer to the question above.

Test the Hypothesis

3 Use the listed materials to build a model of each simple machine: inclined plane, lever, wheel and axle, pulley, screw, and wedge. Describe and draw each model.

4 Design a compound machine by using the materials listed. You may design a machine that already exists, or you may invent your own machine. Be creative!

5 After your teacher approves your design, build your compound machine.

Analyze the Results

1 List a possible use for each of your simple machines.

2 How many simple machines are in your compound machine? List them.

3 Compare your compound machine with those created by your classmates.

4 What is a possible use for your compound machine? Why did you design it as you did?

5 A compound machine is listed in the materials list. What is it?

Applying Your Data

Design a compound machine that has all the simple machines in it. Explain what the machine will do and how it will make work easier. With your teacher's approval, build your machine.

MATERIALS

- bottle caps
- cardboard
- clay, modeling
- craft sticks
- glue
- paper
- pencils
- rubber bands
- scissors
- shoe boxes
- stones
- straws
- string
- tape
- thread spools, empty
- other materials available in your classroom that are approved by your teacher

SAFETY

Skills Practice Lab

Energy of a Pendulum

A pendulum clock is a compound machine that uses stored energy to do work. A spring stores energy, and with each swing of the pendulum, some of that stored energy is used to move the hands of the clock. In this lab, you will take a close look at the energy conversions that occur as a pendulum swings.

MATERIALS

- marker
- mass, hooked, 100 g
- meterstick
- string, 1 m

SAFETY

Procedure

1. Make a pendulum by tying the string around the hook of the mass. Use the marker and the meterstick to mark points on the string that are 50 cm, 70 cm, and 90 cm away from the mass.

2. Hold the string at the 50 cm mark. Gently pull the mass to the side, and release it without pushing it. Observe at least 10 swings of the pendulum.

3. Record your observations. Be sure to note how fast and how high the pendulum swings.

4. Repeat steps 2 and 3 while holding the string at the 70 cm mark and again while holding the string at the 90 cm mark.

Analyze the Results

1. List similarities and differences in the motion of the pendulum during all three trials.

2. At which point (or points) of the swing was the pendulum moving the slowest? the fastest?

Draw Conclusions

3. In each trial, at which point (or points) of the swing did the pendulum have the greatest potential energy? the least potential energy? (Hint: Think about your answers to question 2.)

4. At which point (or points) of the swing did the pendulum have the greatest kinetic energy? the least kinetic energy? Explain your answers.

5. Describe the relationship between the pendulum's potential energy and its kinetic energy on its way down. Explain.

6. What improvements might reduce the amount of energy used to overcome friction so that the pendulum would swing for a longer period of time?

Inquiry Lab

Save the Cube!

The biggest enemy of an ice cube is the transfer of thermal energy—heat. Energy can be transferred to an ice cube in three ways: conduction (the transfer of energy through direct contact), convection (the transfer of energy by the movement of a liquid or gas), and radiation (the transfer of energy through matter or space). Your challenge in this activity is to design a way to protect an ice cube as much as possible from all three types of energy transfer.

MATERIALS

- bag, plastic, small
- balance, metric
- cup, plastic or paper, small
- ice cube
- milk carton, empty, half-pint
- assorted materials provided by your teacher

Ask a Question

1 What materials prevent energy transfer most efficiently?

Form a Hypothesis

2 Design a system that protects an ice cube against each type of energy transfer. Describe your proposed design.

Test the Hypothesis

3 Use a plastic bag to hold the ice cube and any water if the ice cube melts. You may use any of the materials to protect the ice cube. The whole system must fit inside a milk carton.

4 Find the mass of the empty cup, and record it. Then, find and record the mass of an empty plastic bag.

5 Find and record the mass of the ice cube and cup together.

6 Quickly wrap the bag (and the ice cube inside) in its protection. Remember that the package must fit in the milk carton.

7 Place your ice cube in the "thermal zone" set up by your teacher. After 10 min, remove the ice cube from the zone.

8 Open the bag. Pour any water into the cup. Find and record the mass of the cup and water together.

9 Find and record the mass of the water by subtracting the mass of the empty cup from the mass of the cup and water.

10 Use the same method to determine the mass of the ice cube.

11 Using the following equation, find and record the percentage of the ice cube that melted:

$$\% \ melted = \frac{mass\ of\ water}{mass\ of\ ice\ cube} \times 100$$

Analyze the Results

1 Compared with other designs in your class, how well did your design protect against each type of energy transfer? How could you improve your design?

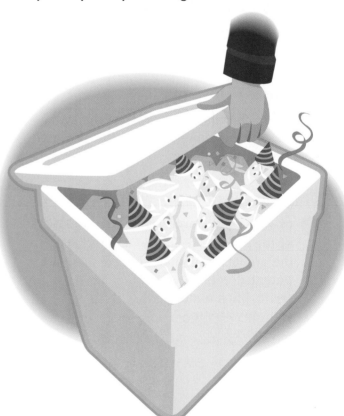

Model-Making Lab

Counting Calories

Energy transferred by heat is often expressed in units called *calories.* **In this lab, you will build a model of a device called a** *calorimeter.* **Scientists often use calorimeters to measure the amount of energy that can be transferred by a substance. In this experiment, you will construct your own calorimeter and test it by measuring the energy released by a hot penny.**

MATERIALS

- cup, plastic-foam, large
- cup, plastic-foam, small, with lid
- graduated cylinder, 100 mL
- heat source
- penny
- stopwatch
- thermometer
- tongs
- water

SAFETY

Procedure

1. Copy the table below.

Data Collection Table									
Seconds	0	15	30	45	60	75	90	105	120
Water temperature (°C)									

DO NOT WRITE IN BOOK

2. Place the lid on the small plastic-foam cup, and insert a thermometer through the hole in the top of the lid. (The thermometer should not touch the bottom of the cup.) Place the small cup inside the large cup to complete the calorimeter.

3. Remove the lid from the small cup, and add 50 mL of room-temperature water to the cup. Measure the water's temperature, and record the value in the first column (0 s) of the table.

4. Using tongs, heat the penny carefully. Add the penny to the water in the small cup, and replace the lid. Start your stopwatch.

5. Every 15 s, measure and record the temperature. Gently swirl the large cup to stir the water, and continue recording temperatures for 2 min (120 s).

Analyze the Results

1. What was the total temperature change of the water after 2 min?

2. The number of calories absorbed by the water is the mass of the water (in grams) multiplied by the temperature change (in °C) of the water. How many calories were absorbed by the water? (Hint: 1 mL water = 1 g water)

3. In terms of heat, explain where the calories to change the water temperature came from.

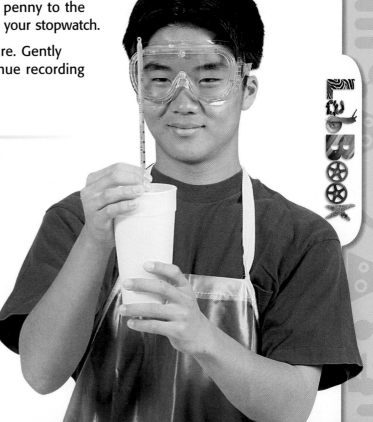

Contents

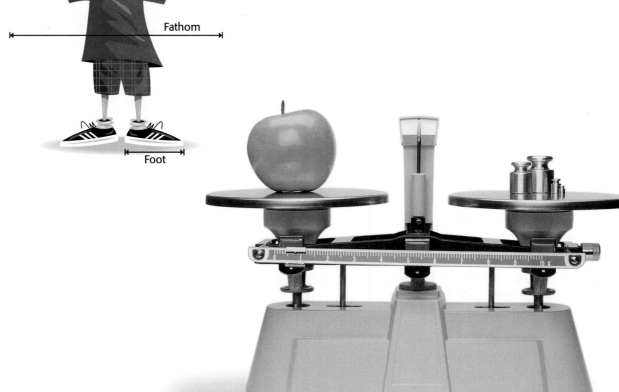

Appendix

✓ *Reading Check* Answers

Chapter 1   Matter in Motion
Section 1
Page 4: A reference point is an object that appears to stay in place.

Page 6: Velocity can change by changing speed or changing direction.

Page 8: The unit for acceleration is meters per second per second (m/s^2).

Section 2
Page 11: If all of the forces act in the same direction, you must add the forces to determine the net force.

Page 12: 2 N north

Section 3
Page 15: Friction is greater between rough surfaces because rough surfaces have more microscopic hills and valleys.

Page 17: *Static* means "not moving."

Page 18: Three common lubricants are oil, grease, and wax.

Section 4
Page 21: You must exert a force to overcome the gravitational force between the object and Earth.

Page 22: Gravitational force increases as mass increases.

Page 24: The weight of an object is a measure of the gravitational force on the object.

Chapter 2   Forces and Motion
Section 1
Page 37: The acceleration due to gravity is 9.8 m/s^2.

Page 38: Air resistance will have more of an effect on the acceleration of a falling leaf.

Page 40: The word *centripetal* means "toward the center."

Page 42: Gravity gives vertical motion to an object in projectile motion.

Section 2
Page 45: When the bus is moving, both you and the bus are in motion. When the bus stops moving, no unbalanced force acts on your body, so your body continues to move forward.

Page 47: The acceleration of an object increases as the force exerted on the object increases.

Page 49: The forces in a force pair are equal in size and opposite in direction.

Page 50: Objects accelerate toward Earth because the force of gravity pulls them toward Earth.

Section 3
Page 53: When two objects collide, some or all of the momentum of each object can be transferred to the other object.

Page 54: After a collision, objects can stick together or can bounce off each other.

Chapter 3   Forces in Fluids
Section 1
Page 67: Two gases in the atmosphere are nitrogen and oxygen.

Page 68: Pressure increases as depth increases.

Page 70: You decrease pressure inside a straw by removing some of the air inside the straw.

Section 2
Page 73: An object is buoyed up if the buoyant force on the object is greater than the object's weight.

Page 74: Helium is less dense than air.

Page 76: Crew members control the density of a submarine by controlling the amount of water in the ballast tanks.

Section 3
Page 79: Lift is an upward force on an object that is moving in a fluid.

Page 81: An irregular or unpredictable flow of fluids is known as *turbulence.*

Page 82: Airplanes can reduce turbulence by changing the shape or area of the wings.

Chapter 4   Work and Machines
Section 1
Page 94: No, work is done on an object only if force causes the object to move in a direction that is parallel to the force.

Page 97: Work is calculated as force times distance.

Page 98: Power is calculated as work done (in joules) divided by the time (in seconds) in which the work was done.

Section 2
Page 101: Machines make work easier by allowing a decreased force to be applied over a greater distance.

Page 102: Machines can change the force or the distance through which force is applied.

Page 104: *mechanical efficiency* = (work output ÷ work input) × 100

Section 3
Page 107: Each class of lever has a different set of mechanical advantage possibilities.

Page 109: the radius of the wheel divided by the radius of the axle

Page 110: a slanted surface that makes the raising of loads easier, such as a ramp

Page 112: They have more moving parts than simple machines do, so they tend to be less efficient than simple machines are.

Chapter 5   Energy and Energy Resources

Section 1

Page 124: Energy is the ability to do work.

Page 127: kinetic energy and potential energy

Page 129: Sound energy consists of vibrations carried through the air.

Page 130: Nuclear energy comes from changes in the nucleus of an atom.

Section 2

Page 133: Elastic potential energy can be stored by stretching a rubber band. Elastic potential energy is released when the rubber band goes back to its original shape.

Page 134: Plants get their energy from the sun.

Page 136: Machines can change the size or direction of the input force.

Section 3

Page 139: Conservation of energy is considered a scientific law because no exception to it has ever been observed.

Page 140: Perpetual motion is impossible because energy conversions always result in the production of waste thermal energy.

Section 4

Page 142: Fossil fuels are nonrenewable resources because they are used up more quickly than they are replaced.

Page 144: Nuclear energy comes from radioactive elements that give off energy during nuclear fission.

Page 146: Geothermal energy comes from the thermal energy given off by underground areas of hot rock.

Chapter 6   Heat and Heat Technology

Section 1

Page 159: Temperature is a measure of the average kinetic energy of the particles of a substance.

Page 160: Thermal expansion makes thermometers work.

Page 163: Expansion joints on a bridge allow the bridge to undergo thermal expansion without breaking.

Section 2

Page 165: If two objects at different temperatures come into contact, thermal energy will be transferred from the higher-temperature object to the lower-temperature object until both objects are at the same temperature.

Page 167: Two objects that are at the same temperature can feel as though they are at different temperatures if one object is a better thermal conductor than the other is. The better conductor will feel colder because it will draw thermal energy away from your hand faster.

Page 168: The greenhouse effect is the trapping of thermal energy from the sun in Earth's atmosphere.

Page 170: Specific heat, mass, and the change in temperature are needed to calculate heat.

Section 3

Page 173: While a substance is undergoing a change of state, the temperature of the substance remains the same.

Page 175: The Calorie is the unit of food energy.

Section 4

Page 177: Insulation helps save energy costs by keeping thermal energy from passing into or escaping from a building.

Page 179: Combustion engines use thermal energy.

Page 181: The inside of a refrigerator is able to stay cooler than the outside because thermal energy inside the refrigerator is continuously being transferred outside of the refrigerator.

Page 182: Sample answer: Thermal pollution can take place when heated water from an electrical generating plant is returned to the river from which the water came. The heated water that is returned to the river raises the temperature of the river water.

Study Skills

FoldNote Instructions

Have you ever tried to study for a test or quiz but didn't know where to start? Or have you read a chapter and found that you can remember only a few ideas? Well, FoldNotes are a fun and exciting way to help you learn and remember the ideas you encounter as you learn science!

FoldNotes are tools that you can use to organize concepts. By focusing on a few main concepts, FoldNotes help you learn and remember how the concepts fit together. They can help you see the "big picture." Below you will find instructions for building 10 different FoldNotes.

Pyramid

1. Place a sheet of paper in front of you. Fold the lower left-hand corner of the paper diagonally to the opposite edge of the paper.

2. Cut off the tab of paper created by the fold (at the top).

3. Open the paper so that it is a square. Fold the lower right-hand corner of the paper diagonally to the opposite corner to form a triangle.

4. Open the paper. The creases of the two folds will have created an X.

5. Using scissors, cut along one of the creases. Start from any corner, and stop at the center point to create two flaps. Use tape or glue to attach one of the flaps on top of the other flap.

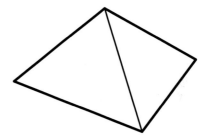

Double Door

1. Fold a sheet of paper in half from the top to the bottom. Then, unfold the paper.

2. Fold the top and bottom edges of the paper to the crease.

Booklet

1. Fold a sheet of paper in half from left to right. Then, unfold the paper.

2. Fold the sheet of paper in half again from the top to the bottom. Then, unfold the paper.

3. Refold the sheet of paper in half from left to right.

4. Fold the top and bottom edges to the center crease.

5. Completely unfold the paper.

6. Refold the paper from top to bottom.

7. Using scissors, cut a slit along the center crease of the sheet from the folded edge to the creases made in step 4. Do not cut the entire sheet in half.

8. Fold the sheet of paper in half from left to right. While holding the bottom and top edges of the paper, push the bottom and top edges together so that the center collapses at the center slit. Fold the four flaps to form a four-page book.

Layered Book

1. Lay one sheet of paper on top of another sheet. Slide the top sheet up so that 2 cm of the bottom sheet is showing.

2. Hold the two sheets together, fold down the top of the two sheets so that you see four 2 cm tabs along the bottom.

3. Using a stapler, staple the top of the FoldNote.

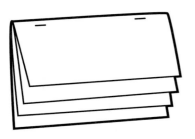

Key-Term Fold

1. Fold a sheet of lined notebook paper in half from left to right.

2. Using scissors, cut along every third line from the right edge of the paper to the center fold to make tabs.

Four-Corner Fold

1. Fold a sheet of paper in half from left to right. Then, unfold the paper.

2. Fold each side of the paper to the crease in the center of the paper.

3. Fold the paper in half from the top to the bottom. Then, unfold the paper.

4. Using scissors, cut the top flap creases made in step 3 to form four flaps.

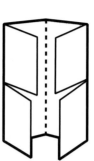

Three-Panel Flip Chart

1. Fold a piece of paper in half from the top to the bottom.

2. Fold the paper in thirds from side to side. Then, unfold the paper so that you can see the three sections.

3. From the top of the paper, cut along each of the vertical fold lines to the fold in the middle of the paper. You will now have three flaps.

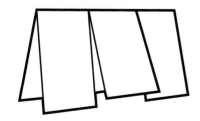

Table Fold

1. Fold a piece of paper in half from the top to the bottom. Then, fold the paper in half again.

2. Fold the paper in thirds from side to side.

3. Unfold the paper completely. Carefully trace the fold lines by using a pen or pencil.

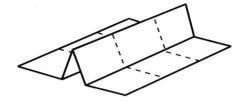

Two-Panel Flip Chart

1. Fold a piece of paper in half from the top to the bottom.

2. Fold the paper in half from side to side. Then, unfold the paper so that you can see the two sections.

3. From the top of the paper, cut along the vertical fold line to the fold in the middle of the paper. You will now have two flaps.

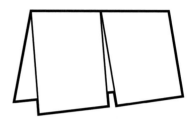

Tri-Fold

1. Fold a piece a paper in thirds from the top to the bottom.

2. Unfold the paper so that you can see the three sections. Then, turn the paper sideways so that the three sections form vertical columns.

3. Trace the fold lines by using a pen or pencil. Label the columns "Know," "Want," and "Learn."

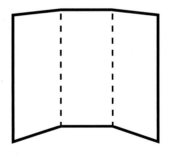

Graphic Organizer Instructions

Have you ever wished that you could "draw out" the many concepts you learn in your science class? Sometimes, being able to *see* how concepts are related really helps you remember what you've learned. Graphic Organizers do just that! They give you a way to draw or map out concepts.

All you need to make a Graphic Organizer is a piece of paper and a pencil. Below you will find instructions for four different Graphic Organizers designed to help you organize the concepts you'll learn in this book.

Spider Map

1. Draw a diagram like the one shown. In the circle, write the main topic.

2. From the circle, draw legs to represent different categories of the main topic. You can have as many categories as you want.

3. From the category legs, draw horizontal lines. As you read the chapter, write details about each category on the horizontal lines.

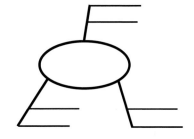

Comparison Table

1. Draw a chart like the one shown. Your chart can have as many columns and rows as you want.

2. In the top row, write the topics that you want to compare.

3. In the left column, write characteristics of the topics that you want to compare. As you read the chapter, fill in the characteristics for each topic in the appropriate boxes.

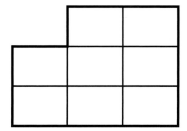

Chain-of-Events-Chart

1. Draw a box. In the box, write the first step of a process or the first event of a timeline.

2. Under the box, draw another box, and use an arrow to connect the two boxes. In the second box, write the next step of the process or the next event in the timeline.

3. Continue adding boxes until the process or timeline is finished.

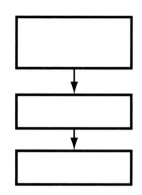

Concept Map

1. Draw a circle in the center of a piece of paper. Write the main idea of the chapter in the center of the circle.

2. From the circle, draw other circles. In those circles, write characteristics of the main idea. Draw arrows from the center circle to the circles that contain the characteristics.

3. From each circle that contains a characteristic, draw other circles. In those circles, write specific details about the characteristic. Draw arrows from each circle that contains a characteristic to the circles that contain specific details. You may draw as many circles as you want.

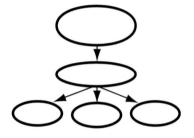

SI Measurement

The International System of Units, or SI, is the standard system of measurement used by many scientists. Using the same standards of measurement makes it easier for scientists to communicate with one another.

SI works by combining prefixes and base units. Each base unit can be used with different prefixes to define smaller and larger quantities. The table below lists common SI prefixes.

SI Prefixes

Prefix	Symbol	Factor	Example
kilo-	k	1,000	kilogram, 1 kg = 1,000 g
hecto-	h	100	hectoliter, 1 hL = 100 L
deka-	da	10	dekameter, 1 dam = 10 m
		1	meter, liter, gram
deci-	d	0.1	decigram, 1 dg = 0.1 g
centi-	c	0.01	centimeter, 1 cm = 0.01 m
milli-	m	0.001	milliliter, 1 mL = 0.001 L
micro-	μ	0.000 001	micrometer, 1 μm = 0.000 001 m

SI Conversion Table

SI units	From SI to English	From English to SI
Length		
kilometer (km) = 1,000 m	1 km = 0.621 mi	1 mi = 1.609 km
meter (m) = 100 cm	1 m = 3.281 ft	1 ft = 0.305 m
centimeter (cm) = 0.01 m	1 cm = 0.394 in.	1 in. = 2.540 cm
millimeter (mm) = 0.001 m	1 mm = 0.039 in.	
micrometer (μm) = 0.000 001 m		
nanometer (nm) = 0.000 000 001 m		
Area		
square kilometer (km^2) = 100 hectares	1 km^2 = 0.386 mi^2	1 mi^2 = 2.590 km^2
hectare (ha) = 10,000 m^2	1 ha = 2.471 acres	1 acre = 0.405 ha
square meter (m^2) = 10,000 cm^2	1 m^2 = 10.764 ft^2	1 ft^2 = 0.093 m^2
square centimeter (cm^2) = 100 mm^2	1 cm^2 = 0.155 in.^{2}	1 in.^{2} = 6.452 cm^2
Volume		
liter (L) = 1,000 mL = 1 dm^3	1 L = 1.057 fl qt	1 fl qt = 0.946 L
milliliter (mL) = 0.001 L = 1 cm^3	1 mL = 0.034 fl oz	1 fl oz = 29.574 mL
microliter (μL) = 0.000 001 L		
Mass		*Equivalent weight at Earth's surface
kilogram (kg) = 1,000 g	1 kg = 2.205 lb*	1 lb* = 0.454 kg
gram (g) = 1,000 mg	1 g = 0.035 oz*	1 oz* = 28.350 g
milligram (mg) = 0.001 g		
microgram (μg) = 0.000 001 g		

Appendix

Scientific Methods

The ways in which scientists answer questions and solve problems are called **scientific methods.** The same steps are often used by scientists as they look for answers. However, there is more than one way to use these steps. Scientists may use all of the steps or just some of the steps during an investigation. They may even repeat some of the steps. The goal of using scientific methods is to come up with reliable answers and solutions.

Six Steps of Scientific Methods

1 Ask a Question Good questions come from careful **observations.** You make observations by using your senses to gather information. Sometimes, you may use instruments, such as microscopes and telescopes, to extend the range of your senses. As you observe the natural world, you will discover that you have many more questions than answers. These questions drive investigations.

Questions beginning with *what, why, how,* and *when* are important in focusing an investigation. Here is an example of a question that could lead to an investigation.

Question: How does acid rain affect plant growth?

2 Form a Hypothesis After you ask a question, you need to form a **hypothesis.** A hypothesis is a clear statement of what you expect the answer to your question to be. Your hypothesis will represent your best "educated guess" based on what you have observed and what you already know. A good hypothesis is testable. Otherwise, the investigation can go no further. Here is a hypothesis based on the question, "How does acid rain affect plant growth?"

Hypothesis: Acid rain slows plant growth.

The hypothesis can lead to predictions. A prediction is what you think the outcome of your experiment or data collection will be. Predictions are usually stated in an if-then format. Here is a sample prediction for the hypothesis that acid rain slows plant growth.

Prediction: If a plant is watered with only acid rain (which has a pH of 4), then the plant will grow at half its normal rate.

3 Test the Hypothesis After you have formed a hypothesis and made a prediction, your hypothesis should be tested. One way to test a hypothesis is with a controlled experiment. A **controlled experiment** tests only one factor at a time. In an experiment to test the effect of acid rain on plant growth, the **control group** would be watered with normal rain water. The **experimental group** would be watered with acid rain. All of the plants should receive the same amount of sunlight and water each day. The air temperature should be the same for all groups. However, the acidity of the water will be a variable. In fact, any factor that is different from one group to another is a **variable.** If your hypothesis is correct, then the acidity of the water and plant growth are *dependant variables.* The amount a plant grows is dependent on the acidity of the water. However, the amount of water each plant receives and the amount of sunlight each plant receives are *independent variables.* Either of these factors could change without affecting the other factor.

Sometimes, the nature of an investigation makes a controlled experiment impossible. For example, the Earth's core is surrounded by thousands of meters of rock. Under such circumstances, a hypothesis may be tested by making detailed observations.

4 Analyze the Results After you have completed your experiments, made your observations, and collected your data, you must analyze all the information you have gathered. Tables and graphs are often used in this step to organize the data.

5 Draw Conclusions

After analyzing your data, you can determine if your results support your hypothesis. If your hypothesis is supported, you (or others) might want to repeat the observations or experiments to verify your results. If your hypothesis is not supported by the data, you may have to check your procedure for errors. You may even have to reject your hypothesis and make a new one. If you cannot draw a conclusion from your results, you may have to try the investigation again or carry out further observations or experiments.

6 Communicate Results

After any scientific investigation, you should report your results. By preparing a written or oral report, you let others know what you have learned. They may repeat your investigation to see if they get the same results. Your report may even lead to another question and then to another investigation.

Scientific Methods in Action

Scientific methods contain loops in which several steps may be repeated over and over again. In some cases, certain steps are unnecessary. Thus, there is not a "straight line" of steps. For example, sometimes scientists find that testing one hypothesis raises new questions and new hypotheses to be tested. And sometimes, testing the hypothesis leads directly to a conclusion. Furthermore, the steps in scientific methods are not always used in the same order. Follow the steps in the diagram, and see how many different directions scientific methods can take you.

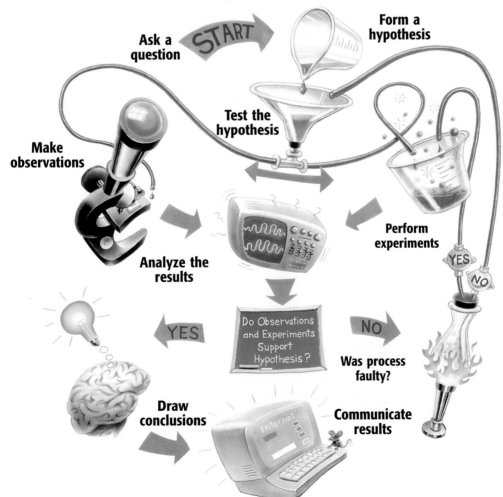

Making Charts and Graphs

Pie Charts

A pie chart shows how each group of data relates to all of the data. Each part of the circle forming the chart represents a category of the data. The entire circle represents all of the data. For example, a biologist studying a hardwood forest in Wisconsin found that there were five different types of trees. The data table at right summarizes the biologist's findings.

Wisconsin Hardwood Trees	
Type of tree	**Number found**
Oak	600
Maple	750
Beech	300
Birch	1,200
Hickory	150
Total	3,000

How to Make a Pie Chart

1 To make a pie chart of these data, first find the percentage of each type of tree. Divide the number of trees of each type by the total number of trees, and multiply by 100.

$$\frac{600 \text{ oak}}{3,000 \text{ trees}} \times 100 = 20\%$$

$$\frac{750 \text{ maple}}{3,000 \text{ trees}} \times 100 = 25\%$$

$$\frac{300 \text{ beech}}{3,000 \text{ trees}} \times 100 = 10\%$$

$$\frac{1,200 \text{ birch}}{3,000 \text{ trees}} \times 100 = 40\%$$

$$\frac{150 \text{ hickory}}{3,000 \text{ trees}} \times 100 = 5\%$$

2 Now, determine the size of the wedges that make up the pie chart. Multiply each percentage by 360°. Remember that a circle contains 360°.

$20\% \times 360° = 72°$ $25\% \times 360° = 90°$

$10\% \times 360° = 36°$ $40\% \times 360° = 144°$

$5\% \times 360° = 18°$

3 Check that the sum of the percentages is 100 and the sum of the degrees is 360.

$20\% + 25\% + 10\% + 40\% + 5\% = 100\%$

$72° + 90° + 36° + 144° + 18° = 360°$

4 Use a compass to draw a circle and mark the center of the circle.

5 Then, use a protractor to draw angles of 72°, 90°, 36°, 144°, and 18° in the circle.

6 Finally, label each part of the chart, and choose an appropriate title.

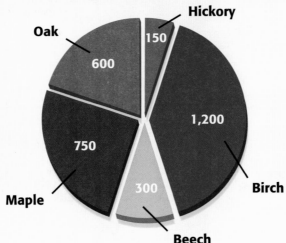

A Community of Wisconsin Hardwood Trees

Line Graphs

Line graphs are most often used to demonstrate continuous change. For example, Mr. Smith's students analyzed the population records for their hometown, Appleton, between 1900 and 2000. Examine the data at right.

Because the year and the population change, they are the *variables*. The population is determined by, or dependent on, the year. Therefore, the population is called the **dependent variable,** and the year is called the **independent variable.** Each set of data is called a **data pair.** To prepare a line graph, you must first organize data pairs into a table like the one at right.

Population of Appleton, 1900–2000	
Year	Population
1900	1,800
1920	2,500
1940	3,200
1960	3,900
1980	4,600
2000	5,300

How to Make a Line Graph

1. Place the independent variable along the horizontal (*x*) axis. Place the dependent variable along the vertical (*y*) axis.

2. Label the *x*-axis "Year" and the *y*-axis "Population." Look at your largest and smallest values for the population. For the *y*-axis, determine a scale that will provide enough space to show these values. You must use the same scale for the entire length of the axis. Next, find an appropriate scale for the *x*-axis.

3. Choose reasonable starting points for each axis.

4. Plot the data pairs as accurately as possible.

5. Choose a title that accurately represents the data.

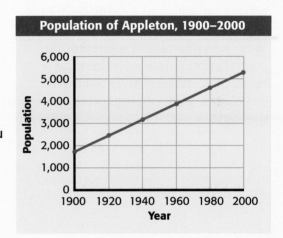

How to Determine Slope

Slope is the ratio of the change in the *y*-value to the change in the *x*-value, or "rise over run."

1. Choose two points on the line graph. For example, the population of Appleton in 2000 was 5,300 people. Therefore, you can define point *a* as (2000, 5,300). In 1900, the population was 1,800 people. You can define point *b* as (1900, 1,800).

2. Find the change in the *y*-value.
(*y* at point *a*) − (*y* at point *b*) =
5,300 people − 1,800 people =
3,500 people

3. Find the change in the *x*-value.
(*x* at point *a*) − (*x* at point *b*) =
2000 − 1900 = 100 years

4. Calculate the slope of the graph by dividing the change in *y* by the change in *x*.

$$slope = \frac{change\ in\ y}{change\ in\ x}$$

$$slope = \frac{3,500\ people}{100\ years}$$

$$slope = 35\ people\ per\ year$$

In this example, the population in Appleton increased by a fixed amount each year. The graph of these data is a straight line. Therefore, the relationship is **linear.** When the graph of a set of data is not a straight line, the relationship is **nonlinear.**

Using Algebra to Determine Slope

The equation in step 4 may also be arranged to be

$$y = kx$$

where y represents the change in the y-value, k represents the slope, and x represents the change in the x-value.

$$slope = \frac{change\ in\ y}{change\ in\ x}$$

$$k = \frac{y}{x}$$

$$k \times x = \frac{y \times x}{x}$$

$$kx = y$$

Bar Graphs

Bar graphs are used to demonstrate change that is not continuous. These graphs can be used to indicate trends when the data cover a long period of time. A meteorologist gathered the precipitation data shown here for Hartford, Connecticut, for April 1–15, 1996, and used a bar graph to represent the data.

Precipitation in Hartford, Connecticut April 1–15, 1996			
Date	Precipitation (cm)	Date	Precipitation (cm)
April 1	0.5	April 9	0.25
April 2	1.25	April 10	0.0
April 3	0.0	April 11	1.0
April 4	0.0	April 12	0.0
April 5	0.0	April 13	0.25
April 6	0.0	April 14	0.0
April 7	0.0	April 15	6.50
April 8	1.75		

How to Make a Bar Graph

1 Use an appropriate scale and a reasonable starting point for each axis.

2 Label the axes, and plot the data.

3 Choose a title that accurately represents the data.

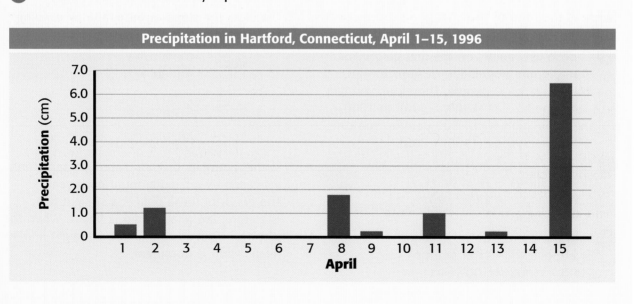

Math Refresher

Science requires an understanding of many math concepts. The following pages will help you review some important math skills.

Averages

An **average**, or **mean**, simplifies a set of numbers into a single number that *approximates* the value of the set.

> **Example:** Find the average of the following set of numbers: 5, 4, 7, and 8.

Step 1: Find the sum.
$$5 + 4 + 7 + 8 = 24$$

Step 2: Divide the sum by the number of numbers in your set. Because there are four numbers in this example, divide the sum by 4.
$$\frac{24}{4} = 6$$

The average, or mean, is **6.**

Ratios

A **ratio** is a comparison between numbers, and it is usually written as a fraction.

> **Example:** Find the ratio of thermometers to students if you have 36 thermometers and 48 students in your class.

Step 1: Make the ratio.
$$\frac{36 \text{ thermometers}}{48 \text{ students}}$$

Step 2: Reduce the fraction to its simplest form.
$$\frac{36}{48} = \frac{36 \div 12}{48 \div 12} = \frac{3}{4}$$

The ratio of thermometers to students is **3 to 4,** or $\frac{3}{4}$. The ratio may also be written in the form 3:4.

Proportions

A **proportion** is an equation that states that two ratios are equal.
$$\frac{3}{1} = \frac{12}{4}$$

To solve a proportion, first multiply across the equal sign. This is called *cross-multiplication*. If you know three of the quantities in a proportion, you can use cross-multiplication to find the fourth.

> **Example:** Imagine that you are making a scale model of the solar system for your science project. The diameter of Jupiter is 11.2 times the diameter of the Earth. If you are using a plastic-foam ball that has a diameter of 2 cm to represent the Earth, what must the diameter of the ball representing Jupiter be?
> $$\frac{11.2}{1} = \frac{x}{2 \text{ cm}}$$

Step 1: Cross-multiply.
$$\frac{11.2}{1} \diagdown \frac{x}{2}$$
$$11.2 \times 2 = x \times 1$$

Step 2: Multiply.
$$22.4 = x \times 1$$

Step 3: Isolate the variable by dividing both sides by 1.
$$x = \frac{22.4}{1}$$
$$x = 22.4 \text{ cm}$$

You will need to use a ball that has a diameter of **22.4** cm to represent Jupiter.

Percentages

A **percentage** is a ratio of a given number to 100.

> **Example:** What is 85% of 40?

Step 1: Rewrite the percentage by moving the decimal point two places to the left.

0.85

Step 2: Multiply the decimal by the number that you are calculating the percentage of.

0.85 × 40 = 34

85% of 40 is **34.**

Decimals

To **add** or **subtract decimals,** line up the digits vertically so that the decimal points line up. Then, add or subtract the columns from right to left. Carry or borrow numbers as necessary.

> **Example:** Add the following numbers: 3.1415 and 2.96.

Step 1: Line up the digits vertically so that the decimal points line up.

3.1415
+ 2.96

Step 2: Add the columns from right to left, and carry when necessary.

```
 1 1
 3.1415
+ 2.96
-------
 6.1015
```

The sum is **6.1015.**

Fractions

Numbers tell you how many; **fractions** tell you *how much of a whole*.

> **Example:** Your class has 24 plants. Your teacher instructs you to put 5 plants in a shady spot. What fraction of the plants in your class will you put in a shady spot?

Step 1: In the denominator, write the total number of parts in the whole.

$$\frac{?}{24}$$

Step 2: In the numerator, write the number of parts of the whole that are being considered.

$$\frac{5}{24}$$

So, $\frac{5}{24}$ of the plants will be in the shade.

Reducing Fractions

It is usually best to express a fraction in its simplest form. Expressing a fraction in its simplest form is called *reducing* a fraction.

> **Example:** Reduce the fraction $\frac{30}{45}$ to its simplest form.

Step 1: Find the largest whole number that will divide evenly into both the numerator and denominator. This number is called the *greatest common factor* (GCF).

Factors of the numerator 30:
   1, 2, 3, 5, 6, 10, **15,** 30

Factors of the denominator 45:
   1, 3, 5, 9, **15,** 45

Step 2: Divide both the numerator and the denominator by the GCF, which in this case is 15.

$$\frac{30}{45} = \frac{30 \div 15}{45 \div 15} = \frac{2}{3}$$

Thus, $\frac{30}{45}$ reduced to its simplest form is $\frac{2}{3}$.

Adding and Subtracting Fractions

To **add** or **subtract fractions** that have the **same denominator,** simply add or subtract the numerators.

Examples:
$$\frac{3}{5} + \frac{1}{5} = ? \text{ and } \frac{3}{4} - \frac{1}{4} = ?$$

Step 1: Add or subtract the numerators.
$$\frac{3}{5} + \frac{1}{5} = \frac{4}{} \text{ and } \frac{3}{4} - \frac{1}{4} = \frac{2}{}$$

Step 2: Write the sum or difference over the denominator.
$$\frac{3}{5} + \frac{1}{5} = \frac{4}{5} \text{ and } \frac{3}{4} - \frac{1}{4} = \frac{2}{4}$$

Step 3: If necessary, reduce the fraction to its simplest form.

$\frac{4}{5}$ cannot be reduced, and $\frac{2}{4} = \frac{1}{2}$.

To **add** or **subtract fractions** that have **different denominators,** first find the least common denominator (LCD).

Examples:
$$\frac{1}{2} + \frac{1}{6} = ? \text{ and } \frac{3}{4} - \frac{2}{3} = ?$$

Step 1: Write the equivalent fractions that have a common denominator.
$$\frac{3}{6} + \frac{1}{6} = ? \text{ and } \frac{9}{12} - \frac{8}{12} = ?$$

Step 2: Add or subtract the fractions.
$$\frac{3}{6} + \frac{1}{6} = \frac{4}{6} \text{ and } \frac{9}{12} - \frac{8}{12} = \frac{1}{12}$$

Step 3: If necessary, reduce the fraction to its simplest form.

The fraction $\frac{4}{6} = \frac{2}{3}$, and $\frac{1}{12}$ cannot be reduced.

Multiplying Fractions

To **multiply fractions,** multiply the numerators and the denominators together, and then reduce the fraction to its simplest form.

Example:
$$\frac{5}{9} \times \frac{7}{10} = ?$$

Step 1: Multiply the numerators and denominators.
$$\frac{5}{9} \times \frac{7}{10} = \frac{5 \times 7}{9 \times 10} = \frac{35}{90}$$

Step 2: Reduce the fraction.
$$\frac{35}{90} = \frac{35 \div 5}{90 \div 5} = \frac{7}{18}$$

Dividing Fractions

To **divide fractions,** first rewrite the divisor (the number you divide by) upside down. This number is called the *reciprocal* of the divisor. Then multiply and reduce if necessary.

Example:
$$\frac{5}{8} \div \frac{3}{2} = ?$$

Step 1: Rewrite the divisor as its reciprocal.
$$\frac{3}{2} \rightarrow \frac{2}{3}$$

Step 2: Multiply the fractions.
$$\frac{5}{8} \times \frac{2}{3} = \frac{5 \times 2}{8 \times 3} = \frac{10}{24}$$

Step 3: Reduce the fraction.
$$\frac{10}{24} = \frac{10 \div 2}{24 \div 2} = \frac{5}{12}$$

Appendix

Scientific Notation

Scientific notation is a short way of representing very large and very small numbers without writing all of the place-holding zeros.

> **Example:** Write 653,000,000 in scientific notation.

Step 1: Write the number without the place-holding zeros.

653

Step 2: Place the decimal point after the first digit.

6.53

Step 3: Find the exponent by counting the number of places that you moved the decimal point.

6.53000000

The decimal point was moved eight places to the left. Therefore, the exponent of 10 is positive 8. If you had moved the decimal point to the right, the exponent would be negative.

Step 4: Write the number in scientific notation.

$$6.53 \times 10^8$$

Area

Area is the number of square units needed to cover the surface of an object.

> **Formulas:**
>
> *area of a square = side × side*
> *area of a rectangle = length × width*
> *area of a triangle = $\frac{1}{2}$ × base × height*
>
> **Examples:** Find the areas.

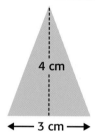

Triangle

area = $\frac{1}{2}$ × base × height

area = $\frac{1}{2}$ × 3 cm × 4 cm

*area = **6 cm²***

4 cm

3 cm

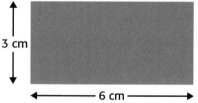

Rectangle

area = length × width

area = 6 cm × 3 cm

*area = **18 cm²***

3 cm

6 cm

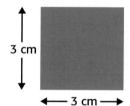

Square

area = side × side

area = 3 cm × 3 cm

*area = **9 cm²***

3 cm

3 cm

Volume

Volume is the amount of space that something occupies.

> **Formulas:**
>
> *volume of a cube =*
> *side × side × side*
>
> *volume of a prism =*
> *area of base × height*
>
> **Examples:**
>
> Find the volume of the solids.

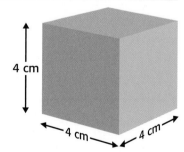

Cube

volume = side × side × side
volume = 4 cm × 4 cm × 4 cm
*volume = **64 cm³***

4 cm

4 cm   4 cm

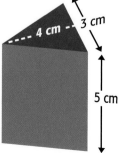

3 cm

4 cm

5 cm

Prism

volume = area of base × height
volume = (area of triangle) × height
volume = ($\frac{1}{2}$ × 3 cm × 4 cm) × 5 cm
volume = 6 cm² × 5 cm
*volume = **30 cm³***

Physical Science Laws and Principles

Law of Conservation of Mass

Mass cannot be created or destroyed during ordinary chemical or physical changes.

The total mass in a closed system is always the same no matter how many physical changes or chemical reactions occur.

Law of Conservation of Energy

Energy can be neither created nor destroyed.

The total amount of energy in a closed system is always the same. Energy can be changed from one form to another, but all of the different forms of energy in a system always add up to the same total amount of energy no matter how many energy conversions occur.

Law of Universal Gravitation

All objects in the universe attract each other by a force called *gravity*. The size of the force depends on the masses of the objects and the distance between the objects.

The first part of the law explains why lifting a bowling ball is much harder than lifting a marble. Because the bowling ball has a much larger mass than the marble does, the amount of gravity between the Earth and the bowling ball is greater than the amount of gravity between the Earth and the marble.

The second part of the law explains why a satellite can remain in orbit around the Earth. The satellite is carefully placed at a distance great enough to prevent the Earth's gravity from immediately pulling the satellite down but small enough to prevent the satellite from completely escaping the Earth's gravity and wandering off into space.

Newton's Laws of Motion

Newton's first law of motion states that an object at rest remains at rest and an object in motion remains in motion at constant speed and in a straight line unless acted on by an unbalanced force.

The first part of the law explains why a football will remain on a tee until it is kicked off or until a gust of wind blows it off.

The second part of the law explains why a bike rider will continue moving forward after the bike comes to an abrupt stop. Gravity and the friction of the sidewalk will eventually stop the rider.

Newton's second law of motion states that the acceleration of an object depends on the mass of the object and the amount of force applied.

The first part of the law explains why the acceleration of a 4 kg bowling ball will be greater than the acceleration of a 6 kg bowling ball if the same force is applied to both balls.

The second part of the law explains why the acceleration of a bowling ball will be larger if a larger force is applied to the bowling ball.

The relationship of acceleration (a) to mass (m) and force (F) can be expressed mathematically by the following equation:

$$acceleration = \frac{force}{mass}, \text{ or } a = \frac{F}{m}$$

This equation is often rearranged to the form

$$force = mass \times acceleration, \text{ or } F = m \times a$$

Newton's third law of motion states that whenever one object exerts a force on a second object, the second object exerts an equal and opposite force on the first.

This law explains that a runner is able to move forward because of the equal and opposite force that the ground exerts on the runner's foot after each step.

Law of Reflection

The law of reflection states that the angle of incidence is equal to the angle of reflection. This law explains why light reflects off a surface at the same angle that the light strikes the surface.

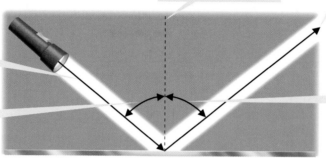

A line perpendicular to the mirror's surface is called the *normal.*

The beam of light reflected off the mirror is called the *reflected beam.*

The beam of light traveling toward the mirror is called the *incident beam.*

The angle between the incident beam and the normal is called the *angle of incidence.*

The angle between the reflected beam and the normal is called the *angle of reflection.*

Charles's Law

Charles's law states that for a fixed amount of gas at a constant pressure, the volume of the gas increases as the temperature of the gas increases. Likewise, the volume of the gas decreases as the temperature of the gas decreases.

If a basketball that was inflated indoors is left outside on a cold winter day, the air particles inside the ball will move more slowly. They will hit the sides of the basketball less often and with less force. The ball will get smaller as the volume of the air decreases.

Boyle's Law

Boyle's law states that for a fixed amount of gas at a constant temperature, the volume of a gas increases as the pressure of the gas decreases. Likewise, the volume of a gas decreases as its pressure increases.

If an inflated balloon is pulled down to the bottom of a swimming pool, the pressure of the water on the balloon increases. The pressure of the air particles inside the balloon must increase to match that of the water outside, so the volume of the air inside the balloon decreases.

Pascal's Principle

Pascal's principle states that a change in pressure at any point in an enclosed fluid will be transmitted equally to all parts of that fluid.

When a mechanic uses a hydraulic jack to raise an automobile off the ground, he or she increases the pressure on the fluid in the jack by pushing on the jack handle. The pressure is transmitted equally to all parts of the fluid-filled jacking system. As fluid presses the jack plate against the frame of the car, the car is lifed off the ground.

Archimedes' Principle

Archimedes' principle states that the buoyant force on an object in a fluid is equal to the weight of the volume of fluid that the object displaces.

A person floating in a swimming pool displaces 20 L of water. The weight of that volume of water is about 200 N. Therefore, the buoyant force on the person is 200 N.

Bernoulli's Principle

Bernoulli's principle states that as the speed of a moving fluid increases, the fluid's pressure decreases.

The lift on an airplane wing or on a Frisbee® can be explained in part by using Bernoulli's principle. Because of the shape of the Frisbee, the air moving over the top of the Frisbee must travel farther than the air below the Frisbee in the same amount of time. In other words, the air above the Frisbee is moving faster than the air below it. This faster-moving air above the Frisbee exerts less pressure than the slower-moving air below it does. The resulting increased pressure below exerts an upward force and pushes the Frisbee up.

Useful Equations

Average speed

$$average\ speed = \frac{total\ distance}{total\ time}$$

Example: A bicycle messenger traveled a distance of 136 km in 8 h. What was the messenger's average speed?

$$\frac{136\ km}{8\ h} = 17\ km/h$$

The messenger's average speed was **17 km/h.**

Average acceleration

$$\frac{average}{acceleration} = \frac{final\ velocity - starting\ velocity}{time\ it\ takes\ to\ change\ velocity}$$

Example: Calculate the average acceleration of an Olympic 100 m dash sprinter who reaches a velocity of 20 m/s south at the finish line. The race was in a straight line and lasted 10 s.

$$\frac{20\ m/s - 0\ m/s}{10s} = 2\ m/s/s$$

The sprinter's average acceleration is **2 m/s/s south.**

Net force

Forces in the Same Direction
When forces are in the same direction, add the forces together to determine the net force.

Example: Calculate the net force on a stalled car that is being pushed by two people. One person is pushing with a force of 13 N northwest, and the other person is pushing with a force of 8 N in the same direction.

$$13\ N + 8\ N = 21\ N$$

The net force is **21 N northwest.**

Forces in Opposite Directions
When forces are in opposite directions, subtract the smaller force from the larger force to determine the net force. The net force will be in the direction of the larger force.

Example: Calculate the net force on a rope that is being pulled on each end. One person is pulling on one end of the rope with a force of 12 N south. Another person is pulling on the opposite end of the rope with a force of 7 N north.

$$12\ N - 7\ N = 5\ N$$

The net force is **5 N south.**

Work

Work is done by exerting a force through a distance. Work has units of joules (J), which are equivalent to Newton-meters.

$$Work = F \times d$$

Example: Calculate the amount of work done by a man who lifts a 100 N toddler 1.5 m off the floor.

$Work = 100 \text{ N} \times 1.5 \text{ m} = 150 \text{ N} \bullet \text{m} = 150 \text{ J}$

The man did **150 J** of work.

Power

Power is the rate at which work is done. Power is measured in watts (W), which are equivalent to joules per second.

$$P = \frac{Work}{t}$$

Example: Calculate the power of a weightlifter who raises a 300 N barbell 2.1 m off the floor in 1.25 s.

$Work = 300 \text{ N} \times 2.1 \text{ m} = 630 \text{ N} \bullet \text{m} = 630 \text{ J}$

$P = \frac{630 \text{ J}}{1.25 \text{ s}} = \frac{504 \text{ J}}{\text{s}} = 504 \text{ W}$

The weightlifter has **504 W** of power.

Pressure

Pressure is the force exerted over a given area. The SI unit for pressure is the pascal (Pa).

$$pressure = \frac{force}{area}$$

Example: Calculate the pressure of the air in a soccer ball if the air exerts a force of 25,000 N over an area of 0.15 m².

$pressure = \frac{25,000 \text{ N}}{0.15 \text{ m}^2} = \frac{167,000 \text{ N}}{\text{m}^2} = 167,000 \text{ Pa}$

The pressure of the air inside the soccer ball is **167,000 Pa.**

Density

$$density = \frac{mass}{volume}$$

Example: Calculate the density of a sponge that has a mass of 10 g and a volume of 40 cm³.

$$\frac{10 \text{ g}}{40 \text{ cm}^3} = \frac{0.25 \text{ g}}{\text{cm}^3}$$

The density of the sponge is $\frac{0.25 \text{ g}}{\text{cm}^3}$.

Concentration

$$concentration = \frac{mass \ of \ solute}{volume \ of \ solvent}$$

Example: Calculate the concentration of a solution in which 10 g of sugar is dissolved in 125 mL of water.

$$\frac{10 \text{ g of sugar}}{125 \text{ mL of water}} = \frac{0.08 \text{ g}}{\text{mL}}$$

The concentration of this solution is $\frac{0.08 \text{ g}}{\text{mL}}$.

Glossary

A

absolute zero the temperature at which molecular energy is at a minimum (0 K on the Kelvin scale or -273.16°C on the Celsius scale) (161)

acceleration (ak SEL uhr AY shuhn) the rate at which velocity changes over time; an object accelerates if its speed, direction, or both change (7)

Archimedes' principle (AHR kuh MEE DEEZ PRIN suh puhl) the principle that states that the buoyant force on an object in a fluid is an upward force equal to the weight of the volume of fluid that the object displaces (72)

atmospheric pressure the pressure caused by the weight of the atmosphere (67)

B

Bernoulli's principle (ber NOO leez PRIN suh puhl) the principle that states that the pressure in a fluid decreases as the fluid's velocity increases (78)

buoyant force (BOY uhnt FAWRS) the upward force that keeps an object immersed in or floating on a liquid (72)

C

change of state the change of a substance from one physical state to another (173)

compound machine a machine made of more than one simple machine (112)

convection the transfer of thermal energy by the circulation or movement of a liquid or gas (167)

D

drag a force parallel to the velocity of the flow; it opposes the direction of an aircraft and, in combination with thrust, determines the speed (81)

E

energy the capacity to do work (10)

energy conversion a change from one form of energy to another (132)

F

fluid a nonsolid state of matter in which the atoms or molecules are free to move past each other, as in a gas or liquid (66)

force a push or a pull exerted on an object in order to change the motion of the object; force has size and direction (10)

fossil fuel a nonrenewable energy resource formed from the remains of organisms that lived long ago (142)

free fall the motion of a body when only the force of gravity is acting on the body (39)

friction a force that opposes motion between two surfaces that are in contact (14)

G

gravity a force of attraction between objects that is due to their masses (20)

H

heat the energy transferred between objects that are at different temperatures (164)

heat engine a machine that transforms heat into mechanical energy, or work (179)

I

inclined plane a simple machine that is a straight, slanted surface, which facilitates the raising of loads; a ramp (110)

inertia (in UHR shuh) the tendency of an object to resist being moved or, if the object is moving, to resist a change in speed or direction until an outside force acts on the object (46)

insulation a substance that reduces the transfer of electricity, heat, or sound (177)

J

joule the unit used to express energy; equivalent to the amount of work done by a force of 1 N acting through a distance of 1 m in the direction of the force (symbol, J) (97)

K

kinetic energy (ki NET ik EN uhr jee) the energy of an object that is due to the object's motion (11)

L

law of conservation of energy the law that states that energy cannot be created or destroyed but can be changed from one form to another (139)

lever a simple machine that consists of a bar that pivots at a fixed point called a *fulcrum* (106)

lift an upward force on an object that moves in a fluid (79)

M

machine a device that helps do work by either overcoming a force or changing the direction of the applied force (100)

mass a measure of the amount of matter in an object (24)

mechanical advantage a number that tells how many times a machine multiplies force (103)

mechanical efficiency (muh KAN i kuhl e FISH uhn see) the ratio of output to input of energy or of power; it can be calculated by dividing work output by work input (104)

mechanical energy the amount of work an object can do because of the object's kinetic and potential energies (127)

momentum (moh MEN tuhm) a quantity defined as the product of the mass and velocity of an object (52)

motion an object's change in position relative to a reference point (4)

N

net force the combination of all of the forces acting on an object (11)

newton the SI unit for force (symbol, N) (10)

nonrenewable resource a resource that forms at a rate that is much slower than the rate at which it is consumed (142)

P

pascal the SI unit of pressure (symbol, Pa) (66)

Pascal's principle the principle that states that a fluid in equilibrium contained in a vessel exerts a pressure of equal intensity in all directions (82)

potential energy the energy that an object has because of the position, shape, or condition of the object (126)

power the rate at which work is done or energy is transformed (98)

pressure the amount of force exerted per unit area of a surface (66)

projectile motion (proh JEK tuhl MOH shuhn) the curved path that an object follows when thrown, launched, or otherwise projected near the surface of Earth (41)

pulley a simple machine that consists of a wheel over which a rope, chain, or wire passes (108)

R

radiation the transfer of energy as electromagnetic waves (168)

renewable resource a natural resource that can be replaced at the same rate at which the resource is consumed (145)

S

screw a simple machine that consists of an inclined plane wrapped around a cylinder (111)

specific heat the quantity of heat required to raise a unit mass of homogeneous material 1 K or 1°C in a specified way given constant pressure and volume (169)

speed the distance traveled divided by the time interval during which the motion occurred (5)

states of matter the physical forms of matter, which include solid, liquid, and gas (172)

T

temperature a measure of how hot (or cold) something is; specifically, a measure of the average kinetic energy of the particles in an object (158)

terminal velocity the constant velocity of a falling object when the force of air resistance is equal in magnitude and opposite in direction to the force of gravity (38)

thermal conduction the transfer of energy as heat through a material (282)

thermal conductor a material through which energy can be transferred as heat (167)

thermal energy the kinetic energy of a substance's atoms (165)

thermal expansion an increase in the size of a substance in response to an increase in the temperature of the substance (46)

thermal insulator a material that reduces or prevents the transfer of heat (167)

thermal pollution a temperature increase in a body of water that is caused by human activity and that has a harmful effect on water quality and on the ability of that body of water to support life (182)

thrust the pushing or pulling force exerted by the engine of an aircraft or rocket (80)

Glossary

V

velocity (vuh LAHS uh tee) the speed of an object in a particular direction (6)

W

watt the unit used to express power; equivalent to joules per second (symbol, W) (98)

wedge a simple machine that is made up of two inclined planes and that moves; often used for cutting (111)

weight a measure of the gravitational force exerted on an object; its value can change with the location of the object in the universe (24)

wheel and axle a simple machine consisting of two circular objects of different sizes; the wheel is the larger of the two circular objects (109)

work the transfer of energy to an object by using a force that causes the object to move in the direction of the force (94)

work input the work done on a machine; the product of the input force and the distance through which the force is exerted (101)

work output the work done by a machine; the product of the output force and the distance through which the force is exerted (101)

Glossary

Spanish Glossary

A

absolute zero/cero absoluto la temperatura a la que la energía molecular es mínima (0 K en la escala de Kelvin ó −273.16°C en la escala de Celsius) (161)

acceleration/aceleración la tasa a la que la velocidad cambia con el tiempo; un objeto acelera si su rapidez cambia, si su dirección cambia, o si tanto su rapidez como su dirección cambian (7)

Archimedes' principle/principio de Arquímedes el principio que establece que la fuerza flotante de un objeto que está en un fluido es una fuerza ascendente cuya magnitud es igual al peso del volumen del fluido que el objeto desplaza (72)

atmospheric pressure/presión atmosférica la presión producida por el peso de la atmósfera (67)

B

Bernoulli's principle/principio de Bernoulli el principio que establece que la presión de un fluido disminuye a medida que la velocidad del fluido aumenta (78)

buoyant force/fuerza boyante la fuerza ascendente que hace que un objeto se mantenga sumergido en un líquido o flotando en él (72)

C

change of state/cambio de estado el cambio de una substancia de un estado físico a otro (173)

compound machine/máquina compuesta una máquina hecha de más de una máquina simple (112)

convection/convección la transferencia de energía térmica mediante la circulación o el movimiento de un líquido o gas (167)

D

drag/resistencia aerodinámica una fuerza paralela a la velocidad del flujo; se opone a la dirección de un avión y, en combinación con el empuje, determina la velocidad del avión (81)

E

energy/energía la capacidad de realizar un trabajo (10)

energy conversion/transformación de energía un cambio de un tipo de energía a otro (132)

F

fluid/fluido un estado no sólido de la materia en el que los átomos o moléculas tienen libertad de movimiento, como en el caso de un gas o un líquido (66)

force/fuerza una acción de empuje o atracción que se ejerce sobre un objeto con el fin de cambiar su movimiento; la fuerza tiene magnitud y dirección (10)

fossil fuel/combustible fósil un recurso energético no renovable formado a partir de los restos de organismos que vivieron hace mucho tiempo (142)

free fall/caída libre el movimiento de un cuerpo cuando la única fuerza que actúa sobre él es la fuerza de gravedad (39)

friction/fricción una fuerza que se opone al movimiento entre dos superficies que están en contacto (14)

G

gravity/gravedad una fuerza de atracción entre dos objetos debido a sus masas (20)

H

heat/calor la transferencia de energía entre objetos que están a temperaturas diferentes (164)

heat engine/motor térmico una máquina que transforma el calor en energía mecánica, o trabajo (179)

I

inclined plane/plano inclinado una máquina simple que es una superficie recta e inclinada, que facilita el levantamiento de cargas; una rampa (110)

inertia/inercia la tendencia de un objeto a no moverse o, si el objeto se está moviendo, la tendencia a resistir un cambio en su rapidez o dirección hasta que una fuerza externa actúe en el objeto (46)

insulation/aislante una substancia que reduce la transferencia de electricidad, calor o sonido (177)

J

joule/joule la unidad que se usa para expresar energía; equivale a la cantidad de trabajo realizada por una fuerza de 1 N que actúa a través de una distancia de 1 m en la dirección de la fuerza (símbolo: J) (97)

K

kinetic energy/energía cinética la energía de un objeto debido al movimiento del objeto (11)

L

law of conservation of energy/ley de la conservación de la energía la ley que establece que la energía ni se crea ni se destruye, sólo se transforma de una forma a otra (139)

lever/palanca una máquina simple formada por una barra que gira en un punto fijo llamado fulcro (106)

lift/propulsión una fuerza hacia arriba en un objeto que se mueve en un fluido (79)

M

machine/máquina un aparato que ayuda a realizar un trabajo, ya sea venciendo una fuerza o cambiando la dirección de la fuerza aplicada (100)

mass/masa una medida de la cantidad de materia que tiene un objeto (24)

mechanical advantage/ventaja mecánica un número que dice cuántas veces una máquina multiplica una fuerza (103)

mechanical efficiency/eficiencia mecánica la relación entre la entrada y la salida de energía o potencia; se calcula dividiendo la salida de trabajo por la entrada de trabajo (104)

mechanical energy/energía mecánica la cantidad de trabajo que un objeto realiza debido a las energías cinética y potencial del objeto (127)

momentum/momento una cantidad que se define como el producto de la masa de un objeto por su velocidad (52)

motion/movimiento el cambio en la posición de un objeto respecto a un punto de referencia (4)

N

net force/fuerza neta la combinación de todas las fuerzas que actúan sobre un objeto (11)

newton/newton la unidad de fuerza del sistema internacional de unidades (símbolo: N) (10)

nonrenewable resource/recurso no renovable un recurso que se forma a una tasa que es mucho más lenta que la tasa a la que se consume (142)

P

pascal/pascal la unidad de presión del sistema internacional de unidades (símbolo: Pa) (66)

Pascal's principle/principio de Pascal el principio que establece que un fluido en equilibro que esté contenido en un recipiente ejerce una presión de igual intensidad en todas las direcciones (82)

potential energy/energía potencial la energía que tiene un objeto debido a su posición, forma o condición (126)

power/potencia la tasa a la que se realiza un trabajo o a la que se transforma la energía (98)

pressure/presión la cantidad de fuerza ejercida en una superficie por unidad de área (66)

projectile motion/movimiento proyectil la trayectoria curva que sigue un objeto cuando es aventado, lanzado o proyectado de cualquier otra manera cerca de la superficie de la Tierra (41)

pulley/polea una máquina simple formada por una rueda sobre la cual pasa una cuerda, cadena o cable (108)

R

radiation/radiación la transferencia de energía en forma de ondas electromagnéticas (168)

renewable resource/recurso renovable un recurso natural que puede reemplazarse a la misma tasa a la que se consume (145)

S

screw/tornillo una máquina simple formada por un plano inclinado enrollado a un cilindro (111)

specific heat/calor específico la cantidad de calor que se requiere para aumentar una unidad de masa de un material homogéneo 1 K ó 1°C de una manera especificada, dados un volumen y una presión constantes (169)

speed/rapidez la distancia que un objeto se desplaza dividida entre el intervalo de tiempo durante el cual ocurrió el movimiento (5)

states of matter/estados de la material las formas físicas de la materia, que son sólida, líquida y gaseosa (172)

T

temperature/temperatura una medida de qué tan caliente (o frío) está algo; específicamente, una medida de la energía cinética promedio de las partículas de un objeto (158)

terminal velocity/velocidad terminal la velocidad constante de un objeto en caída cuando la fuerza de resistencia del aire es igual en magnitud y opuesta en dirección a la fuerza de gravedad (38)

thermal conduction/conducción térmica la transferencia de energía en forma de calor a través de un material (282)

thermal conductor/conductor térmico un material a través del cual es posible transferir energía en forma de calor (167)

thermal energy/energía térmica la energía cinética de los átomos de una sustancia (165)

thermal expansion/expansión térmica un aumento en el tamaño de una sustancia en respuesta a un aumento en la temperatura de la sustancia (46)

thermal insulator/aislante térmico un material que reduce o evita la transferencia de calor (167)

thermal pollution/contaminación térmica un aumento en la temperatura de una masa de agua, producido por las actividades humanas y que tieneun efecto dañino en la calidad del agua y en la capacidad de esa masa de agua para permitir que se desarrolle la vida (182)

thrust/empuje la fuerza de empuje o arrastre ejercida por el motor de un avión o cohete (80)

V

velocity/velocidad la rapidez de un objeto en una dirección dada (6)

W

watt/watt (o vatio) la unidad que se usa para expresar potencia; es equivalente a un joule por segundo (símbolo: W) (98)

wedge/cuña una máquina simple que está formada por dos planos inclinados y que se mueve; normalmente se usa para cortar (111)

weight/peso una medida de la fuerza gravitacional ejercida sobre un objeto; su valor puede cambiar en función de la ubicación del objeto en el universo (24)

wheel and axle/eje y rueda una máquina simple que está formada por dos objetos circulares de diferente tamaño; la rueda es el mayor de los dos objetos circulares (109)

work/trabajo la transferencia de energía a un objeto mediante una fuerza que hace que el objeto se mueva en la dirección de la fuerza (94)

work input/trabajo de entrada el trabajo realizado en una máquina; el producto de la fuerza de entrada por la distancia a través de la que se ejerce la fuerza (101)

work output/trabajo producido el trabajo realizado por una máquina; el producto de la fuerza de salida por la distancia a través de la que se ejerce la fuerza (101)

Index

Boldface page numbers refer to illustrative material, such as figures, tables, margin elements, photographs, and illustrations.

Index — vertical tab on left margin

Index

Index

Index

Credits

Abbreviations used: (t) top, (c) center, (b) bottom, (l) left, (r) right, (bkgd) background

PHOTOGRAPHY

Front Cover Daryl Benson/Masterfile

Skills Practice Lab Teens Sam Dudgeon/HRW

Connection to Astronomy Corbis Images; **Connection to Biology** David M. Phillips/Visuals Unlimited; **Connection to Chemistry** Digital Image copyright © 2005 PhotoDisc; **Connection to Environment** Digital Image copyright © 2005 PhotoDisc; **Connection to Geology** Letraset Phototone; **Connection to Language Arts** Digital Image copyright © 2005 PhotoDisc; **Connection to Meteorology** Digital Image copyright © 2005 PhotoDisc; **Connection to Oceanography** © ICONOTEC; **Connection to Physics** Digital Image copyright © 2005 PhotoDisc

Table of Contents iv (cl), age fotostock/Fabio Cardoso; v (tl), Larry L. Miller/Photo Researchers, Inc.; v (tr), CORBIS Images/HRW; v (cl), © Galen Rowell/CORBIS; vi, Victoria Smith/HRW; x (bl), Sam Dudgeon/HRW; xi (tl), John Langford/HRW; xi (b), Sam Dudgeon/HRW; xii (tl), Victoria Smith/HRW; xii (bl), Stephanie Morris/HRW; xii (br), Sam Dudgeon/HRW; xiii (tl), Patti Murray/Animals, Animals; xiii (tr), Jana Birchum/HRW; xiii (b), Peter Van Steen/HRW

Chapter One 2–3 (all), © AFP/CORBIS; 4 (all), © SuperStock; 6 (bl), Robert Ginn/PhotoEdit; 8 (t), Sergio Purtell/Foca; 9 (tr), Digital Image copyright © 2005 PhotoDisc; 10 (b), Michelle Bridwell/HRW; 11 (b), Michelle Bridwell/HRW; 11 (tr), © Roger Ressmeyer/CORBIS; 12 (t), Daniel Schaefer/HRW; 12 (bl), Sam Dudgeon/HRW; 13 (tr), age fotostock/Fabio Cardoso; 16 (bl, br), Michelle Bridwell/HRW; 16 (inset), Stephanie Morris/HRW; 18 (br), © Annie Griffiths Belt/CORBIS; 19 (tr), Sam Dudgeon/HRW; 19 (cr), Victoria Smith/HRW; 20 (br), NASA; 25 (tr), Digital Image copyright © 2005 PhotoDisc; 26 (bl), Sam Dudgeon/HRW; 27 (b), Sam Dudgeon/HRW; 28 (br), © Roger Ressmeyer/CORBIS; 28 (tl), Digital Image copyright © 2005 PhotoDisc; 29 (br), Sam Dudgeon/HRW; 32 (tl, c), Sam Dudgeon/HRW; 32 (tr), Justin Sullivan/Getty Images; 33 (bl), Allsport Concepts/Getty Images; 33 (cr), Courtesy Dartmouth University

Chapter Two 34–35 (all), NASA; 35 (br), NASA; 36 (bl), Richard Megna/Fundamental Photographs; 38 (cl), Toby Rankin/Masterfile; 39 (tr), James Sugar/Black Star; 39 (bl), NASA; 41 (bl), Michelle Bridwell/Frontera Fotos; 41 (br), Image copyright © 2005 PhotoDisc, Inc.; 42 (tc), Richard Megna/Fundamental Photographs; 43 (tr), Toby Rankin/Masterfile; 44 (b), John Langford/HRW; 46 (br), Mavournea Hay/HRW; 46 (bc), Michelle Bridwell/Frontera Fotos; 47 (all), Victoria Smith/HRW; 48 (all), Image copyright © 2005 PhotoDisc, Inc.; 49 (b), David Madison; 50 (tc), Gerard Lacz/Animals Animals/Earth Scenes; 50 (tr), Sam Dudgeon/HRW; 50 (tr), Image copyright © 2005 PhotoDisc, Inc.; 50 (tl), NASA; 51 (br), Lance Schriner/HRW; 51 (tr), Victoria Smith/HRW; 53 (all), Michelle Bridwell/HRW; 54 (br), Zigy Kaluzny/Getty Images; 54 (bl), © SuperStock; 55 (cl), Michelle Bridwell/HRW; 56 (bl), Image ©2001 PhotoDisc, Inc.; 57 (all), Sam Dudgeon/HRW; 58 (tc), Gerard Lacz/Animals Animals/Earth Scenes; 59 (all), Sam Dudgeon/HRW; 62 (tl), AP Photo/Martyn Hayhow; 62 (tr), Junko Kimura/Getty Images/NewsCom; 63 (tr), Steve Okamoto; 63 (br), Lee Schwabe

Chapter Three 64–65 (all), © Nicholas Pinturas/Getty Images; 68 (tl), © Royalty Free/CORBIS; 68 (tcl), David R. Frazier Photolibrary; 68 (cl), Dieter and Mary Plage/Bruce Coleman, Inc.; 68 (bcl), Wolfgang Kaehler/CORBIS; 68 (bl), © Martin Barraud/Getty Images; 69 (tr), © SuperStock; 69 (tcr), Daniel A. Nord; 69 (cr), © Ken Marschall/Madison Press Books; 69 (bcr), Dr. Paul A. Zahl/Photo Researchers, Inc.; 69 (br), CORBIS/Bettman; 71 (tr), © Charles Doswell III/Getty Images; 74 (tl), Bruno P. Zehnder/Peter Arnold, Inc.; 78 (br), Richard Megna/Fundamental Photographs/HRW Photo; 80 (tl), Larry L. Miller/Photo Researchers, Inc.; 80 (tr), Richard Neville/Check Six; 82 (tr), John Neubauer/PhotoEdit; 83 (br), Check Six; 85 (b), Sam Dudgeon/HRW; 86 (tr), © SuperStock; 90 (tc), © Victor Malafronte; 90 (tl), Sam Dudgeon/HRW; 91 (bl), Corbis Images; 91 (tr), Courtesy of Alisha Bracken

Chapter Four 92–93 (all), age fotostock/Photographer, Year; 94 (bl), John Langford/HRW; 95 (all), John Langford/HRW; 96 (all), © Galen Rowell/CORBIS; 97 (all), Sam Dudgeon/HRW; 98 (all), John Langford/HRW; 100 (cr), Scott Van Osdol/HRW; 100 (br), Robert Wolf/HRW; 100 (bc), Digital Image copyright © 2005 Artville; 101 (br), Sam Dudgeon/HRW; 102 (all), Scott Van Osdol/HRW; 103 (tr, cr), Sam Dudgeon/HRW; 103 (tl), John Langford/HRW; 104 (br), CC Studio/Science Photo Library/Photo Researchers, Inc.; 105 (tr), © Reuters NewMedia Inc./CORBIS; 106 (bc), Victoria Smith/HRW; 106 (br), Robert Wolf/HRW; 107 (tr), Robert Wolf/HRW; 107 (br), Scott Van Osdol/HRW; 107 (bc), Sam Dudgeon/HRW; 107 (tc), John Langford/HRW; 109 (t), Robert Wolf/HRW; 110 (tr), Lisa Davis/HRW; 111 (tl, cr), Sam Dudgeon/HRW; 111 (br), Peter Van Steen/HRW ; 112 (b), Robert Wolf/HRW; 113 (tr), Robert Wolf/HRW; 113 (br), John Langford/HRW; 114 (bl), Stephanie Morris/HRW; 115 (br), Paul Dance/Getty Images; 116 (tl), John Langford/HRW; 117 (cl), Helmut Gritscher/Peter Arnold, Inc.; 117 (tr), Robert Wolf/HRW; 117 (cr), John Langford/HRW; 117 (br), Stephanie Morris/HRW; 120 (tr), © Visuals Unlimited; 120 (tl), Wayne Sorce; 121 (cr), A.W. Stegmeyer/Upstream; 121 (bl), Digital Image copyright © 2005 PhotoDisc

Chapter Five 122–123 (all), © AFP/CORBIS; 124 (br), Tim Kiusalaas/Masterfile; 125 (cr), Sam Dudgeon/HRW; 126 (tl), Earl Kowall/CORBIS; 127 (br), Sam Dudgeon/HRW; 128 (tl), John Langford/HRW; 128 (tc), Corbis Images; 128 (tr), David Phillips/HRW; 129 (br), Sam Dudgeon/HRW; 129 (cr), Peter Van Steen/HRW; 130 (tr), John Langford/HRW; 130 (bl), NASA; 131 (cr), Peter Van Steen/HRW; 132 (br), © Duomo/CORBIS; 133(bl, br), John Langford/HRW; 133 (tr), Peter Van Steen/HRW; 136 (all), John Langford/HRW; 137 (tr), © Martin Bond/Photo Researchers, Inc.; 140 (bl), Sam Dudgeon/HRW; 141 (all), Courtesy of Honda; 143 (tl), Robert Brook/Photo Researchers, Inc.; 143 (cl), Sam Dudgeon/HRW; 143 (bl), John Langford/HRW; 144 (bl), D.O.E./Science Source/Photo Researchers, Inc.; 145 (tr), © John D. Cunningham/Visuals Unlimited; 145 (b), CORBIS Images/HRW; 146 (tl), Digital Image copyright © 2005 PhotoDisc; 150 (tl), Courtesy of Honda; 150 (bc), Digital Image copyright © 2005 PhotoDisc; 151 (bl), © Patrik Giardino/CORBIS; 154 (bl), Courtesy Pursuit Dynamics; 154 (tr), © Bettman/CORBIS; 155 (all), Robert Wolf/HRW

Chapter Six 156–157 (all), © Vandystadt/Allsport/Getty Images; 159 (br), John Langford/HRW; 161 (br), Michelle Bridwell/HRW; 162 (tl), Mark Burnett/Photo Researchers, Inc.; 163 (tr), AP Photo/Joe Giblin; 164 (all), Sam Dudgeon/HRW; 165 (all), John Langford/HRW; 166 (b), John Langford/HRW; 168 (cl), John Langford/HRW; 169 (tr), Sam Dudgeon/HRW; 170 (tl), John Langford/HRW; 171 (cr), © Simon Watson/FoodPix/Getty Images; 172 (bc), Sam Dudgeon/HRW; 173 (all), John Langford/HRW; 174 (cl), John Langford/HRW; 175 (tr), Peter Van Steen/HRW; 177 (br), John Langford/HRW; 180 (tr), Dorling Kindersley Ltd.; 180 (bl), © COMSTOCK; 183 (tr), John Langford/HRW; 185 (br), Victoria Smith/HRW; 186 (tl), John Langford/HRW; 187 (bl), AP Photo/Joe Giblin; 190 (tl), Dan Winters/Discover Magazine; 191 (b), Solar Survival Architecture; 191 (tr), Singeli Agnew/Taos News

Lab Book/Appendix "LabBook Header", "L", Corbis Images; "a", Letraset Phototone; "b", and "B", HRW; "o", and "k", images ©2006 PhotoDisc/HRW; 192 (all), Sam Dudgeon/HRW; 193 (tl), Sam Dudgeon/HRW; 195 (c), Sam Dudgeon/HRW; 200 (br), Sam Dudgeon/HRW; 201 (bl), Sam Dudgeon/HRW; 202 (br), John Langford/HRW; 204 (tr, cr), Robert Wolf; 204 (br), John Langford/HRW; 205 (br), Victoria Smith/HRW; 207 (br), Sam Dudgeon/HRW; 212 (br), Victoria Smith; 213 (br), Victoria Smith; 229 (tr), Sam Dudgeon/HRW